and a little bittersweet as well: with every set of pencils, I felt like "Wow – this *would've* worked as a movie…"

And starting from issue one, I'd get in last-licks – which was mostly cleaning up dopey, out-dated dialogue from the six year old script. Joe Rybandt at Dynamite kept me honest, as far as a timeline, to ensure that the book stayed on a monthly schedule (it's made all the difference for me as a reader of the book). And, Jesus: those COVERS! Suddenly, in a very unlikely pairing, Alex Ross and I were on a book together. In fact, it was Alex who redesigned the Hornet, Kato, and the Black Beauty, as well as provided those jizz-worthy splashes before you even open each issue.

But Nick really deserves the most credit, as well as my sincere thanks. It's not often in life our failures can be redeemed and turned into successes: snatching victory from the jaws of defeat, as it were. The HORNET had long been a sore spot for me… until the Dynamite series that Nick engineered. Now, whenever I think of the HORNET, I think about all the love the book's gotten on Twitter, or the strong sales as folks still turned out for the 80 year old crime-fighter. Nick took my blooper and made that shit *super*. Taking a page from THIS book, he was Old Man Kato to my brash, hot-headed Britt Jr.

Which would make Hester Clutch Kato – the mechanic who builds the wonderful toys. And Jonathan would be Mulan Kato – sexy and Asian.

Let's roll, Kato.

Um…

That was NOT meant to be a pass at Lau.

Unless he's interested…

Kevin Smith
Backdoor HORNET writer
July 17, 2010

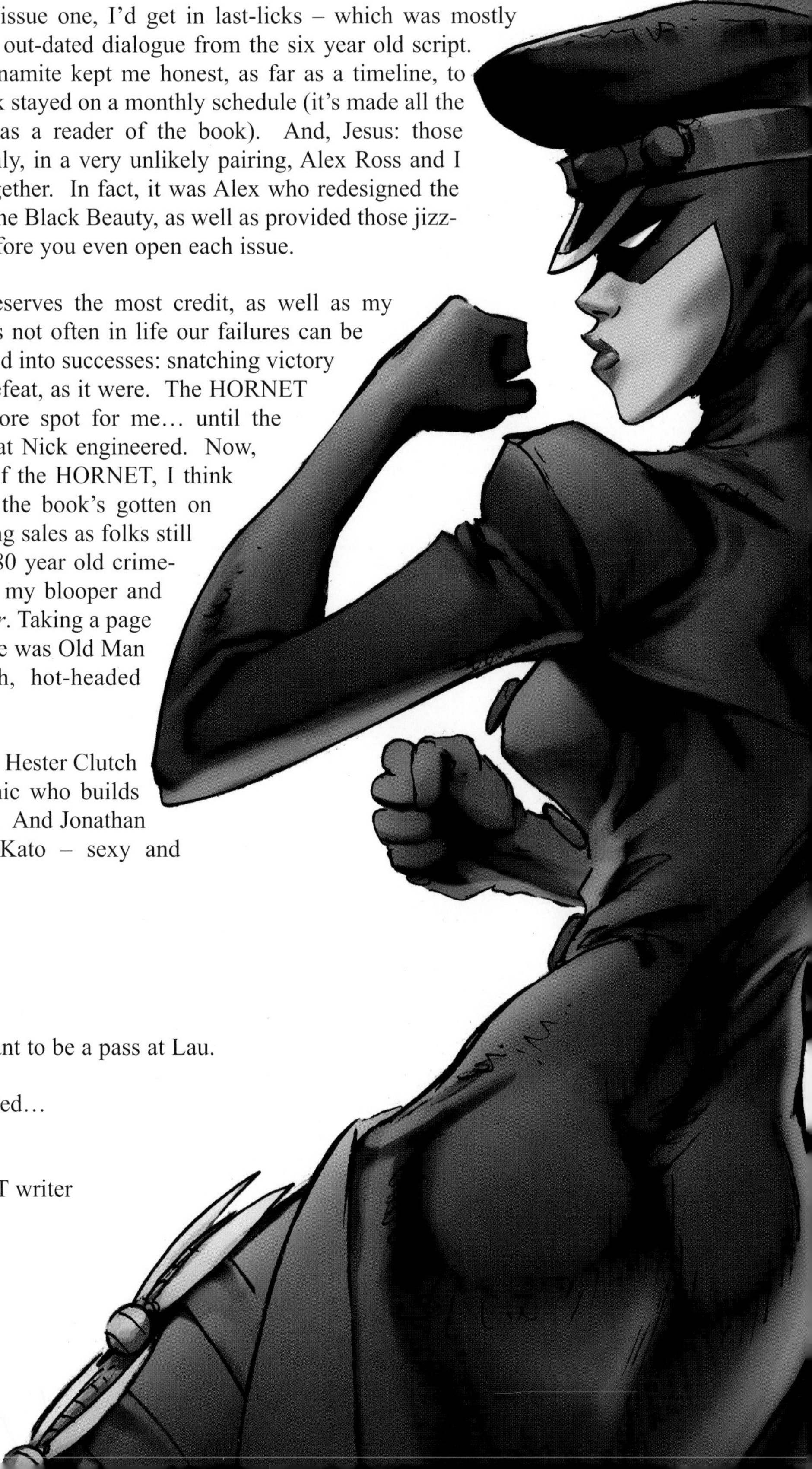

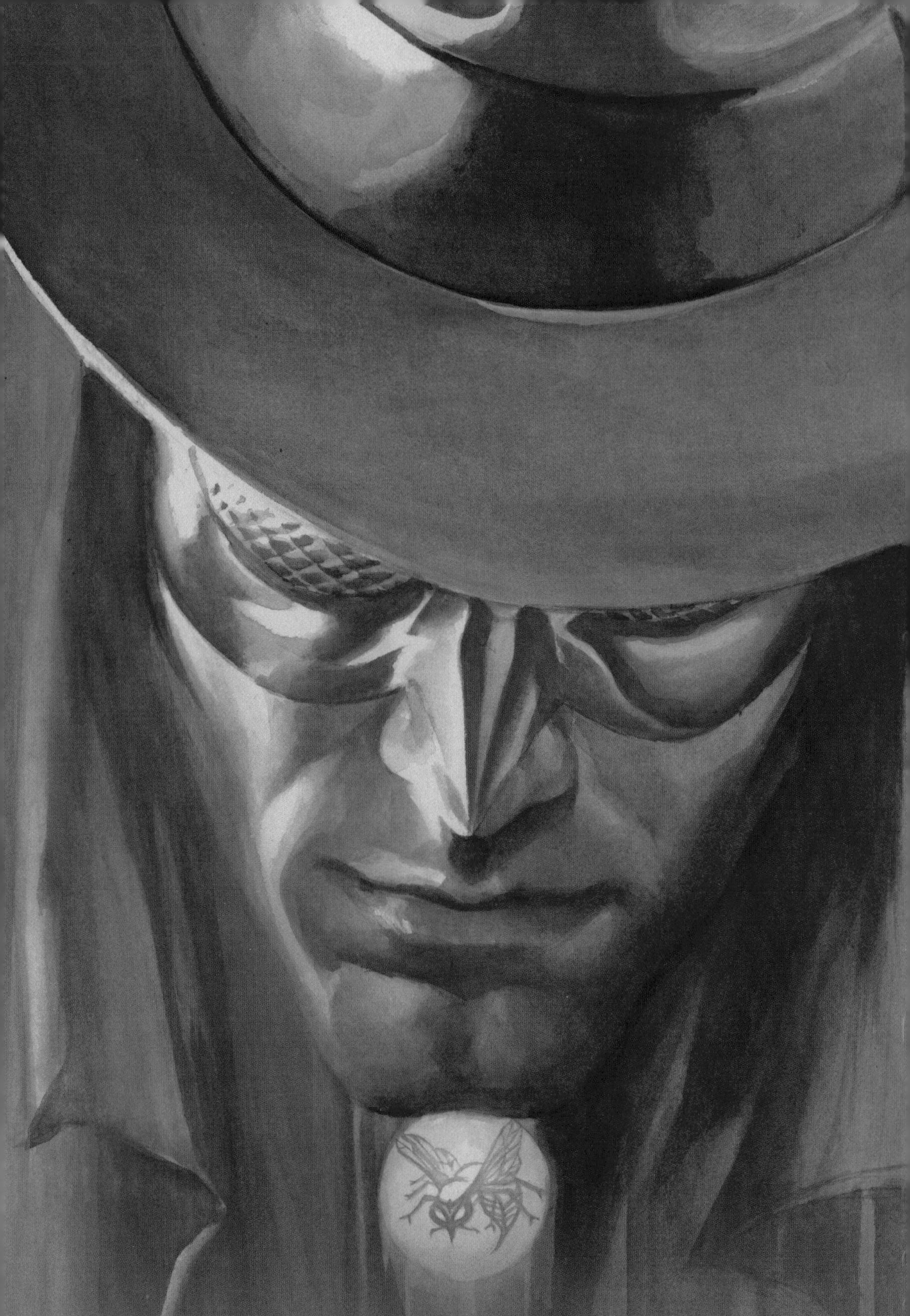

EPISODE ONE: NIGHT AND DAY

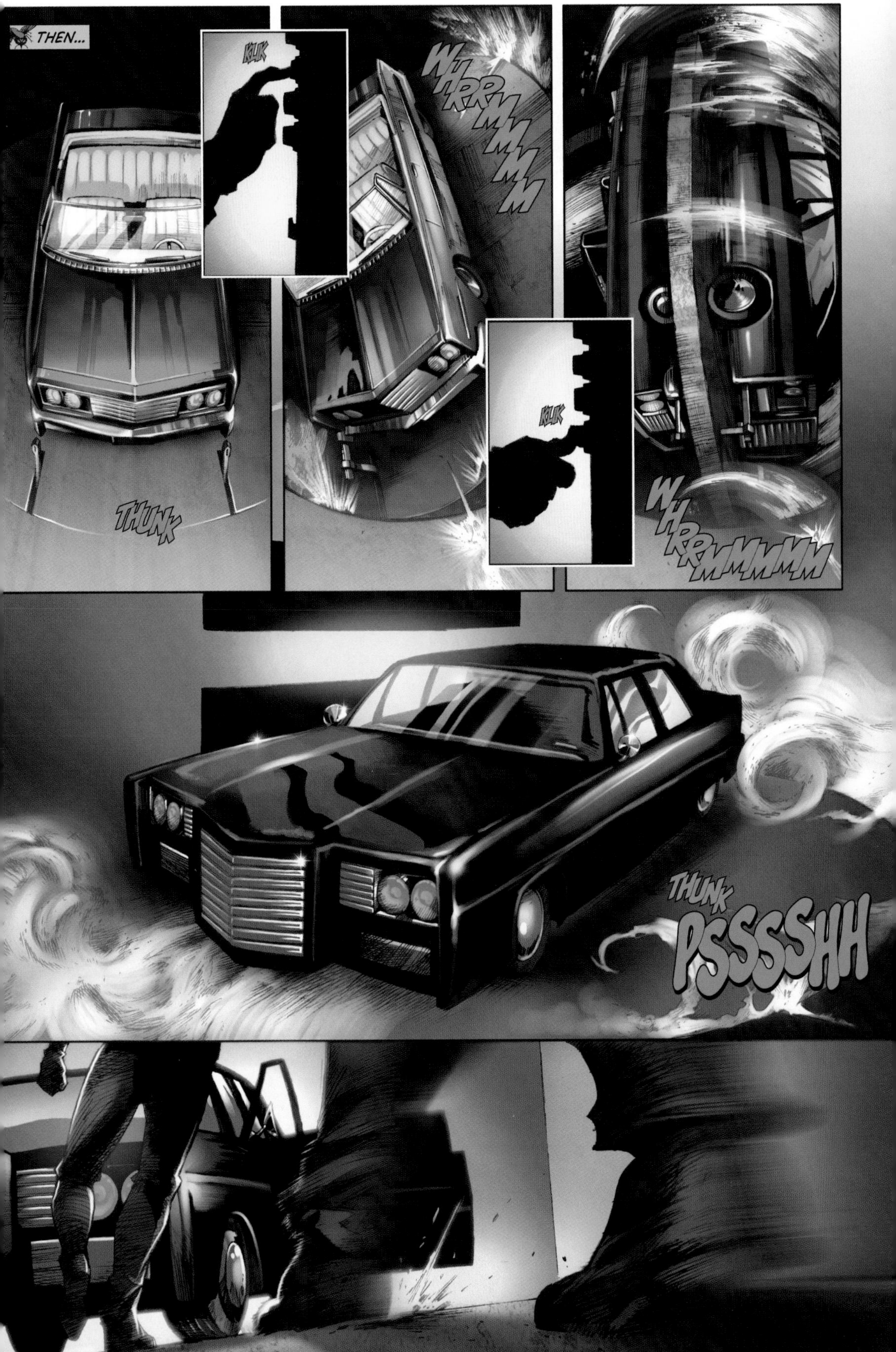
THEN...
THUNK
KLIK
WHRRMMMMM
KLIK
WHRRMMMMMM
THUNK
PSSSSHH

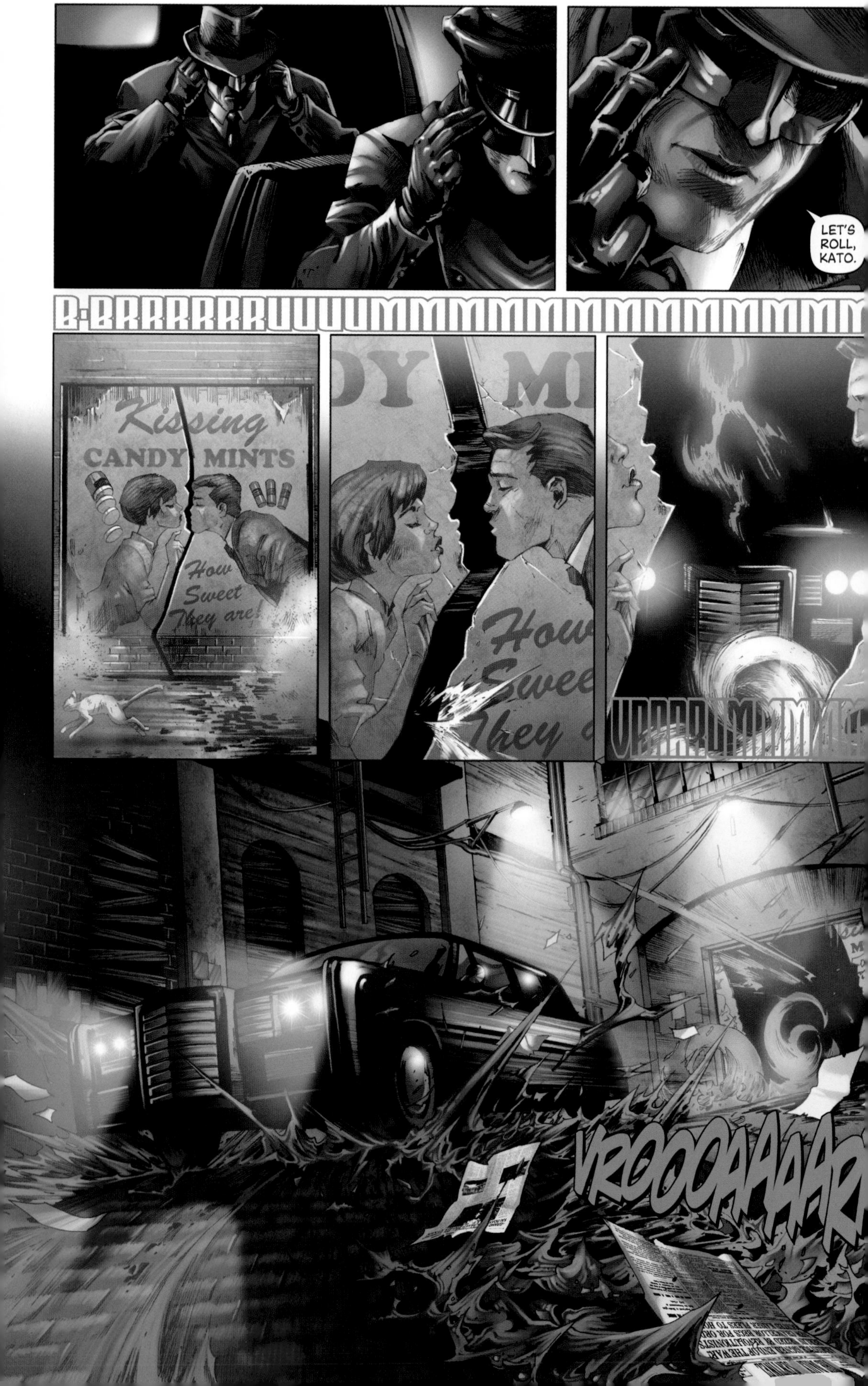
LET'S ROLL, KATO.
B-BRRRRRRUUUUMMMMMMMMMMMMMM
Kissing
CANDY MINTS
How Sweet They are!
VRRRRUMMMMM
VROOOAAAAR

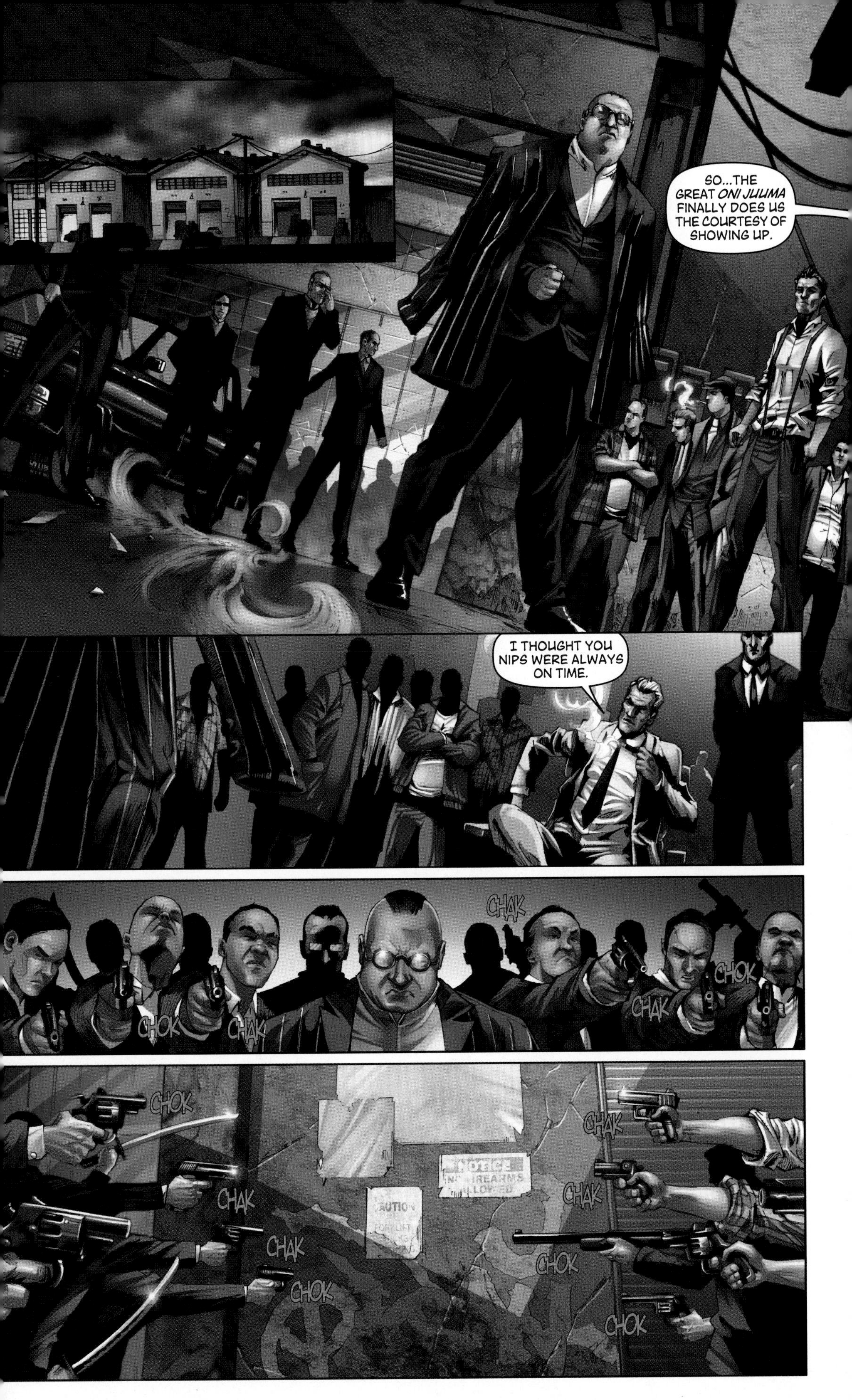
SO...THE GREAT *ONI JUUMA* FINALLY DOES US THE COURTESY OF SHOWING UP.
I THOUGHT YOU NIPS WERE ALWAYS ON TIME.
CHAK
CHOK
CHAK
CHOK
CHAK
CHOK
CHAK
CHAK
CHOK
NOTICE
CAUTION
CHAK
CHAK
CHOK
CHOK

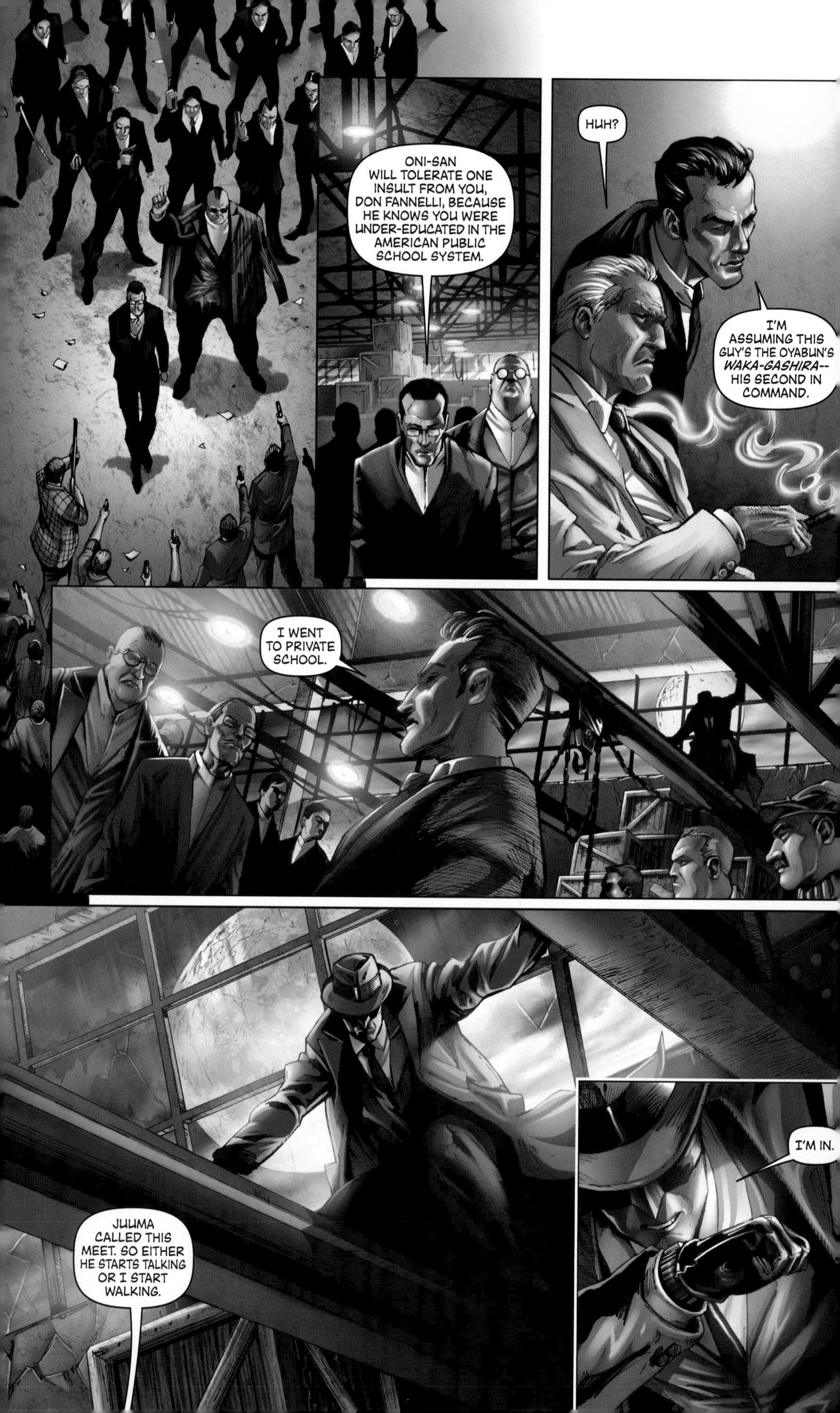
ONI-SAN WILL TOLERATE ONE INSULT FROM YOU, DON FANNELLI, BECAUSE HE KNOWS YOU WERE UNDER-EDUCATED IN THE AMERICAN PUBLIC SCHOOL SYSTEM.
HUH?
I'M ASSUMING THIS GUY'S THE OYABUN'S *WAKA-GASHIRA*-- HIS SECOND IN COMMAND.
I WENT TO PRIVATE SCHOOL.
JUUMA CALLED THIS MEET. SO EITHER HE STARTS TALKING OR I START WALKING.
I'M IN.

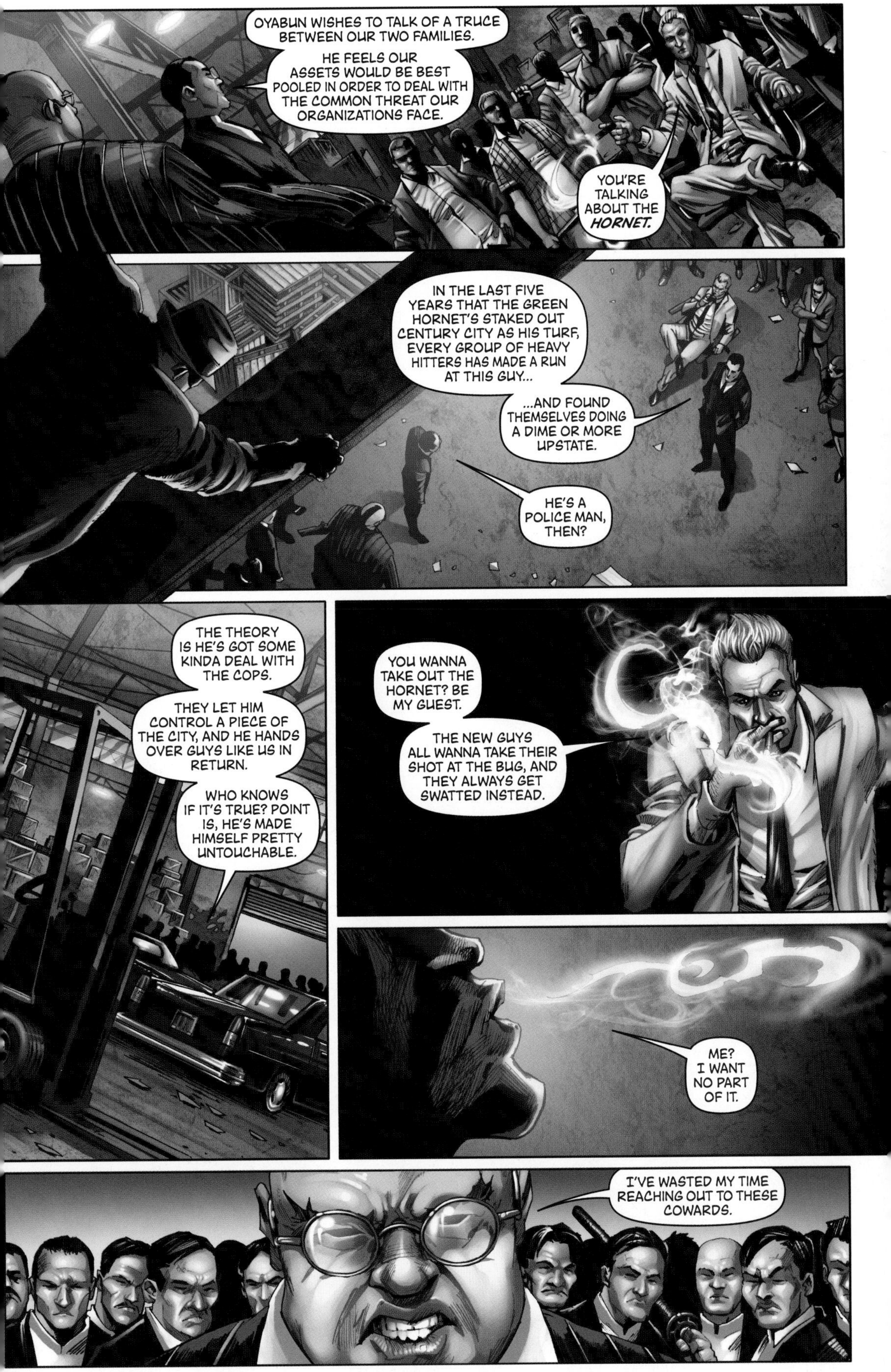
OYABUN WISHES TO TALK OF A TRUCE BETWEEN OUR TWO FAMILIES.
HE FEELS OUR ASSETS WOULD BE BEST POOLED IN ORDER TO DEAL WITH THE COMMON THREAT OUR ORGANIZATIONS FACE.
YOU'RE TALKING ABOUT THE *HORNET.*
IN THE LAST FIVE YEARS THAT THE GREEN HORNET'S STAKED OUT CENTURY CITY AS HIS TURF, EVERY GROUP OF HEAVY HITTERS HAS MADE A RUN AT THIS GUY...
...AND FOUND THEMSELVES DOING A DIME OR MORE UPSTATE.
HE'S A POLICE MAN, THEN?
THE THEORY IS HE'S GOT SOME KINDA DEAL WITH THE COPS.
THEY LET HIM CONTROL A PIECE OF THE CITY, AND HE HANDS OVER GUYS LIKE US IN RETURN.
WHO KNOWS IF IT'S TRUE? POINT IS, HE'S MADE HIMSELF PRETTY UNTOUCHABLE.
YOU WANNA TAKE OUT THE HORNET? BE MY GUEST.
THE NEW GUYS ALL WANNA TAKE THEIR SHOT AT THE BUG, AND THEY ALWAYS GET SWATTED INSTEAD.
ME? I WANT NO PART OF IT.
I'VE WASTED MY TIME REACHING OUT TO THESE COWARDS.

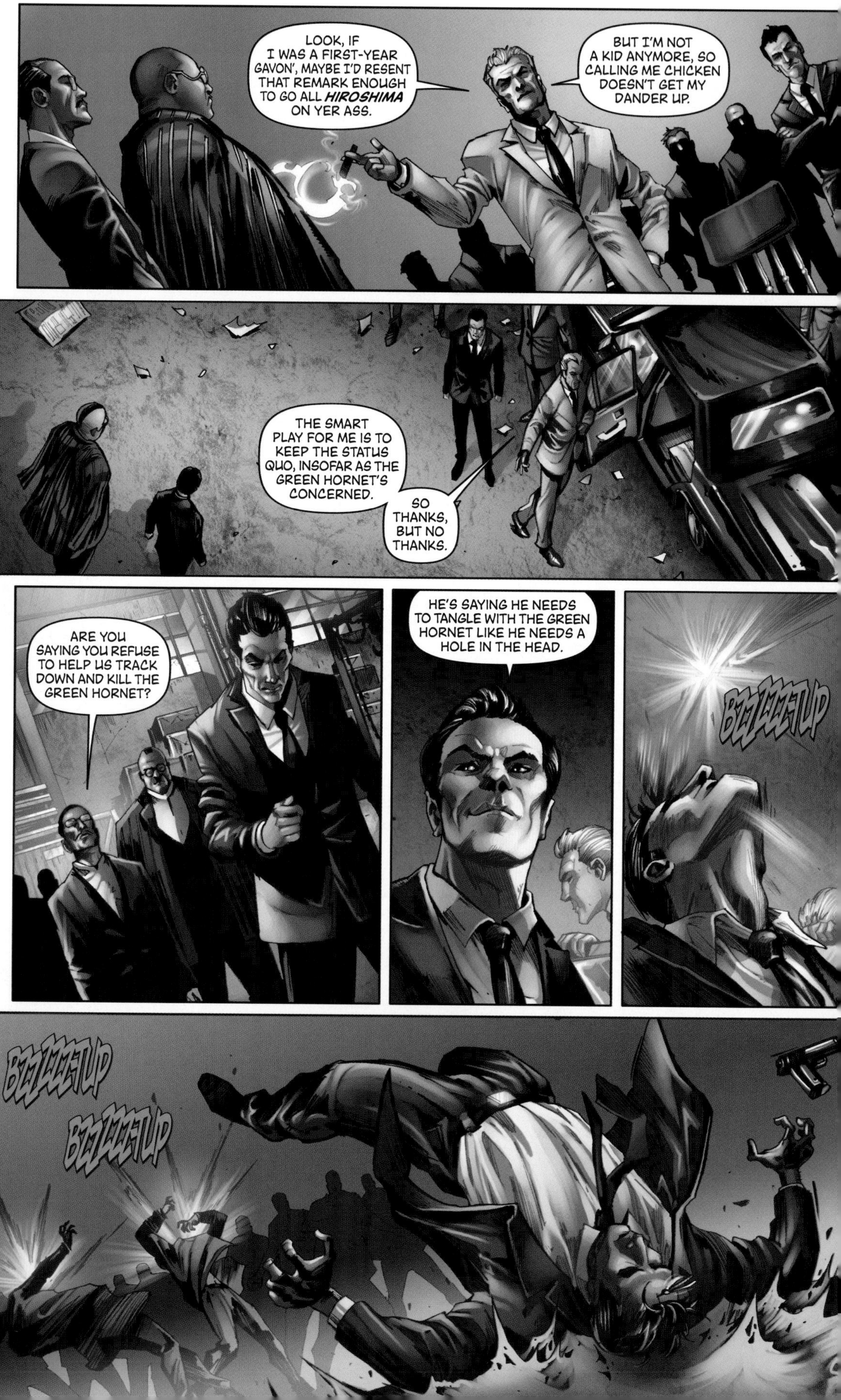
LOOK, IF I WAS A FIRST-YEAR GAVON', MAYBE I'D RESENT THAT REMARK ENOUGH TO GO ALL *HIROSHIMA* ON YER ASS.
BUT I'M NOT A KID ANYMORE, SO CALLING ME CHICKEN DOESN'T GET MY DANDER UP.
THE SMART PLAY FOR ME IS TO KEEP THE STATUS QUO, INSOFAR AS THE GREEN HORNET'S CONCERNED.
SO THANKS, BUT NO THANKS.
ARE YOU SAYING YOU REFUSE TO HELP US TRACK DOWN AND KILL THE GREEN HORNET?
HE'S SAYING HE NEEDS TO TANGLE WITH THE GREEN HORNET LIKE HE NEEDS A HOLE IN THE HEAD.
BZZZZTUP
BZZZZTUP
BZZZZTUP

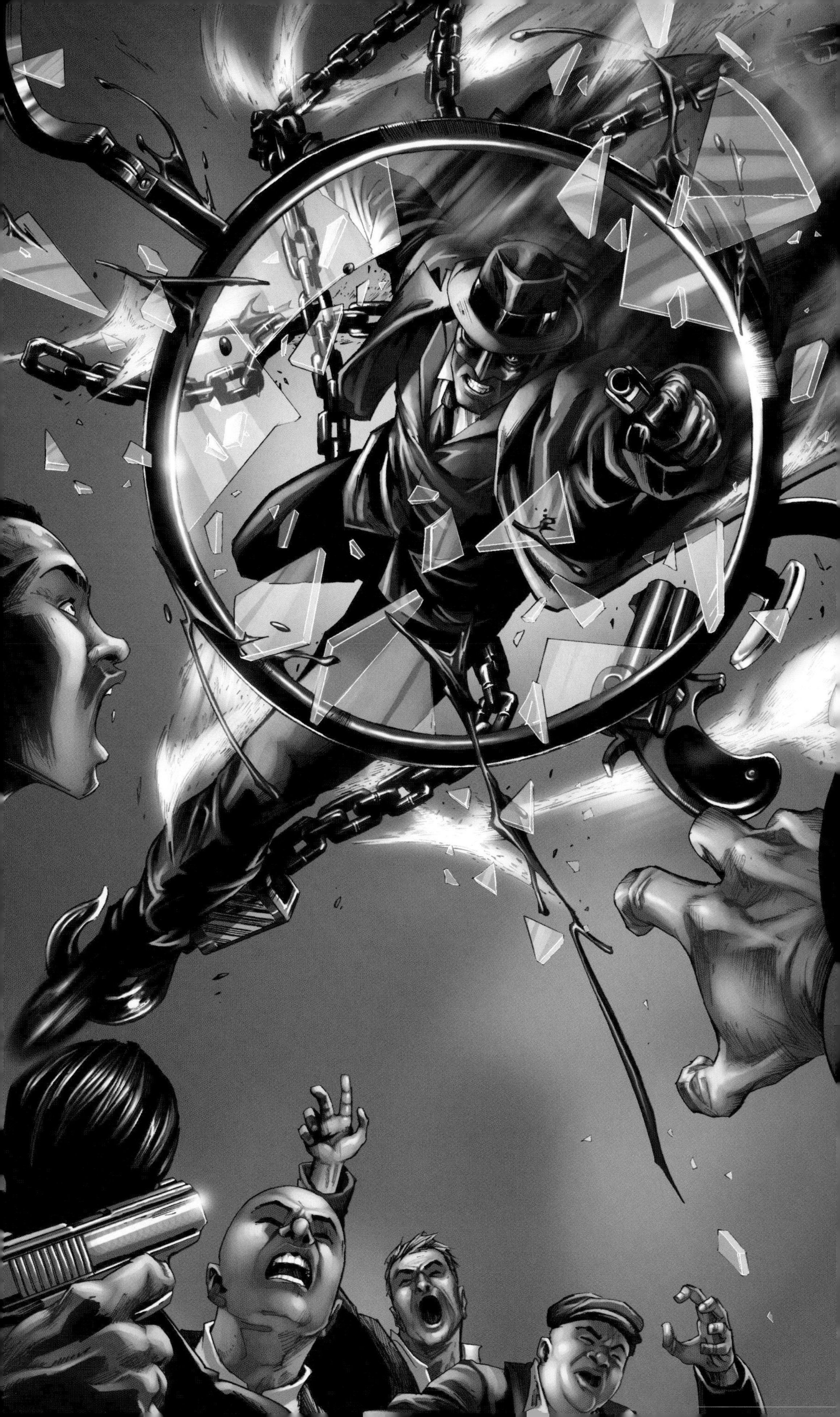

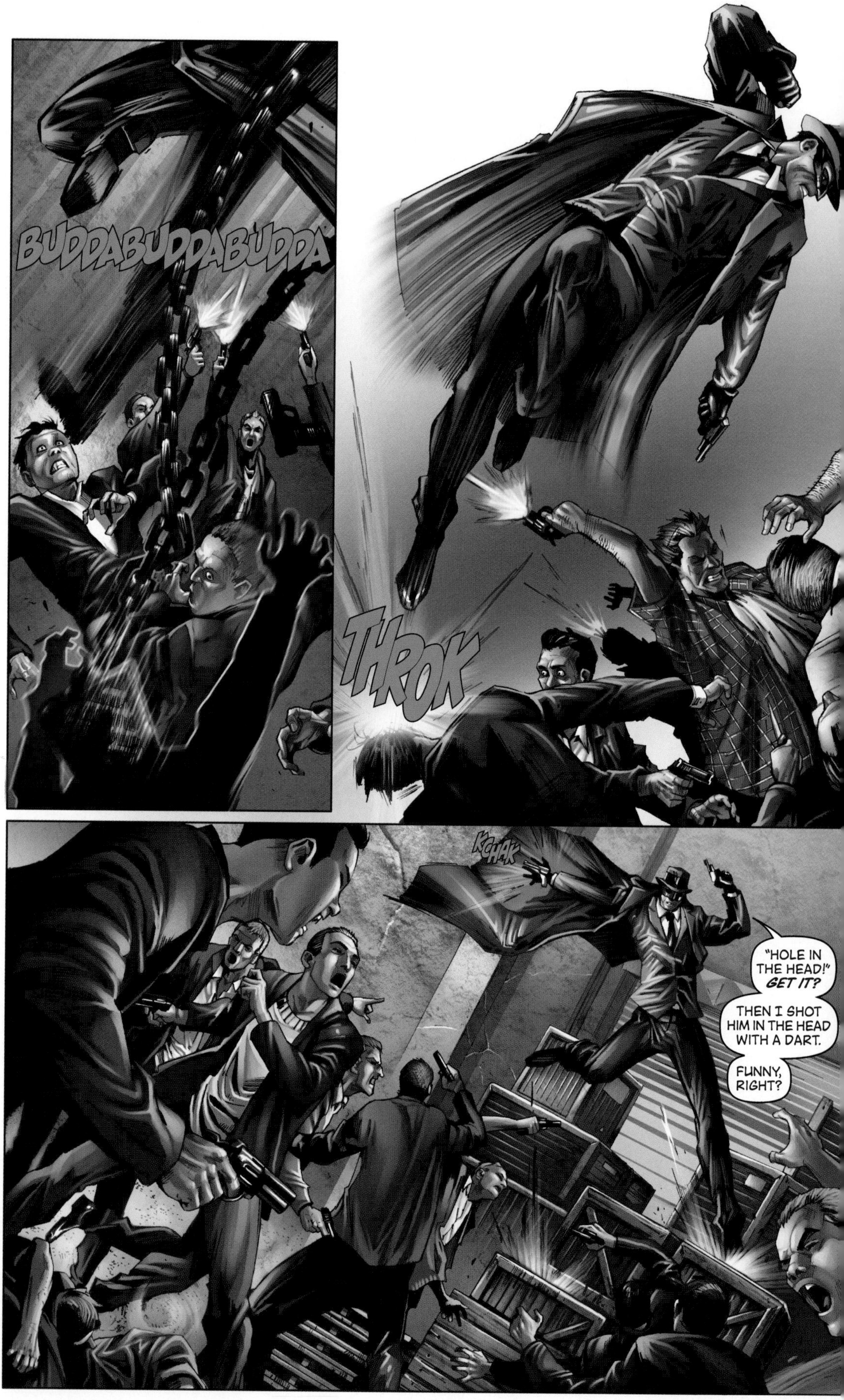
BUDDABUDDABUDDA
THROK
KCHAK
"HOLE IN THE HEAD!" GET IT?
THEN I SHOT HIM IN THE HEAD WITH A DART.
FUNNY, RIGHT?

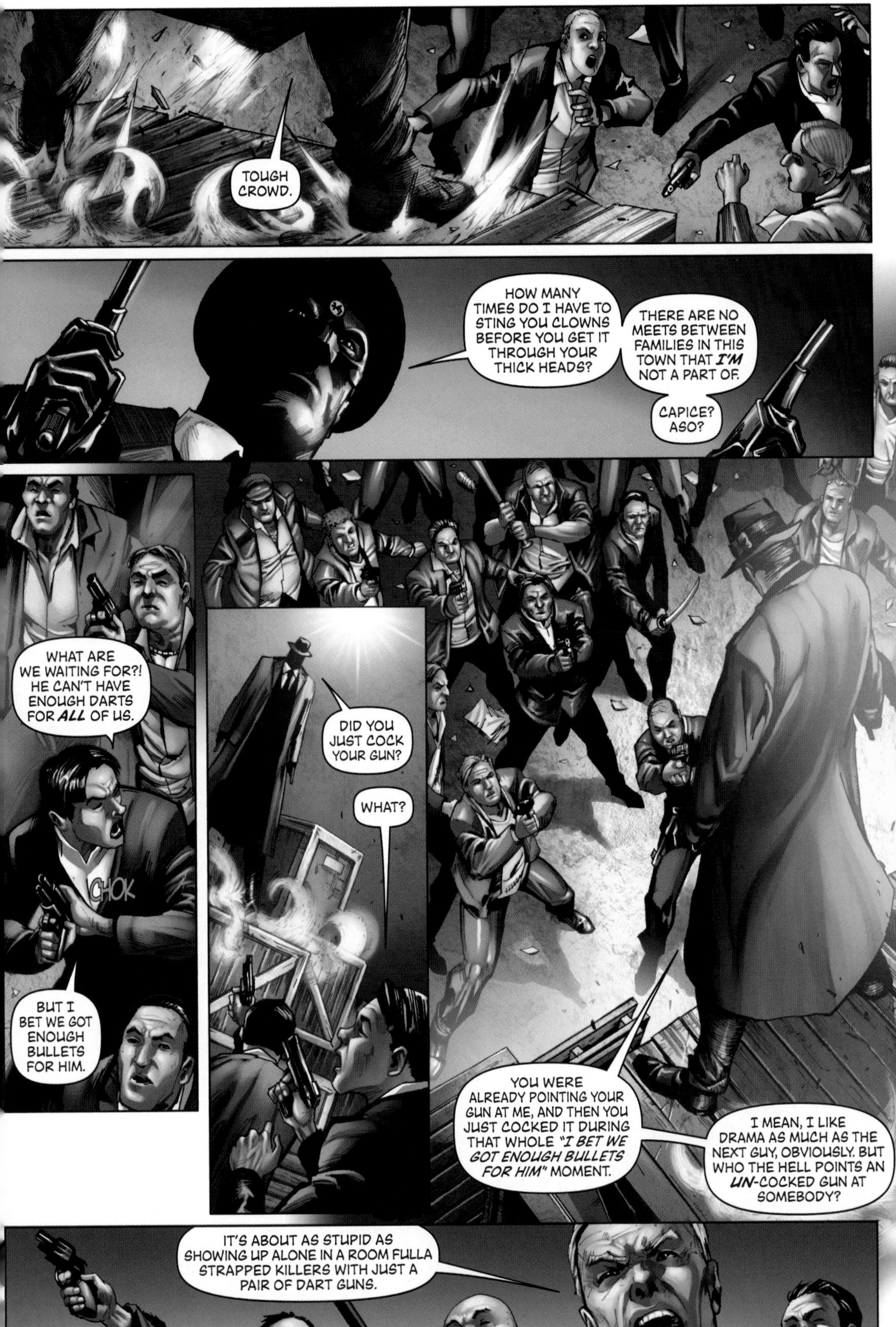
TOUGH CROWD.
HOW MANY TIMES DO I HAVE TO STING YOU CLOWNS BEFORE YOU GET IT THROUGH YOUR THICK HEADS?
THERE ARE NO MEETS BETWEEN FAMILIES IN THIS TOWN THAT *I'M* NOT A PART OF.
CAPICE? ASO?
WHAT ARE WE WAITING FOR?! HE CAN'T HAVE ENOUGH DARTS FOR ***ALL*** OF US.
CHOK
BUT I BET WE GOT ENOUGH BULLETS FOR HIM.
DID YOU JUST COCK YOUR GUN?
WHAT?
YOU WERE ALREADY POINTING YOUR GUN AT ME, AND THEN YOU JUST COCKED IT DURING THAT WHOLE *"I BET WE GOT ENOUGH BULLETS FOR HIM"* MOMENT.
I MEAN, I LIKE DRAMA AS MUCH AS THE NEXT GUY, OBVIOUSLY. BUT WHO THE HELL POINTS AN ***UN***-COCKED GUN AT SOMEBODY?
IT'S ABOUT AS STUPID AS SHOWING UP ALONE IN A ROOM FULLA STRAPPED KILLERS WITH JUST A PAIR OF DART GUNS.

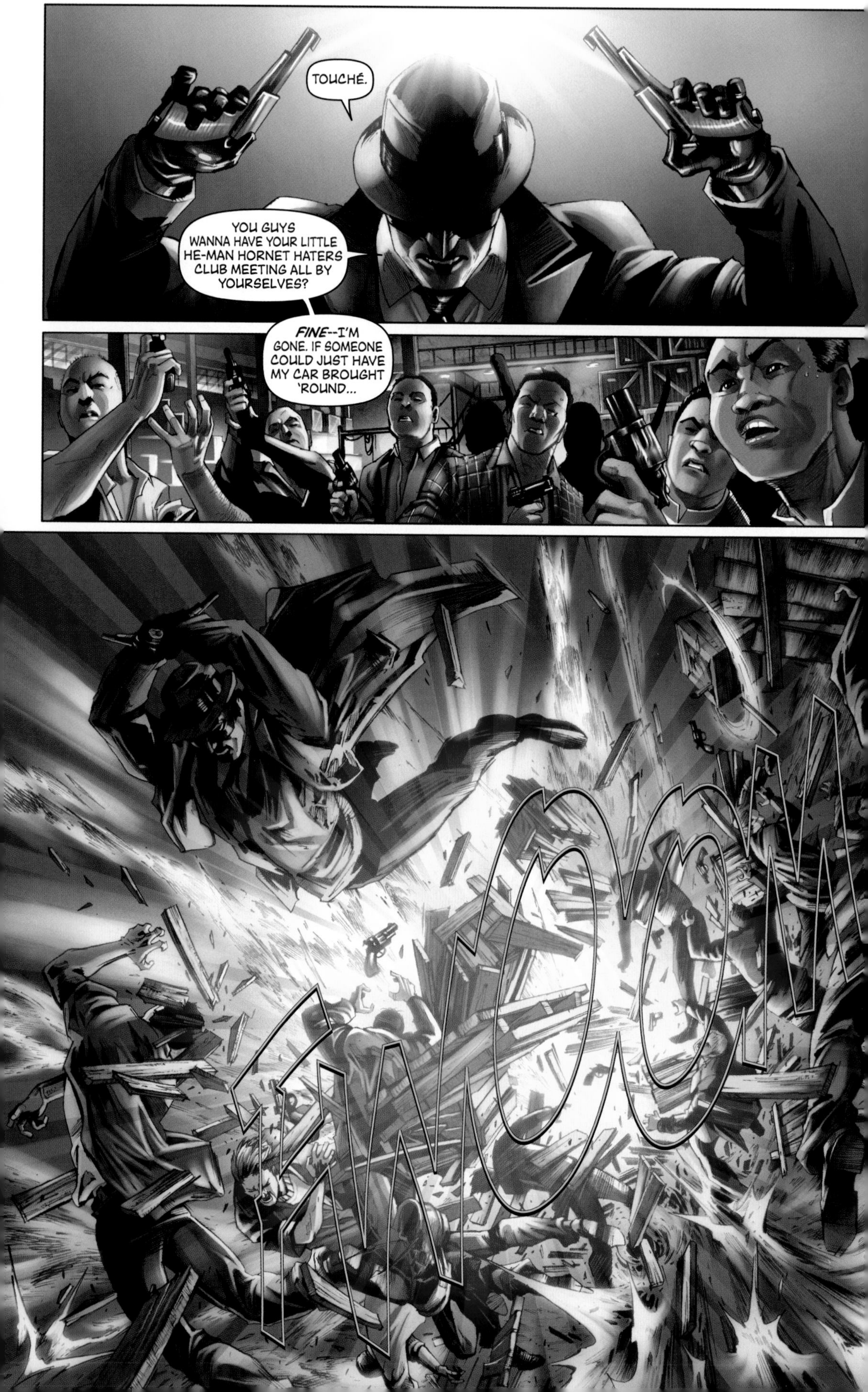
TOUCHÉ.
YOU GUYS WANNA HAVE YOUR LITTLE HE-MAN HORNET HATERS CLUB MEETING ALL BY YOURSELVES?
FINE--I'M GONE. IF SOMEONE COULD JUST HAVE MY CAR BROUGHT 'ROUND...
KA-WOOOOM

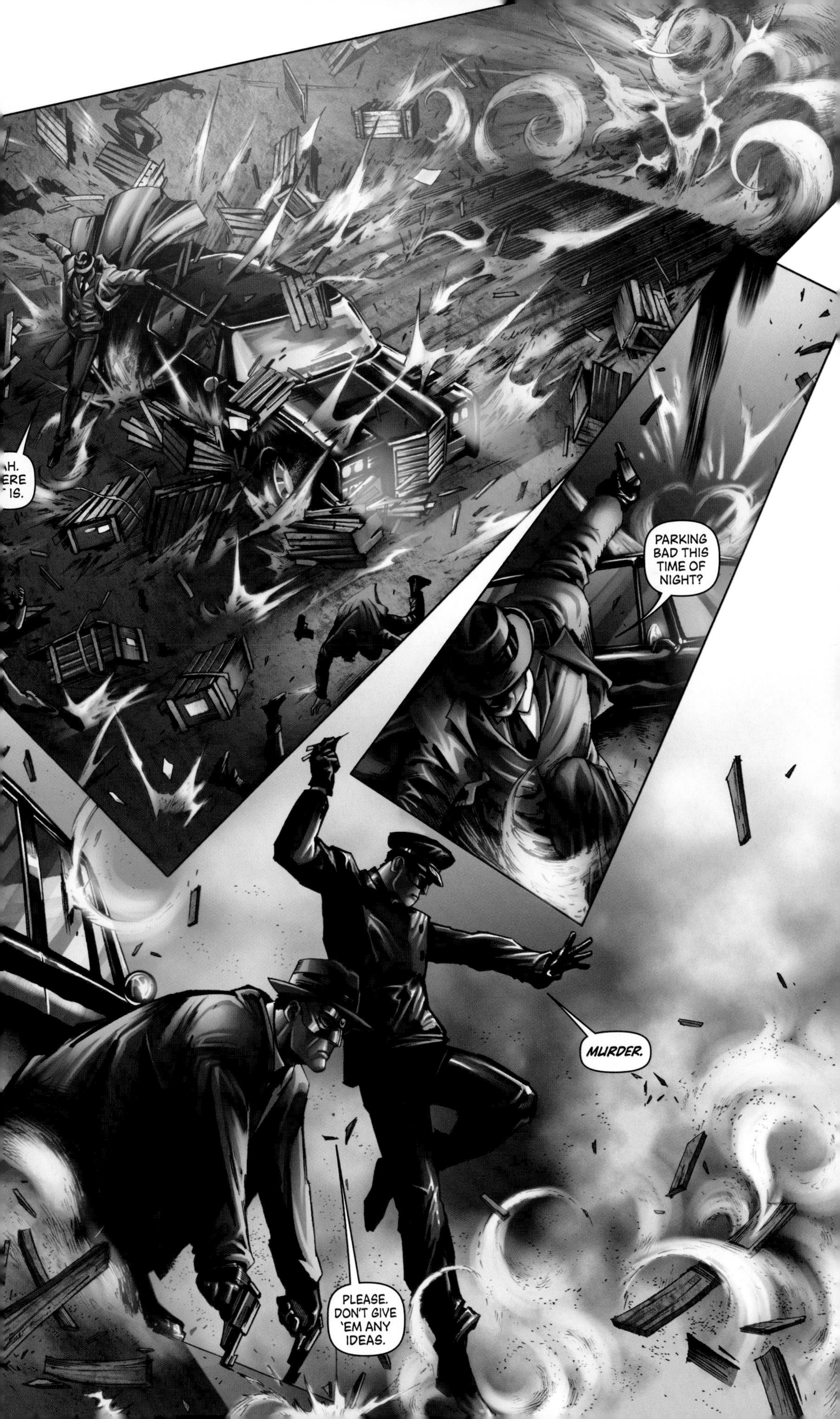
PARKING BAD THIS TIME OF NIGHT?
MURDER.
PLEASE. DON'T GIVE 'EM ANY IDEAS.

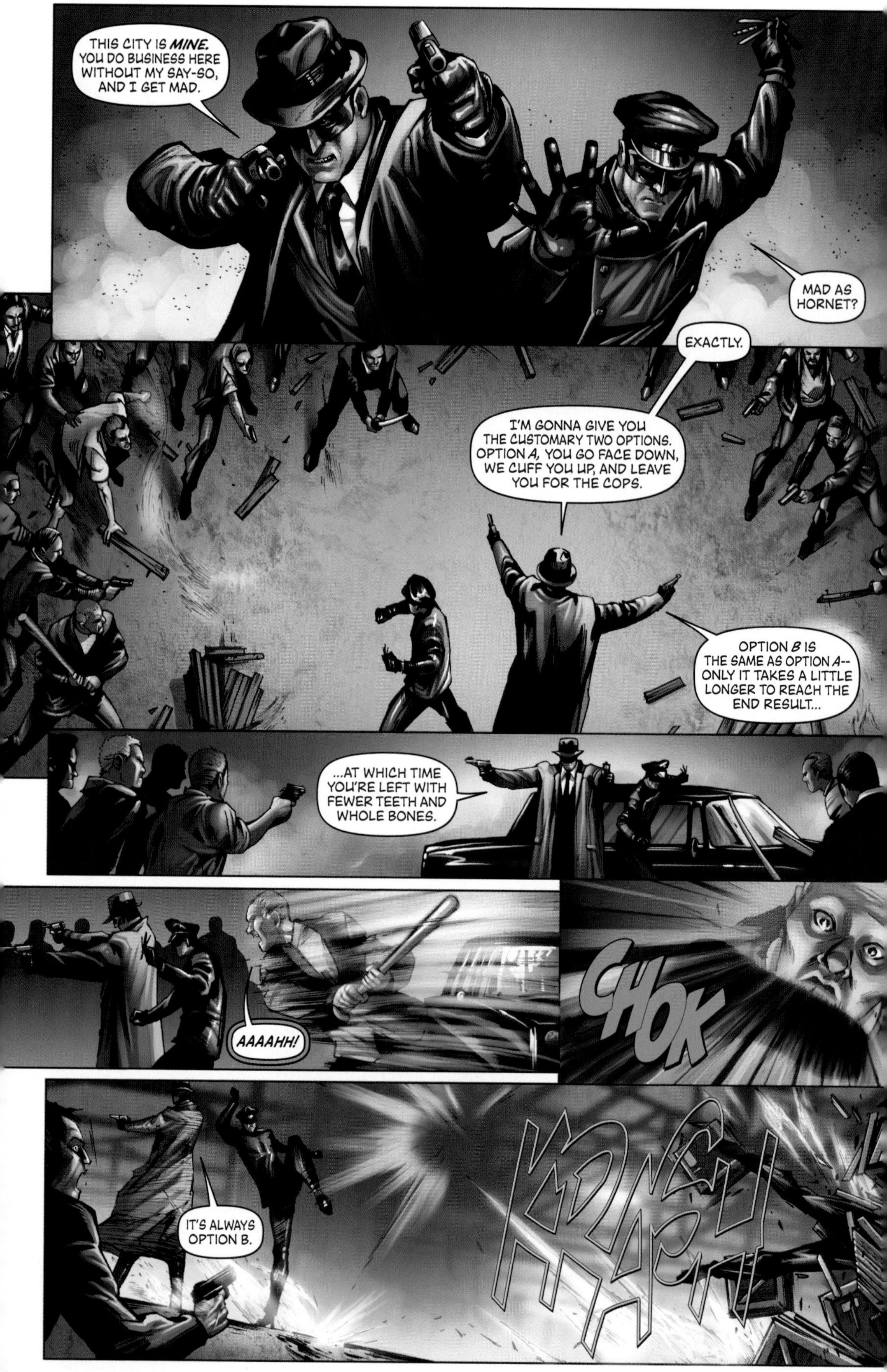
THIS CITY IS *MINE.* YOU DO BUSINESS HERE WITHOUT MY SAY-SO, AND I GET MAD.
MAD AS HORNET?
EXACTLY.
I'M GONNA GIVE YOU THE CUSTOMARY TWO OPTIONS. OPTION *A,* YOU GO FACE DOWN, WE CUFF YOU UP, AND LEAVE YOU FOR THE COPS.
OPTION *B* IS THE SAME AS OPTION *A*-- ONLY IT TAKES A LITTLE LONGER TO REACH THE END RESULT...
...AT WHICH TIME YOU'RE LEFT WITH FEWER TEETH AND WHOLE BONES.
AAAAHH!
CHOK
IT'S ALWAYS OPTION B.
KRUNCH

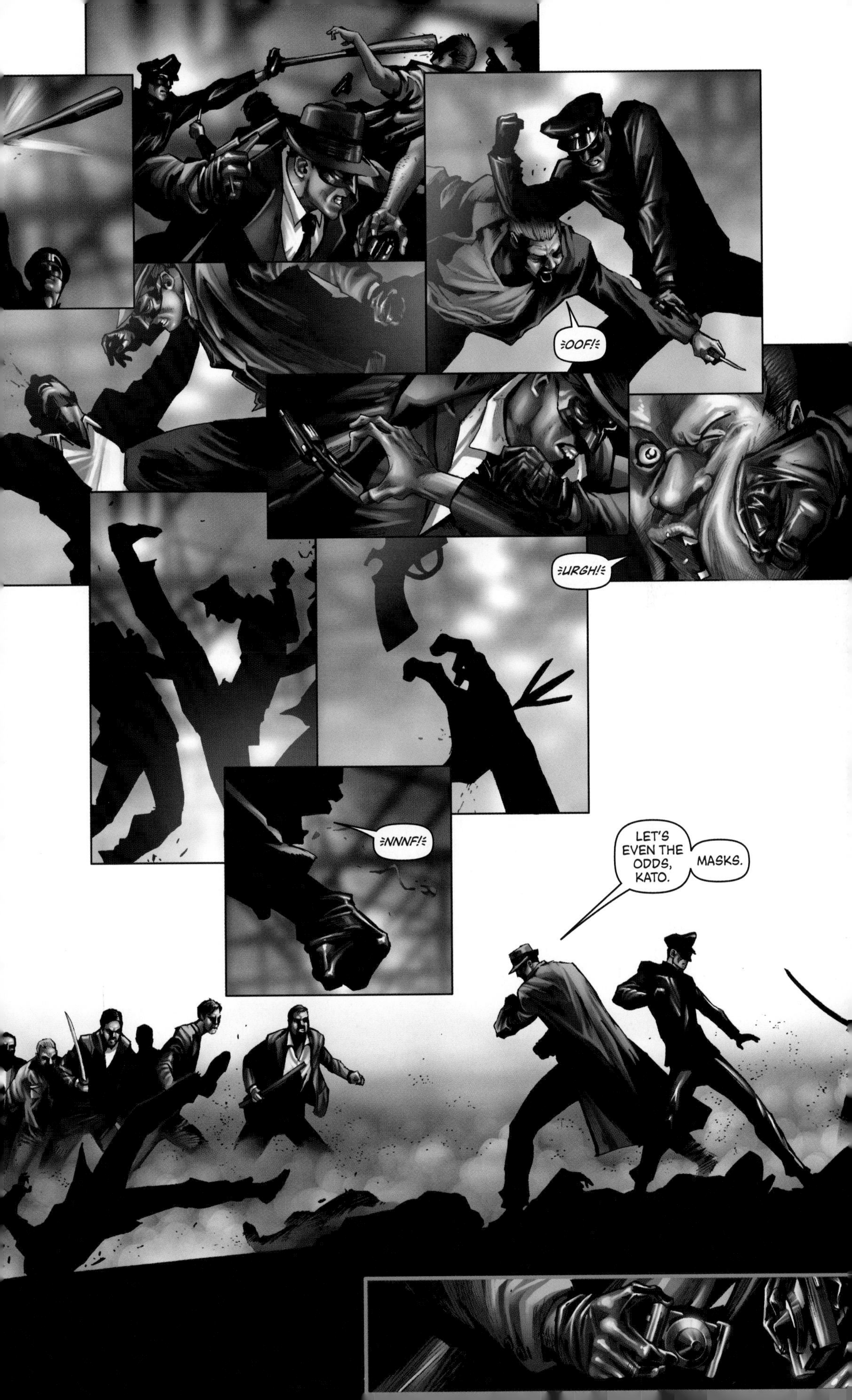
OOF!
URGH!
NNNF!
LET'S EVEN THE ODDS, KATO.
MASKS.

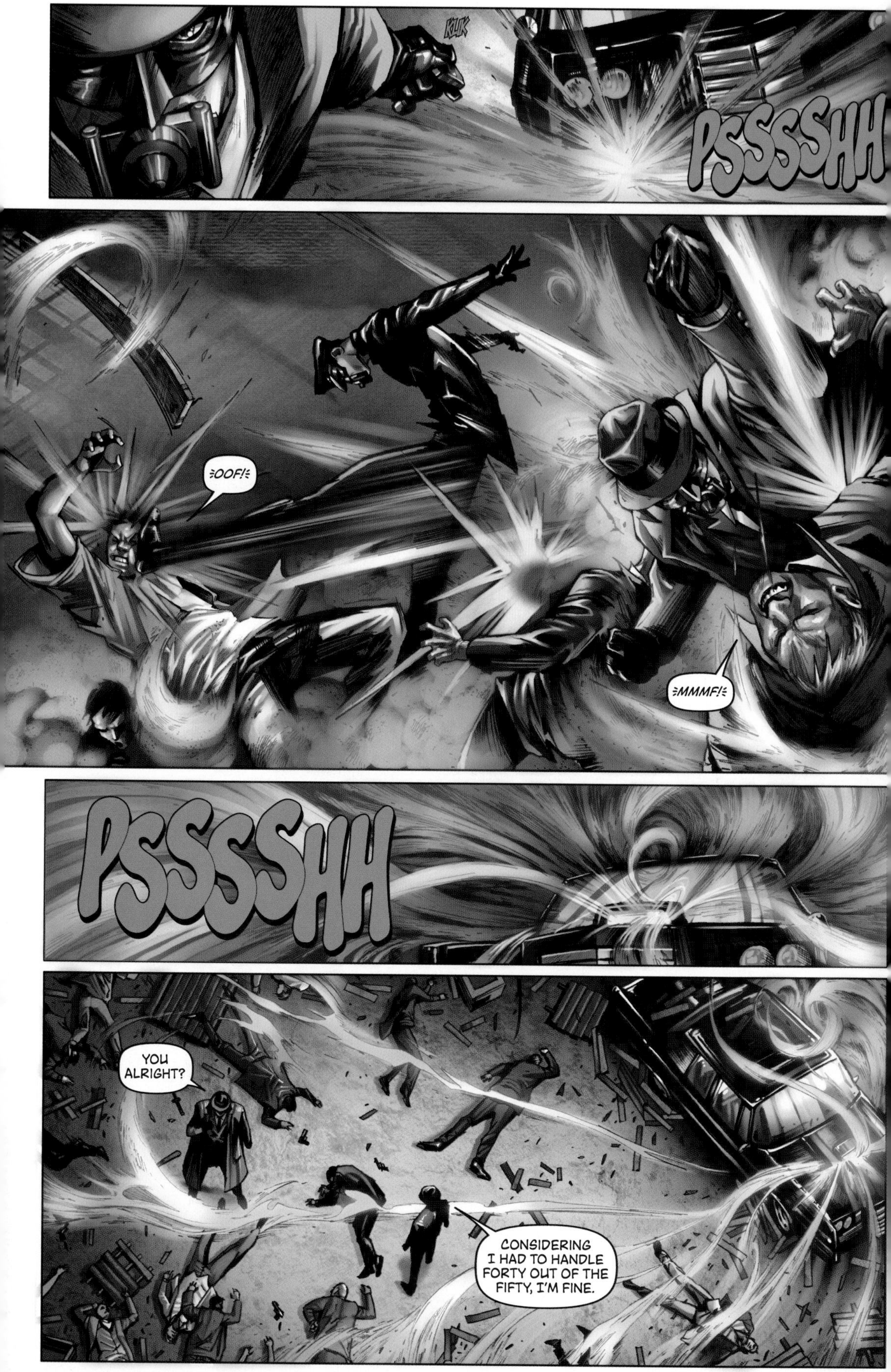
KLIK
PSSSSHH
OOF!
MMMF!
PSSSSHH
YOU ALRIGHT?
CONSIDERING I HAD TO HANDLE FORTY OUT OF THE FIFTY, I'M FINE.

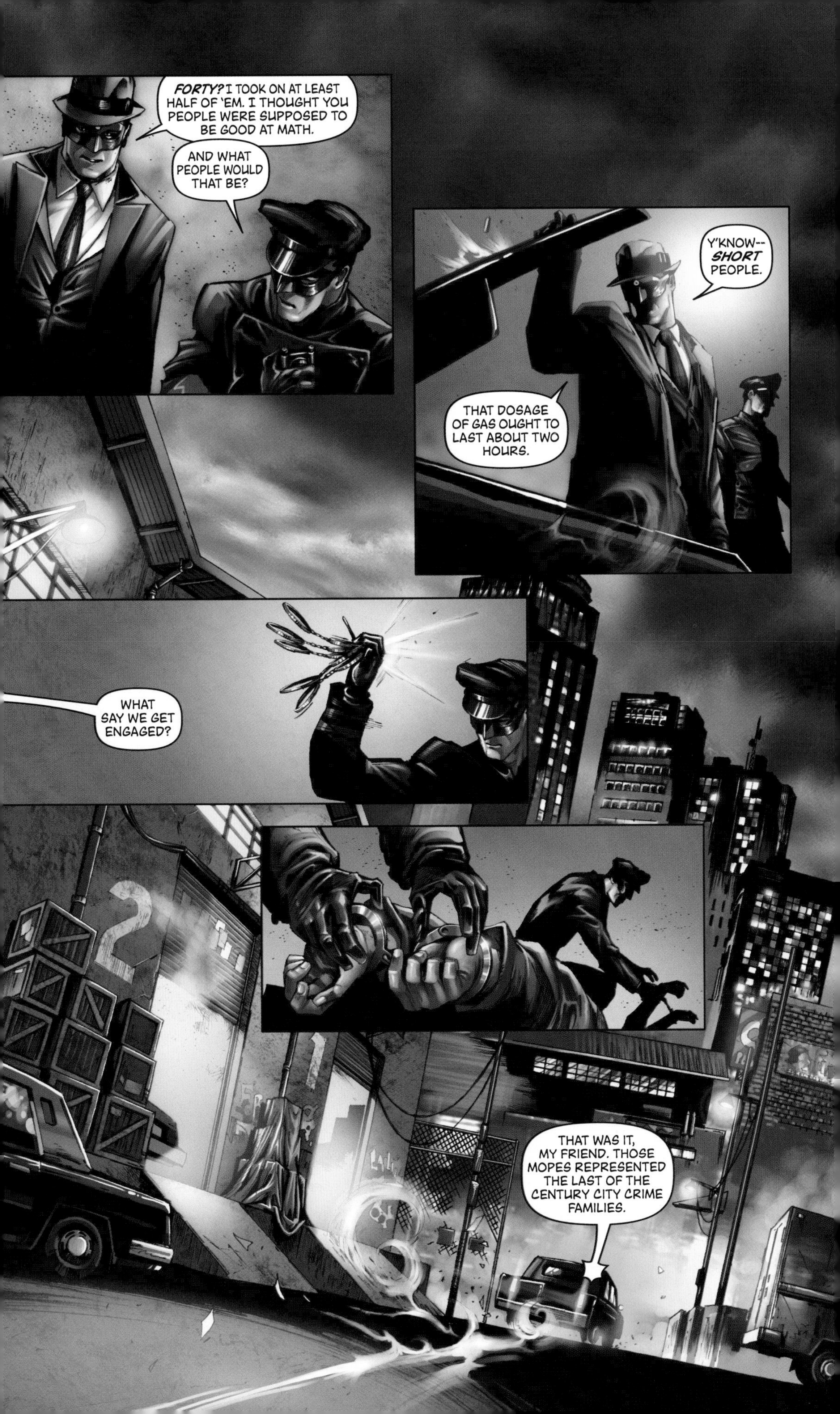

FORTY? I TOOK ON AT LEAST HALF OF 'EM. I THOUGHT YOU PEOPLE WERE SUPPOSED TO BE GOOD AT MATH.
AND WHAT PEOPLE WOULD THAT BE?
Y'KNOW-- SHORT PEOPLE.
THAT DOSAGE OF GAS OUGHT TO LAST ABOUT TWO HOURS.
WHAT SAY WE GET ENGAGED?
THAT WAS IT, MY FRIEND. THOSE MOPES REPRESENTED THE LAST OF THE CENTURY CITY CRIME FAMILIES.

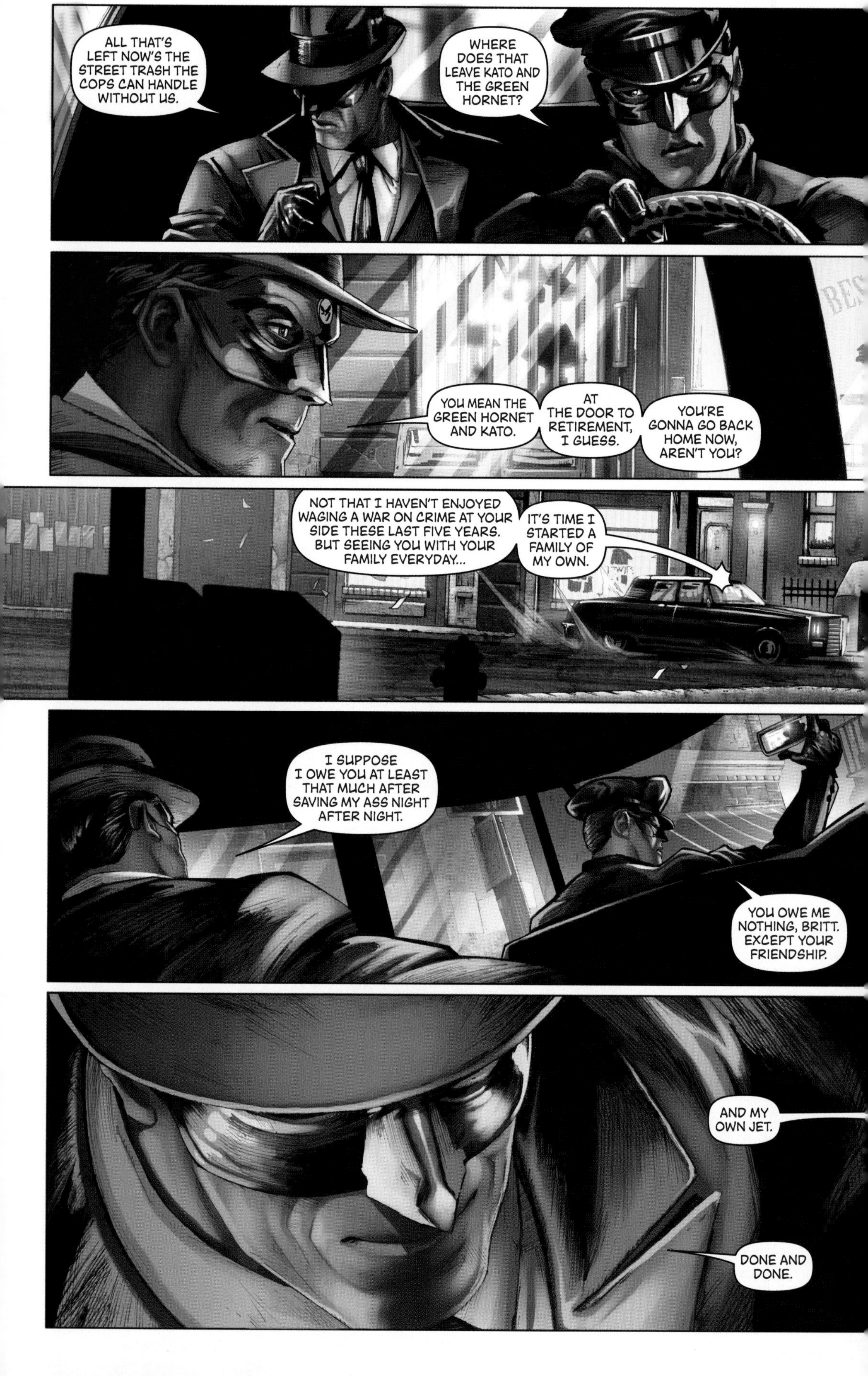
ALL THAT'S LEFT NOW'S THE STREET TRASH THE COPS CAN HANDLE WITHOUT US.
WHERE DOES THAT LEAVE KATO AND THE GREEN HORNET?
YOU MEAN THE GREEN HORNET AND KATO.
AT THE DOOR TO RETIREMENT, I GUESS.
YOU'RE GONNA GO BACK HOME NOW, AREN'T YOU?
NOT THAT I HAVEN'T ENJOYED WAGING A WAR ON CRIME AT YOUR SIDE THESE LAST FIVE YEARS. BUT SEEING YOU WITH YOUR FAMILY EVERYDAY...
IT'S TIME I STARTED A FAMILY OF MY OWN.
I SUPPOSE I OWE YOU AT LEAST THAT MUCH AFTER SAVING MY ASS NIGHT AFTER NIGHT.
YOU OWE ME NOTHING, BRITT. EXCEPT YOUR FRIENDSHIP.
AND MY OWN JET.
DONE AND DONE.

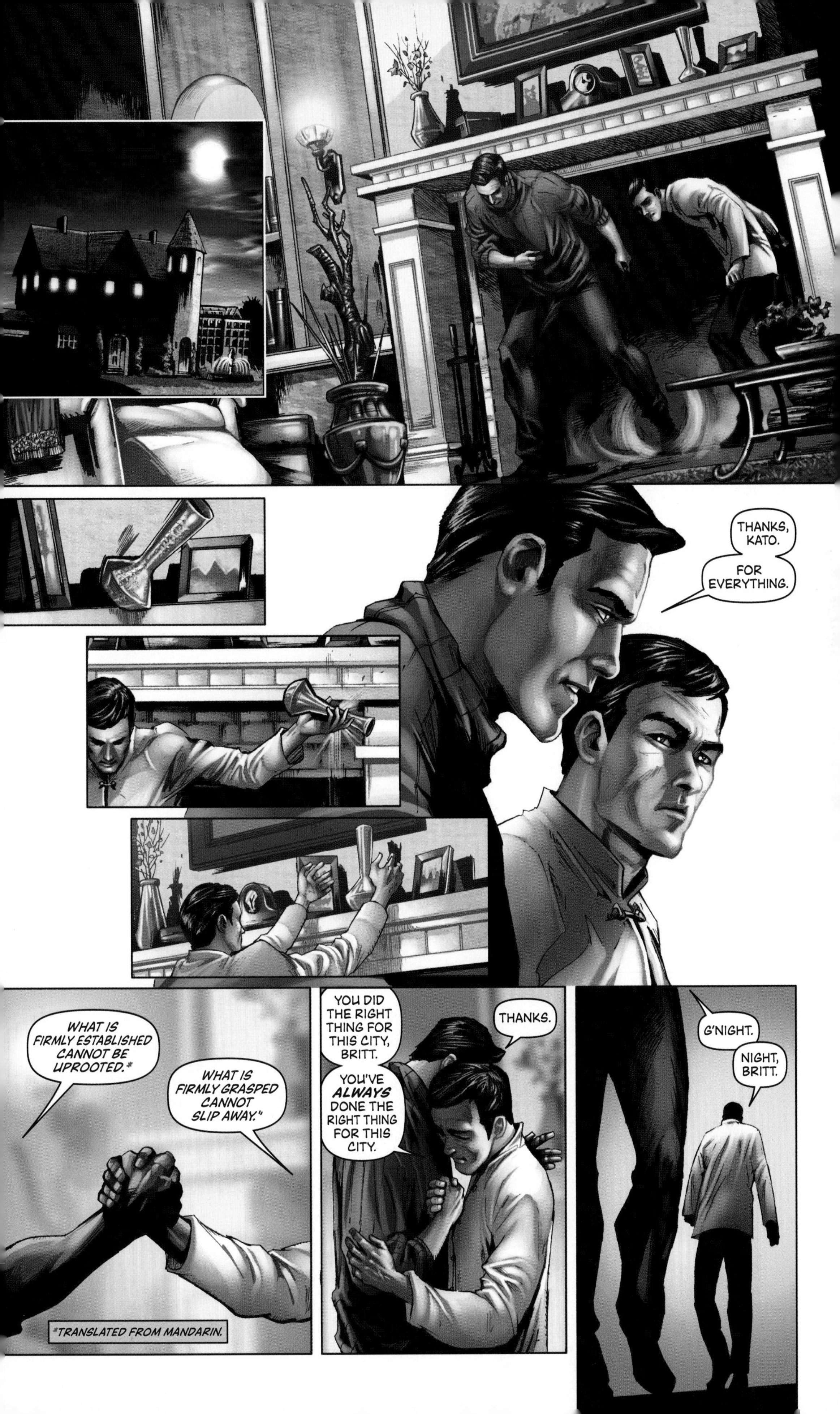
THANKS, KATO.
FOR EVERYTHING.
WHAT IS FIRMLY ESTABLISHED CANNOT BE UPROOTED.*
WHAT IS FIRMLY GRASPED CANNOT SLIP AWAY."
*TRANSLATED FROM MANDARIN.
YOU DID THE RIGHT THING FOR THIS CITY, BRITT.
YOU'VE ALWAYS DONE THE RIGHT THING FOR THIS CITY.
THANKS.
G'NIGHT.
NIGHT, BRITT.

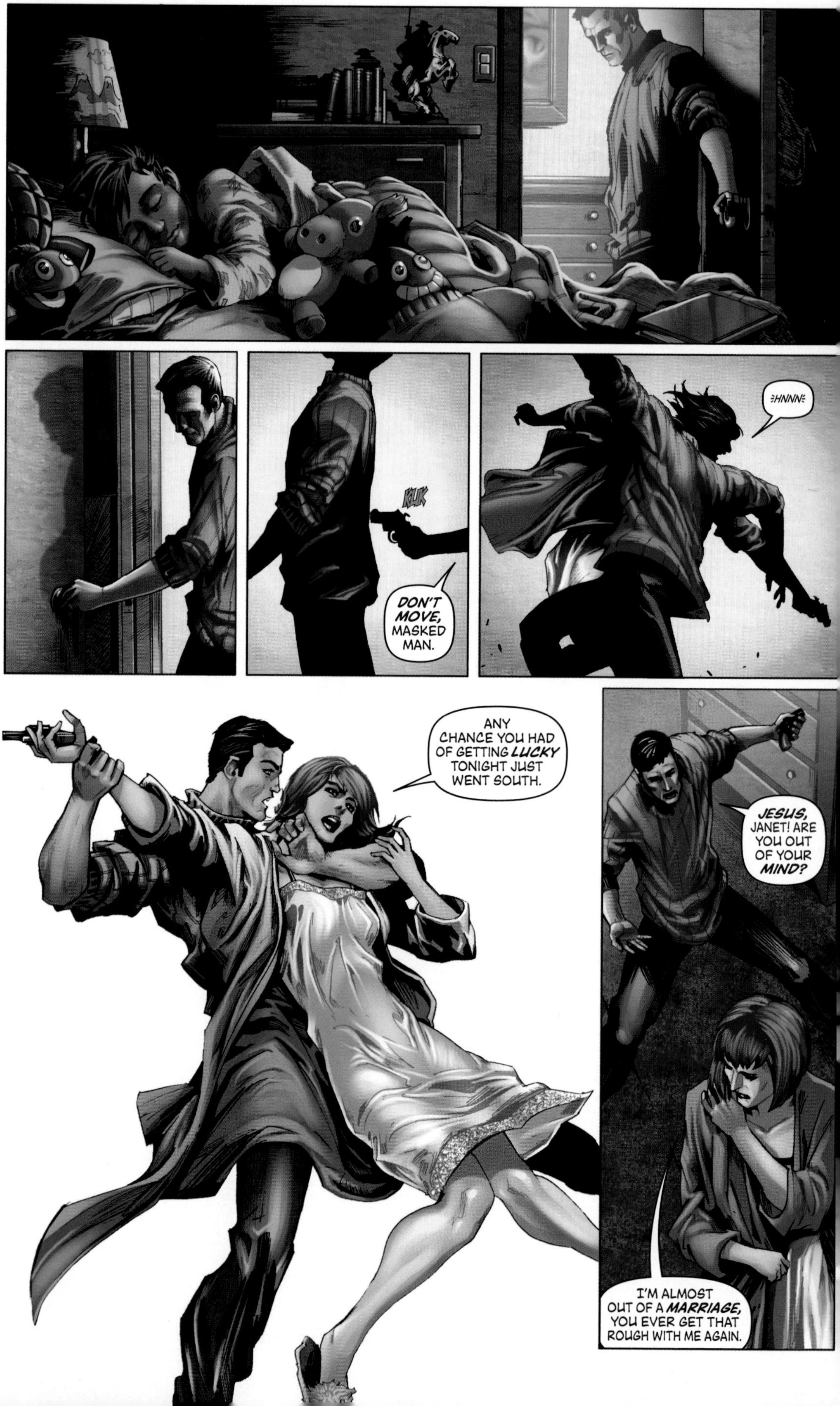
KLIK
DON'T MOVE, MASKED MAN.
HNNN
ANY CHANCE YOU HAD OF GETTING LUCKY TONIGHT JUST WENT SOUTH.
JESUS, JANET! ARE YOU OUT OF YOUR MIND?
I'M ALMOST OUT OF A MARRIAGE, YOU EVER GET THAT ROUGH WITH ME AGAIN.

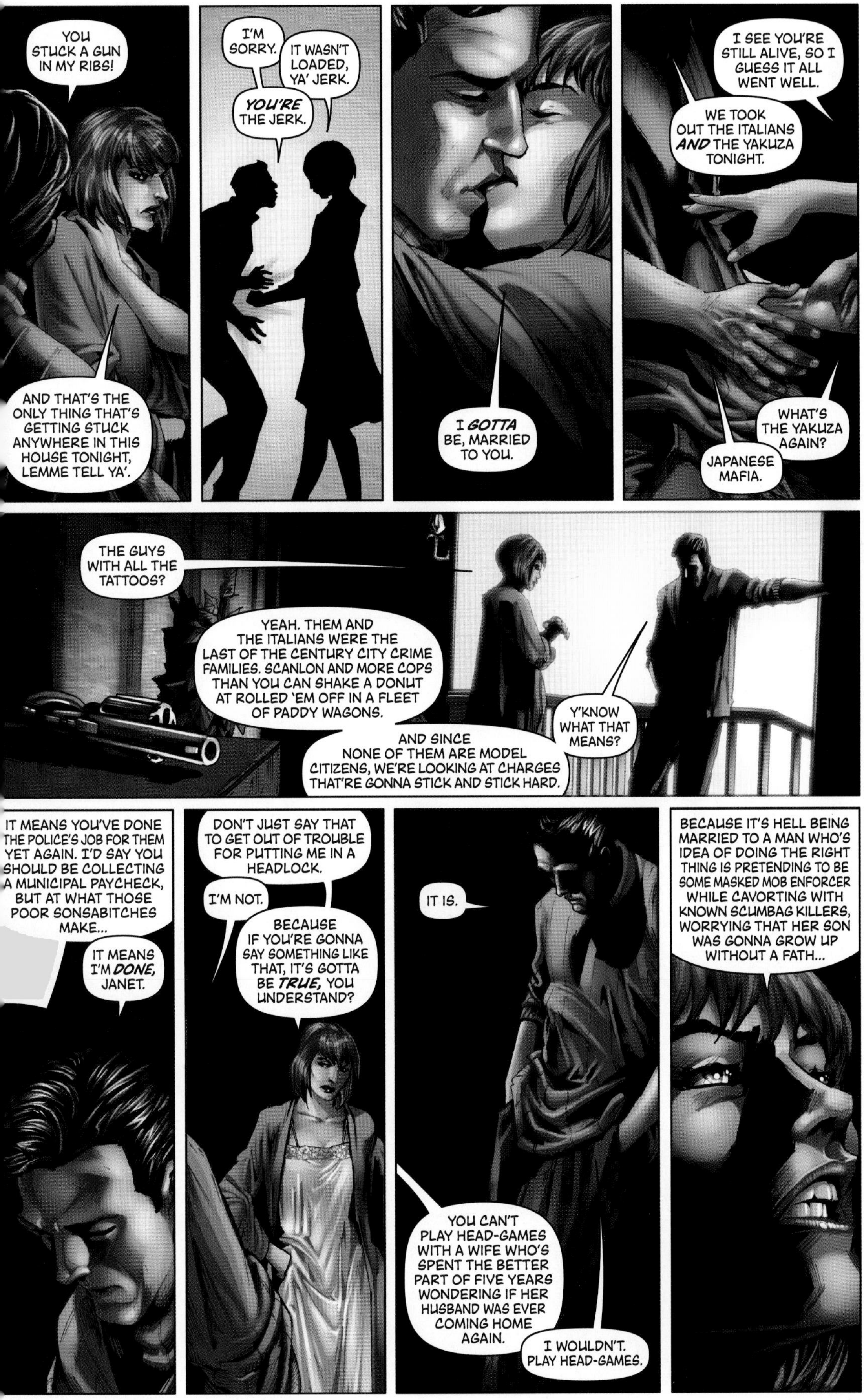
YOU STUCK A GUN IN MY RIBS!
AND THAT'S THE ONLY THING THAT'S GETTING STUCK ANYWHERE IN THIS HOUSE TONIGHT, LEMME TELL YA'.
I'M SORRY.
IT WASN'T LOADED, YA' JERK.
YOU'RE THE JERK.
I GOTTA BE, MARRIED TO YOU.
I SEE YOU'RE STILL ALIVE, SO I GUESS IT ALL WENT WELL.
WE TOOK OUT THE ITALIANS AND THE YAKUZA TONIGHT.
WHAT'S THE YAKUZA AGAIN?
JAPANESE MAFIA.
THE GUYS WITH ALL THE TATTOOS?
YEAH. THEM AND THE ITALIANS WERE THE LAST OF THE CENTURY CITY CRIME FAMILIES. SCANLON AND MORE COPS THAN YOU CAN SHAKE A DONUT AT ROLLED 'EM OFF IN A FLEET OF PADDY WAGONS.
AND SINCE NONE OF THEM ARE MODEL CITIZENS, WE'RE LOOKING AT CHARGES THAT'RE GONNA STICK AND STICK HARD.
Y'KNOW WHAT THAT MEANS?
IT MEANS YOU'VE DONE THE POLICE'S JOB FOR THEM YET AGAIN. I'D SAY YOU SHOULD BE COLLECTING A MUNICIPAL PAYCHECK, BUT AT WHAT THOSE POOR SONSABITCHES MAKE...
IT MEANS I'M DONE, JANET.
DON'T JUST SAY THAT TO GET OUT OF TROUBLE FOR PUTTING ME IN A HEADLOCK.
I'M NOT.
BECAUSE IF YOU'RE GONNA SAY SOMETHING LIKE THAT, IT'S GOTTA BE TRUE, YOU UNDERSTAND?
IT IS.
YOU CAN'T PLAY HEAD-GAMES WITH A WIFE WHO'S SPENT THE BETTER PART OF FIVE YEARS WONDERING IF HER HUSBAND WAS EVER COMING HOME AGAIN.
I WOULDN'T. PLAY HEAD-GAMES.
BECAUSE IT'S HELL BEING MARRIED TO A MAN WHO'S IDEA OF DOING THE RIGHT THING IS PRETENDING TO BE SOME MASKED MOB ENFORCER WHILE CAVORTING WITH KNOWN SCUMBAG KILLERS, WORRYING THAT HER SON WAS GONNA GROW UP WITHOUT A FATH...

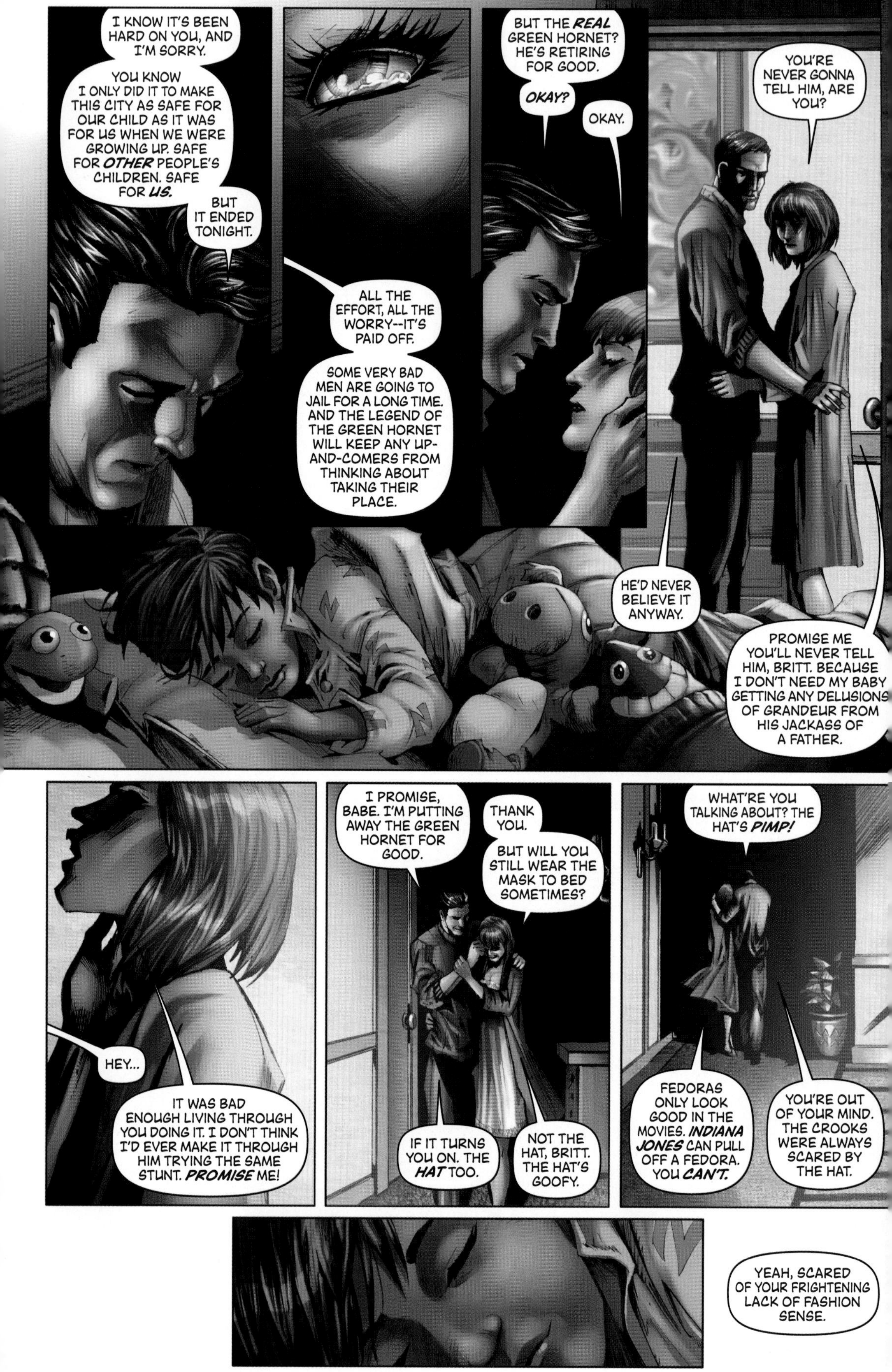
I KNOW IT'S BEEN HARD ON YOU, AND I'M SORRY.
YOU KNOW I ONLY DID IT TO MAKE THIS CITY AS SAFE FOR OUR CHILD AS IT WAS FOR US WHEN WE WERE GROWING UP. SAFE FOR *OTHER* PEOPLE'S CHILDREN. SAFE FOR *US.*
BUT IT ENDED TONIGHT.
ALL THE EFFORT, ALL THE WORRY--IT'S PAID OFF.
SOME VERY BAD MEN ARE GOING TO JAIL FOR A LONG TIME. AND THE LEGEND OF THE GREEN HORNET WILL KEEP ANY UP-AND-COMERS FROM THINKING ABOUT TAKING THEIR PLACE.
BUT THE *REAL* GREEN HORNET? HE'S RETIRING FOR GOOD.
OKAY?
OKAY.
YOU'RE NEVER GONNA TELL HIM, ARE YOU?
HE'D NEVER BELIEVE IT ANYWAY.
PROMISE ME YOU'LL NEVER TELL HIM, BRITT. BECAUSE I DON'T NEED MY BABY GETTING ANY DELUSIONS OF GRANDEUR FROM HIS JACKASS OF A FATHER.
HEY...
IT WAS BAD ENOUGH LIVING THROUGH YOU DOING IT. I DON'T THINK I'D EVER MAKE IT THROUGH HIM TRYING THE SAME STUNT. *PROMISE* ME!
I PROMISE, BABE. I'M PUTTING AWAY THE GREEN HORNET FOR GOOD.
THANK YOU.
BUT WILL YOU STILL WEAR THE MASK TO BED SOMETIMES?
IF IT TURNS YOU ON. THE *HAT* TOO.
NOT THE HAT, BRITT. THE HAT'S GOOFY.
WHAT'RE YOU TALKING ABOUT? THE HAT'S *PIMP!*
FEDORAS ONLY LOOK GOOD IN THE MOVIES. *INDIANA JONES* CAN PULL OFF A FEDORA. YOU *CAN'T.*
YOU'RE OUT OF YOUR MIND. THE CROOKS WERE ALWAYS SCARED BY THE HAT.
YEAH, SCARED OF YOUR FRIGHTENING LACK OF FASHION SENSE.

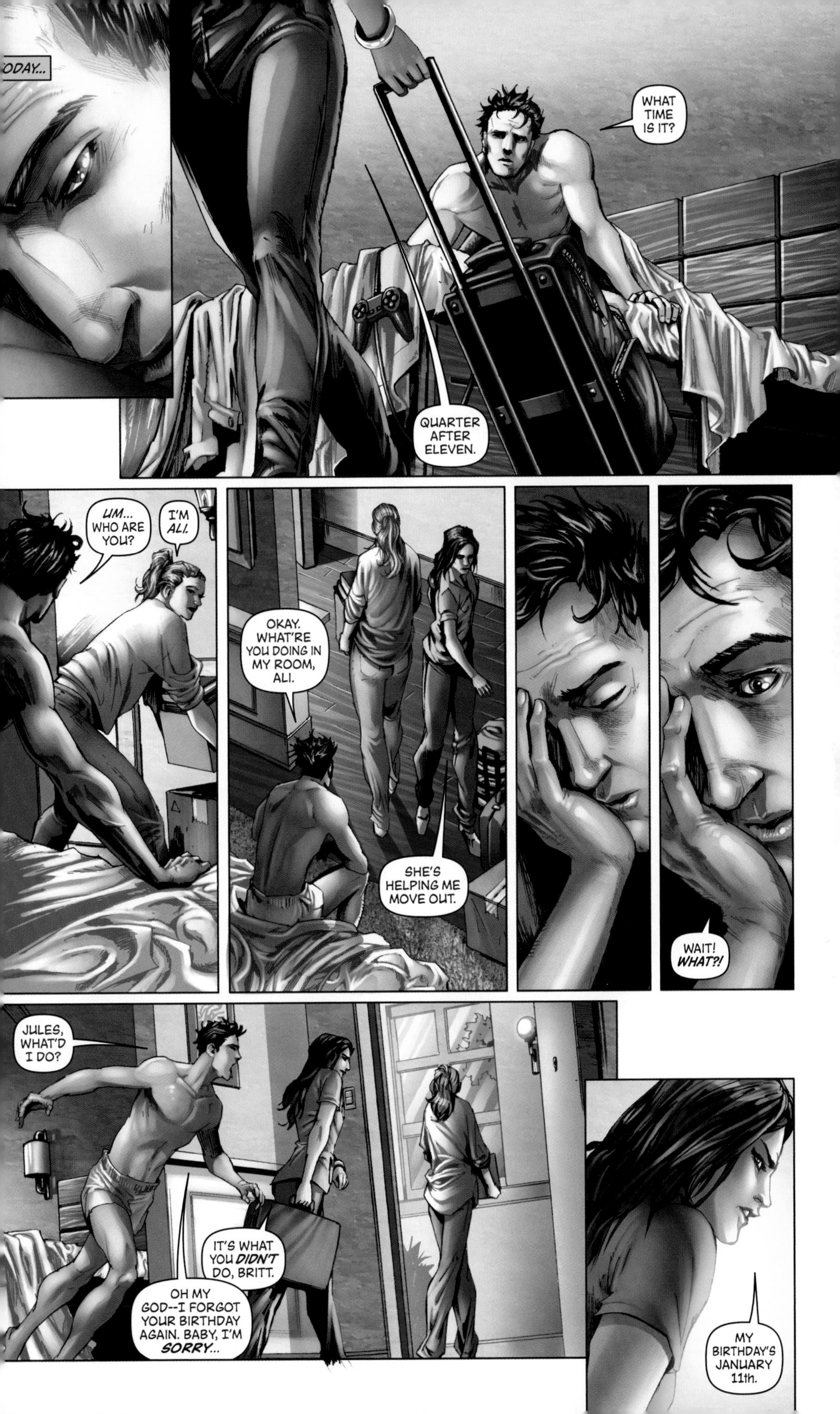
ODAY...
WHAT TIME IS IT?
QUARTER AFTER ELEVEN.
UM... WHO ARE YOU?
I'M ALI.
OKAY. WHAT'RE YOU DOING IN MY ROOM, ALI.
SHE'S HELPING ME MOVE OUT.
WAIT! WHAT?!
JULES, WHAT'D I DO?
IT'S WHAT YOU DIDN'T DO, BRITT.
OH MY GOD--I FORGOT YOUR BIRTHDAY AGAIN. BABY, I'M SORRY...
MY BIRTHDAY'S JANUARY 11th.

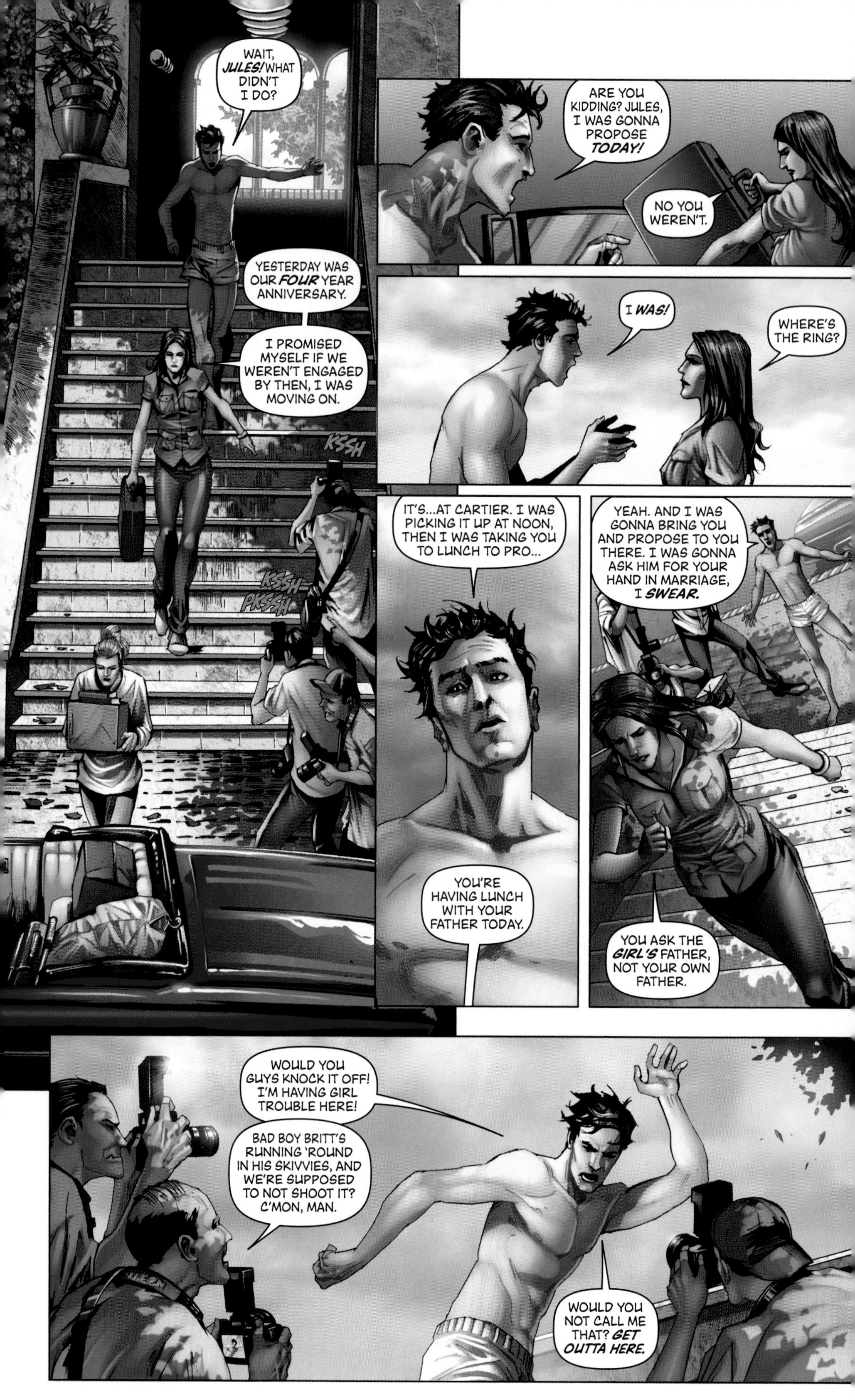
WAIT, JULES! WHAT DIDN'T I DO?
YESTERDAY WAS OUR FOUR YEAR ANNIVERSARY.
I PROMISED MYSELF IF WE WEREN'T ENGAGED BY THEN, I WAS MOVING ON.
KSSH
KSSH
PKSSH
ARE YOU KIDDING? JULES, I WAS GONNA PROPOSE TODAY!
NO YOU WEREN'T.
I WAS!
WHERE'S THE RING?
IT'S...AT CARTIER. I WAS PICKING IT UP AT NOON, THEN I WAS TAKING YOU TO LUNCH TO PRO...
YOU'RE HAVING LUNCH WITH YOUR FATHER TODAY.
YEAH. AND I WAS GONNA BRING YOU AND PROPOSE TO YOU THERE. I WAS GONNA ASK HIM FOR YOUR HAND IN MARRIAGE, I SWEAR.
YOU ASK THE GIRL'S FATHER, NOT YOUR OWN FATHER.
WOULD YOU GUYS KNOCK IT OFF! I'M HAVING GIRL TROUBLE HERE!
BAD BOY BRITT'S RUNNING 'ROUND IN HIS SKIVVIES, AND WE'RE SUPPOSED TO NOT SHOOT IT? C'MON, MAN.
WOULD YOU NOT CALL ME THAT? GET OUTTA HERE.

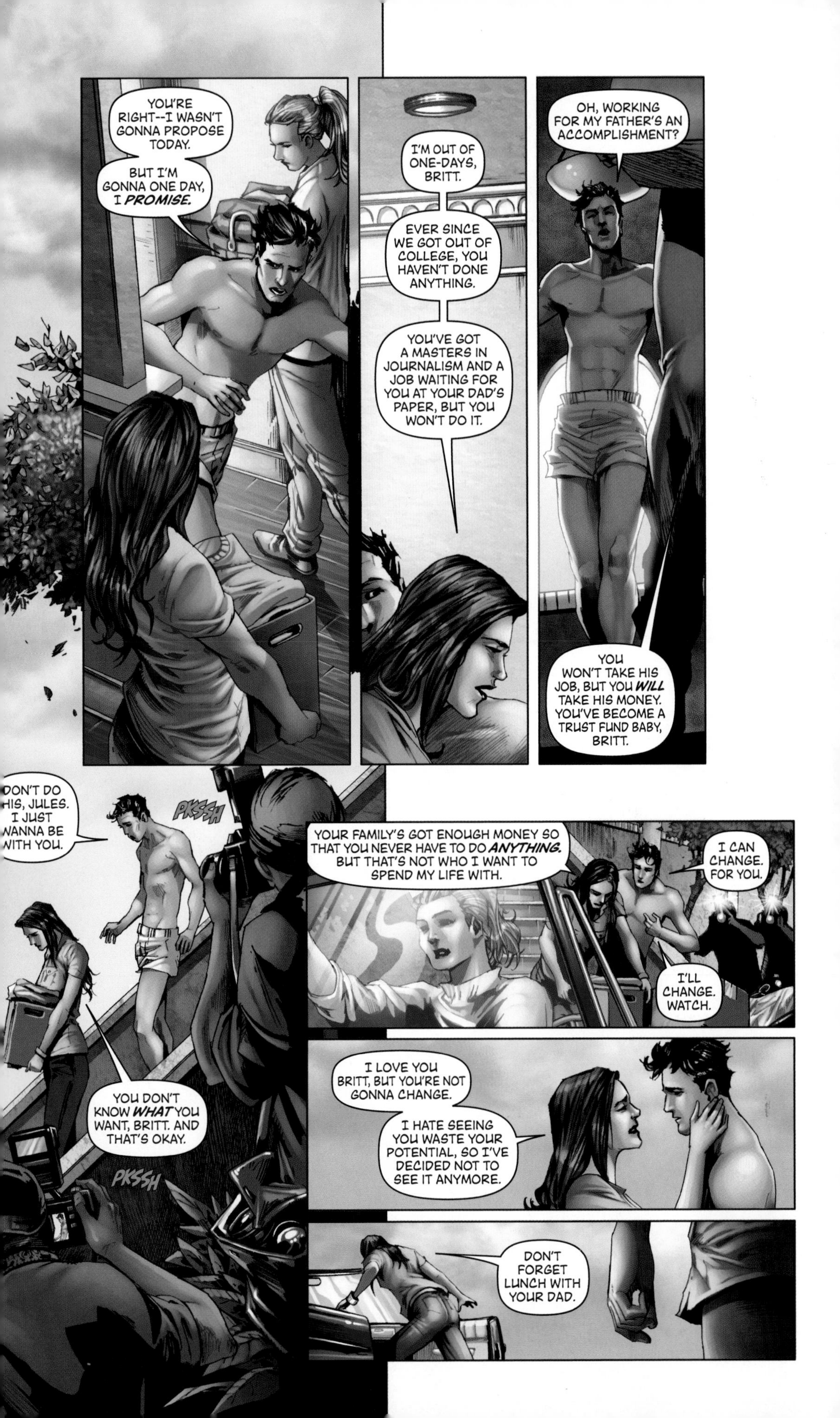
YOU'RE RIGHT--I WASN'T GONNA PROPOSE TODAY.
BUT I'M GONNA ONE DAY, I *PROMISE.*
I'M OUT OF ONE-DAYS, BRITT.
EVER SINCE WE GOT OUT OF COLLEGE, YOU HAVEN'T DONE ANYTHING.
YOU'VE GOT A MASTERS IN JOURNALISM AND A JOB WAITING FOR YOU AT YOUR DAD'S PAPER, BUT YOU WON'T DO IT.
OH, WORKING FOR MY FATHER'S AN ACCOMPLISHMENT?
YOU WON'T TAKE HIS JOB, BUT YOU *WILL* TAKE HIS MONEY. YOU'VE BECOME A TRUST FUND BABY, BRITT.
DON'T DO HIS, JULES. I JUST WANNA BE WITH YOU.
PKSSH
YOU DON'T KNOW *WHAT* YOU WANT, BRITT. AND THAT'S OKAY.
PKSSH
YOUR FAMILY'S GOT ENOUGH MONEY SO THAT YOU NEVER HAVE TO DO *ANYTHING.* BUT THAT'S NOT WHO I WANT TO SPEND MY LIFE WITH.
I CAN CHANGE. FOR YOU.
I'LL CHANGE. WATCH.
I LOVE YOU BRITT, BUT YOU'RE NOT GONNA CHANGE.
I HATE SEEING YOU WASTE YOUR POTENTIAL, SO I'VE DECIDED NOT TO SEE IT ANYMORE.
DON'T FORGET LUNCH WITH YOUR DAD.

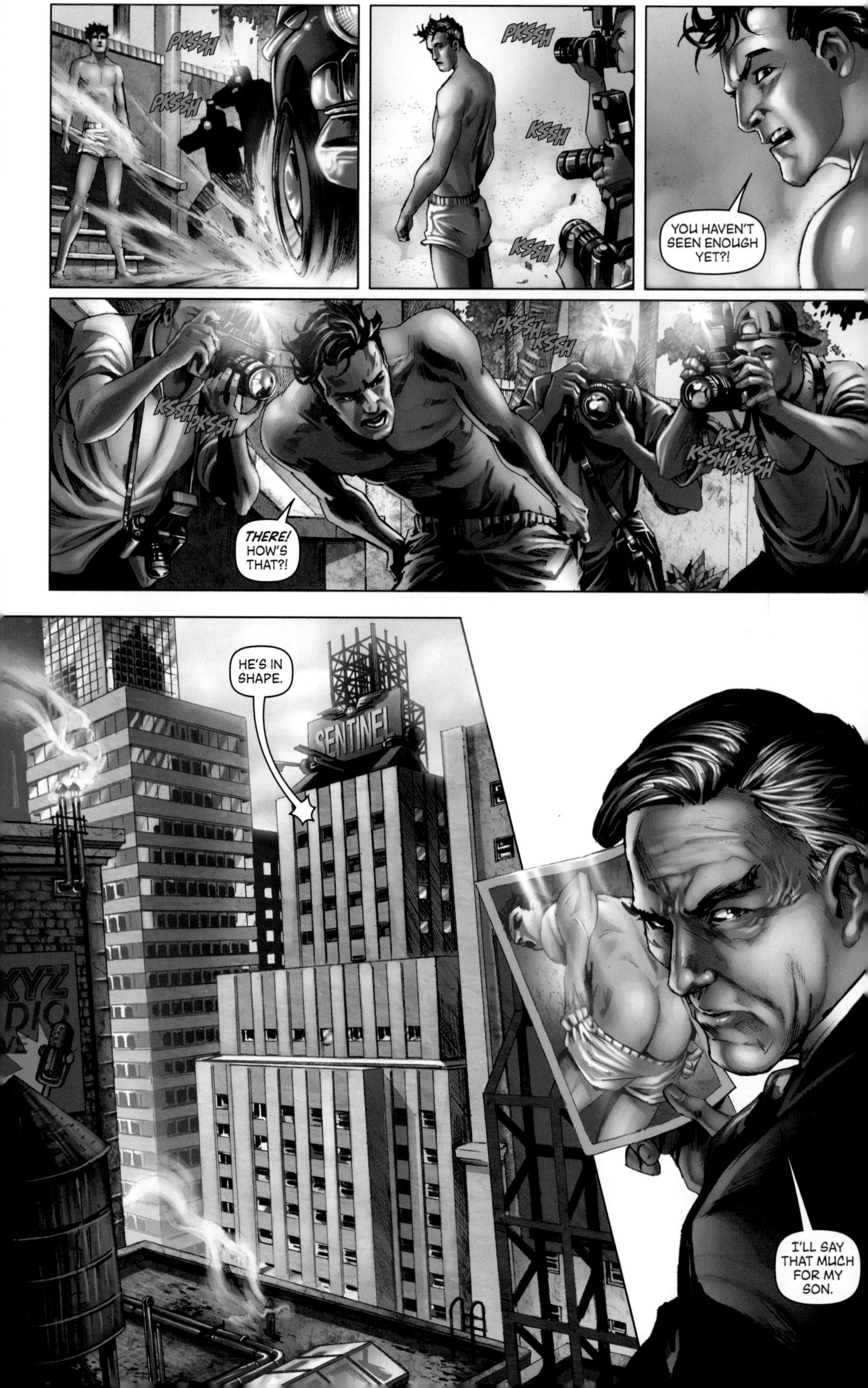
PKSSH
PKSSH
PKSSH
KSSH
KSSH
YOU HAVEN'T SEEN ENOUGH YET?!
KSSH PKSSH
PKSSH KSSH
KSSH KSSHPKSSH
THERE! HOW'S THAT?!
HE'S IN SHAPE.
SENTINEL
I'LL SAY THAT MUCH FOR MY SON.

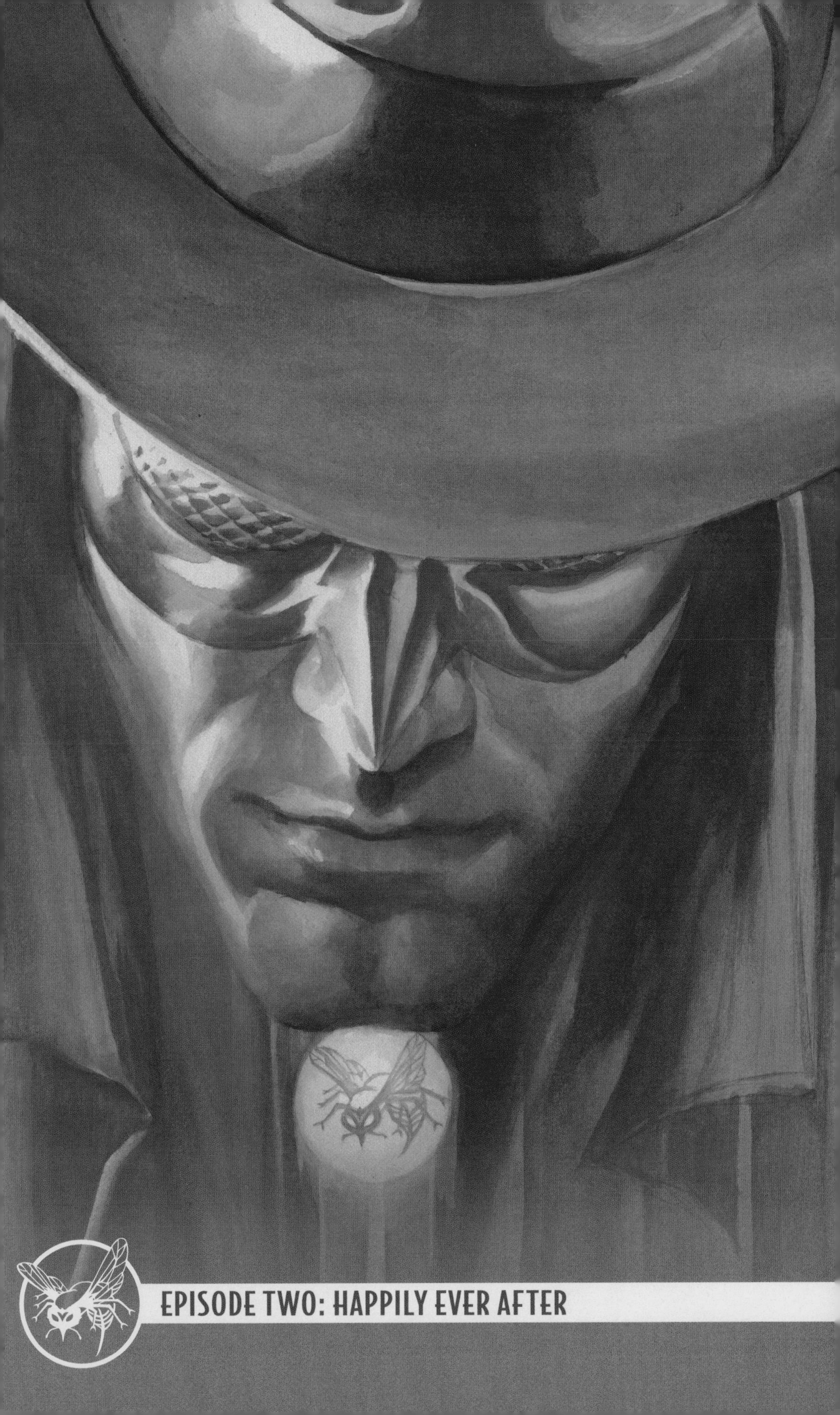

EPISODE TWO: HAPPILY EVER AFTER

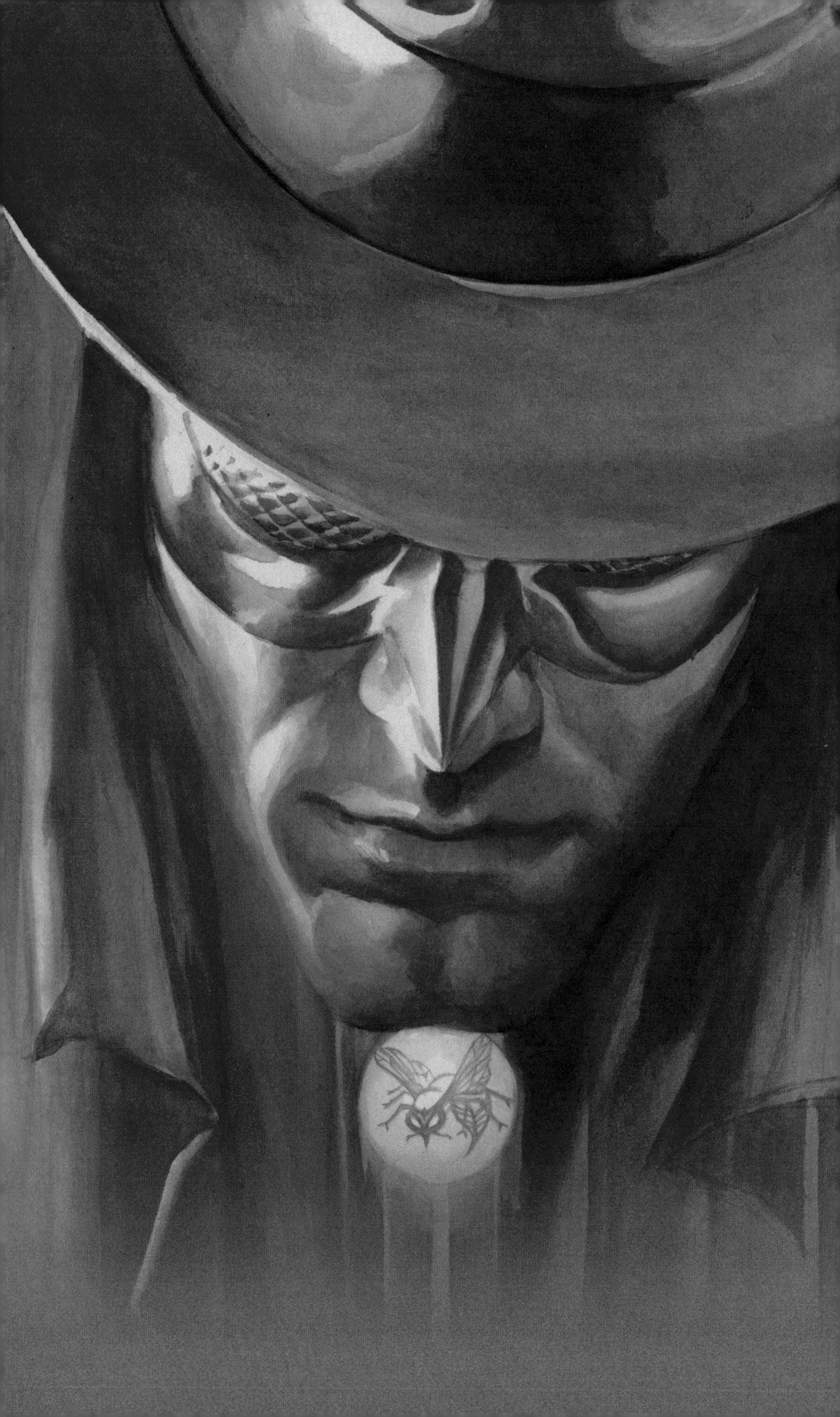

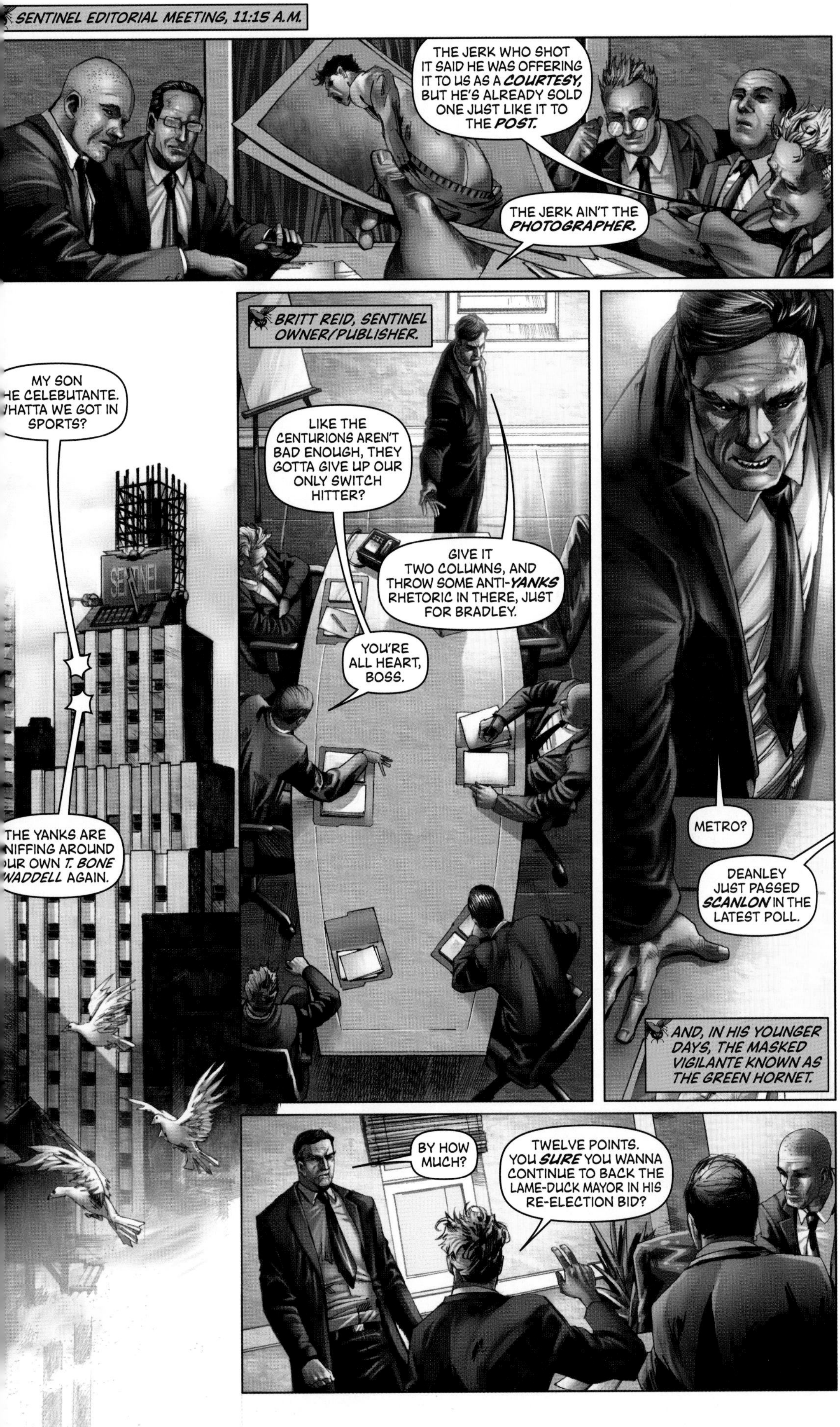
SENTINEL EDITORIAL MEETING, 11:15 A.M.
THE JERK WHO SHOT IT SAID HE WAS OFFERING IT TO US AS A *COURTESY*, BUT HE'S ALREADY SOLD ONE JUST LIKE IT TO THE *POST.*
THE JERK AIN'T THE *PHOTOGRAPHER.*
MY SON HE CELEBUTANTE. HATTA WE GOT IN SPORTS?
THE YANKS ARE NIFFING AROUND UR OWN *T. BONE WADDELL* AGAIN.
SENTINEL
BRITT REID, SENTINEL OWNER/PUBLISHER.
LIKE THE CENTURIONS AREN'T BAD ENOUGH, THEY GOTTA GIVE UP OUR ONLY SWITCH HITTER?
GIVE IT TWO COLUMNS, AND THROW SOME ANTI-*YANKS* RHETORIC IN THERE, JUST FOR BRADLEY.
YOU'RE ALL HEART, BOSS.
METRO?
DEANLEY JUST PASSED *SCANLON* IN THE LATEST POLL.
AND, IN HIS YOUNGER DAYS, THE MASKED VIGILANTE KNOWN AS THE GREEN HORNET.
BY HOW MUCH?
TWELVE POINTS. YOU *SURE* YOU WANNA CONTINUE TO BACK THE LAME-DUCK MAYOR IN HIS RE-ELECTION BID?

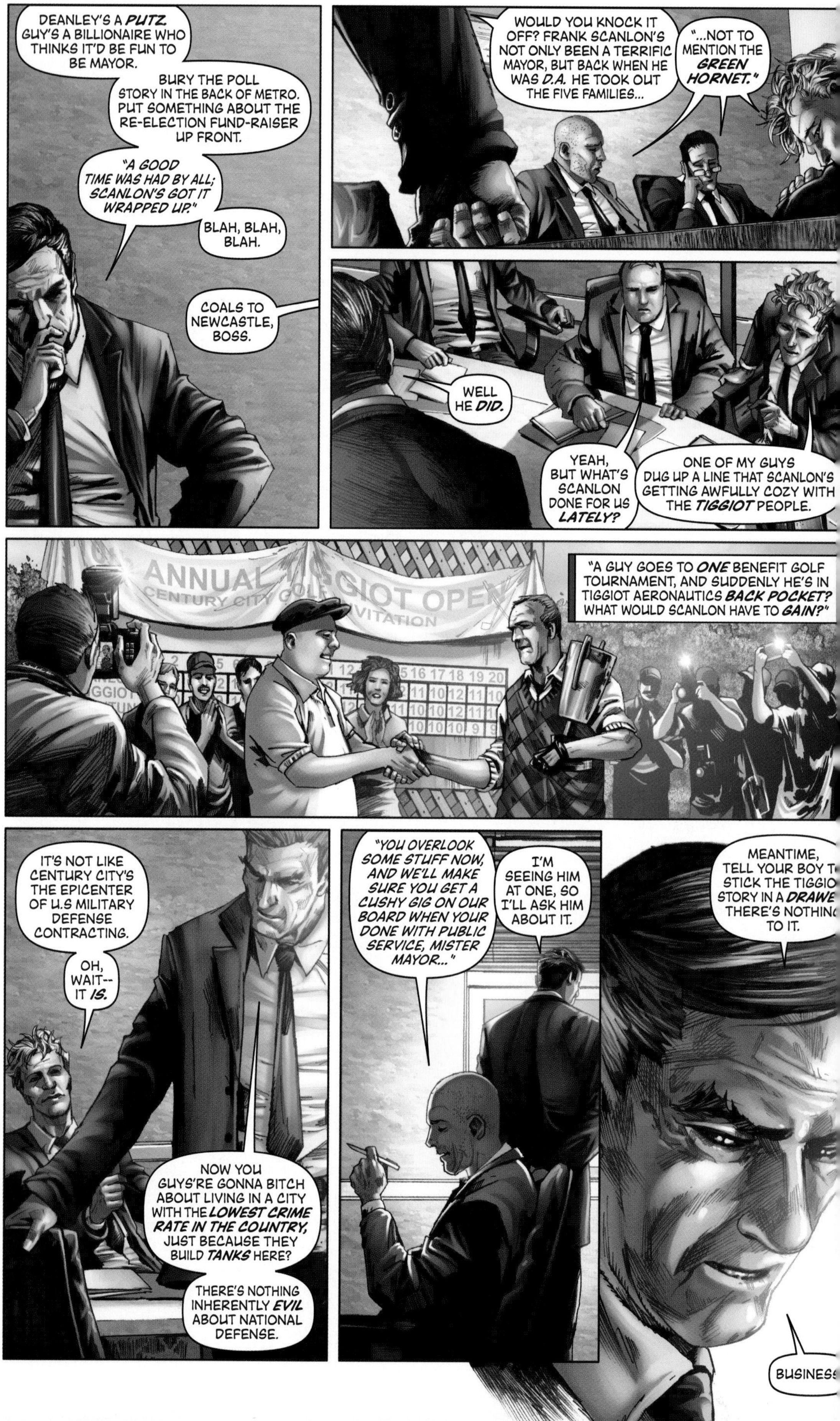
DEANLEY'S A *PUTZ.* GUY'S A BILLIONAIRE WHO THINKS IT'D BE FUN TO BE MAYOR.
BURY THE POLL STORY IN THE BACK OF METRO. PUT SOMETHING ABOUT THE RE-ELECTION FUND-RAISER UP FRONT.
"A GOOD TIME WAS HAD BY ALL; SCANLON'S GOT IT WRAPPED UP."
BLAH, BLAH, BLAH.
COALS TO NEWCASTLE, BOSS.
WOULD YOU KNOCK IT OFF? FRANK SCANLON'S NOT ONLY BEEN A TERRIFIC MAYOR, BUT BACK WHEN HE WAS *D.A.* HE TOOK OUT THE FIVE FAMILIES...
"...NOT TO MENTION THE *GREEN HORNET."*
WELL HE *DID.*
YEAH, BUT WHAT'S SCANLON DONE FOR US *LATELY?*
ONE OF MY GUYS DUG UP A LINE THAT SCANLON'S GETTING AWFULLY COZY WITH THE *TIGGIOT* PEOPLE.
ANNUAL TIGGIOT OPEN
CENTURY CITY GOLF INVITATION
"A GUY GOES TO *ONE* BENEFIT GOLF TOURNAMENT, AND SUDDENLY HE'S IN TIGGIOT AERONAUTICS *BACK POCKET?* WHAT WOULD SCANLON HAVE TO *GAIN?"*
IT'S NOT LIKE CENTURY CITY'S THE EPICENTER OF U.S MILITARY DEFENSE CONTRACTING.
OH, WAIT-- IT *IS.*
NOW YOU GUYS'RE GONNA BITCH ABOUT LIVING IN A CITY WITH THE *LOWEST CRIME RATE IN THE COUNTRY,* JUST BECAUSE THEY BUILD *TANKS* HERE?
THERE'S NOTHING INHERENTLY *EVIL* ABOUT NATIONAL DEFENSE.
"YOU OVERLOOK SOME STUFF NOW, AND WE'LL MAKE SURE YOU GET A CUSHY GIG ON OUR BOARD WHEN YOUR DONE WITH PUBLIC SERVICE, MISTER MAYOR..."
I'M SEEING HIM AT ONE, SO I'LL ASK HIM ABOUT IT.
MEANTIME, TELL YOUR BOY T STICK THE TIGGIO STORY IN A *DRAWE* THERE'S NOTHIN TO IT.
BUSINES

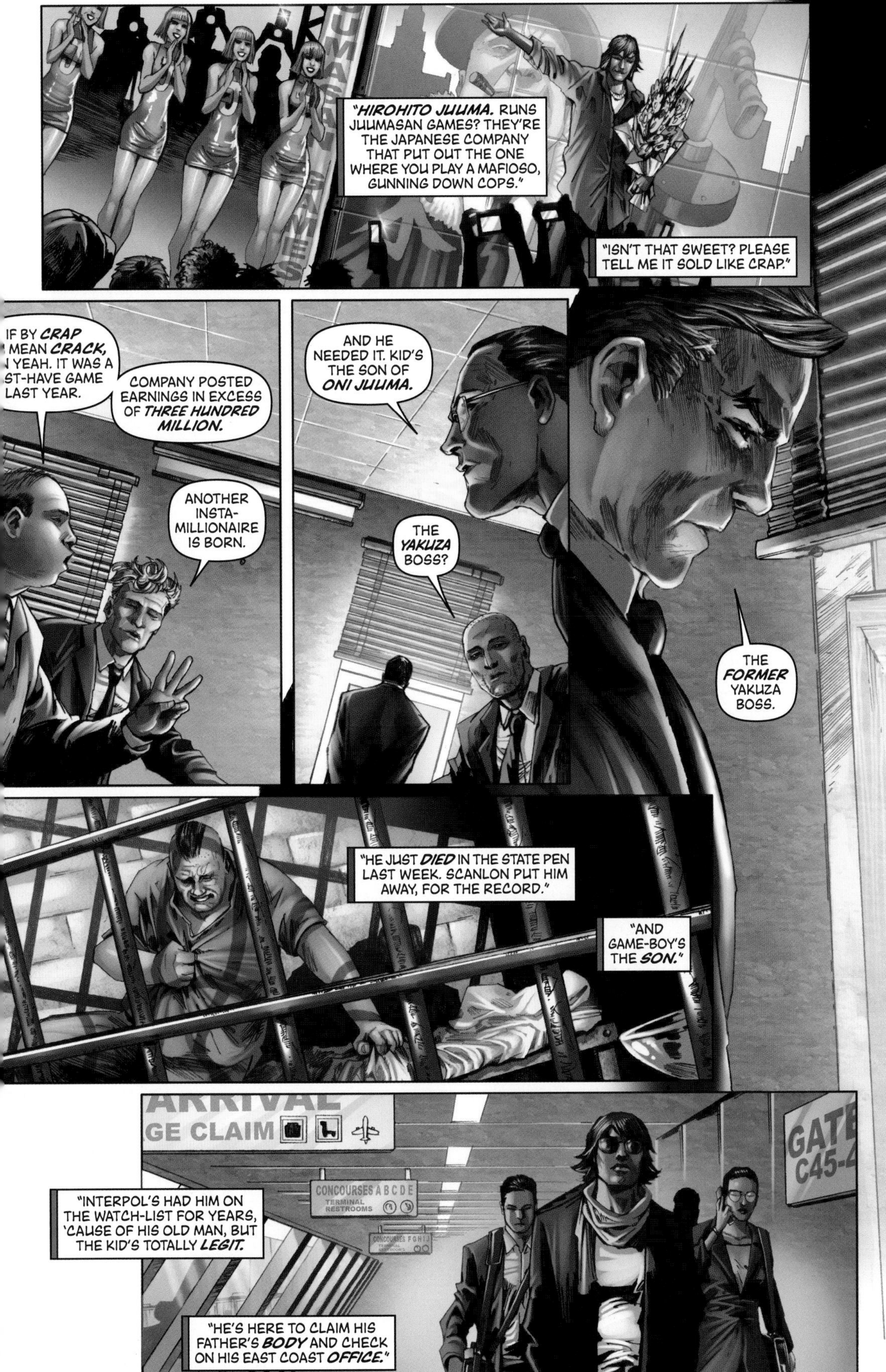
"HIROHITO JUUMA. RUNS JUUMASAN GAMES? THEY'RE THE JAPANESE COMPANY THAT PUT OUT THE ONE WHERE YOU PLAY A MAFIOSO, GUNNING DOWN COPS."
"ISN'T THAT SWEET? PLEASE TELL ME IT SOLD LIKE CRAP."
IF BY CRAP MEAN CRACK, N YEAH. IT WAS A ST-HAVE GAME LAST YEAR.
COMPANY POSTED EARNINGS IN EXCESS OF THREE HUNDRED MILLION.
ANOTHER INSTA-MILLIONAIRE IS BORN.
AND HE NEEDED IT. KID'S THE SON OF ONI JUUMA.
THE YAKUZA BOSS?
THE FORMER YAKUZA BOSS.
"HE JUST DIED IN THE STATE PEN LAST WEEK. SCANLON PUT HIM AWAY, FOR THE RECORD."
"AND GAME-BOY'S THE SON."
GE CLAIM
CONCOURSES A B C D E
TERMINAL RESTROOMS
GATE C45-4
"INTERPOL'S HAD HIM ON THE WATCH-LIST FOR YEARS, 'CAUSE OF HIS OLD MAN, BUT THE KID'S TOTALLY LEGIT.
"HE'S HERE TO CLAIM HIS FATHER'S BODY AND CHECK ON HIS EAST COAST OFFICE."

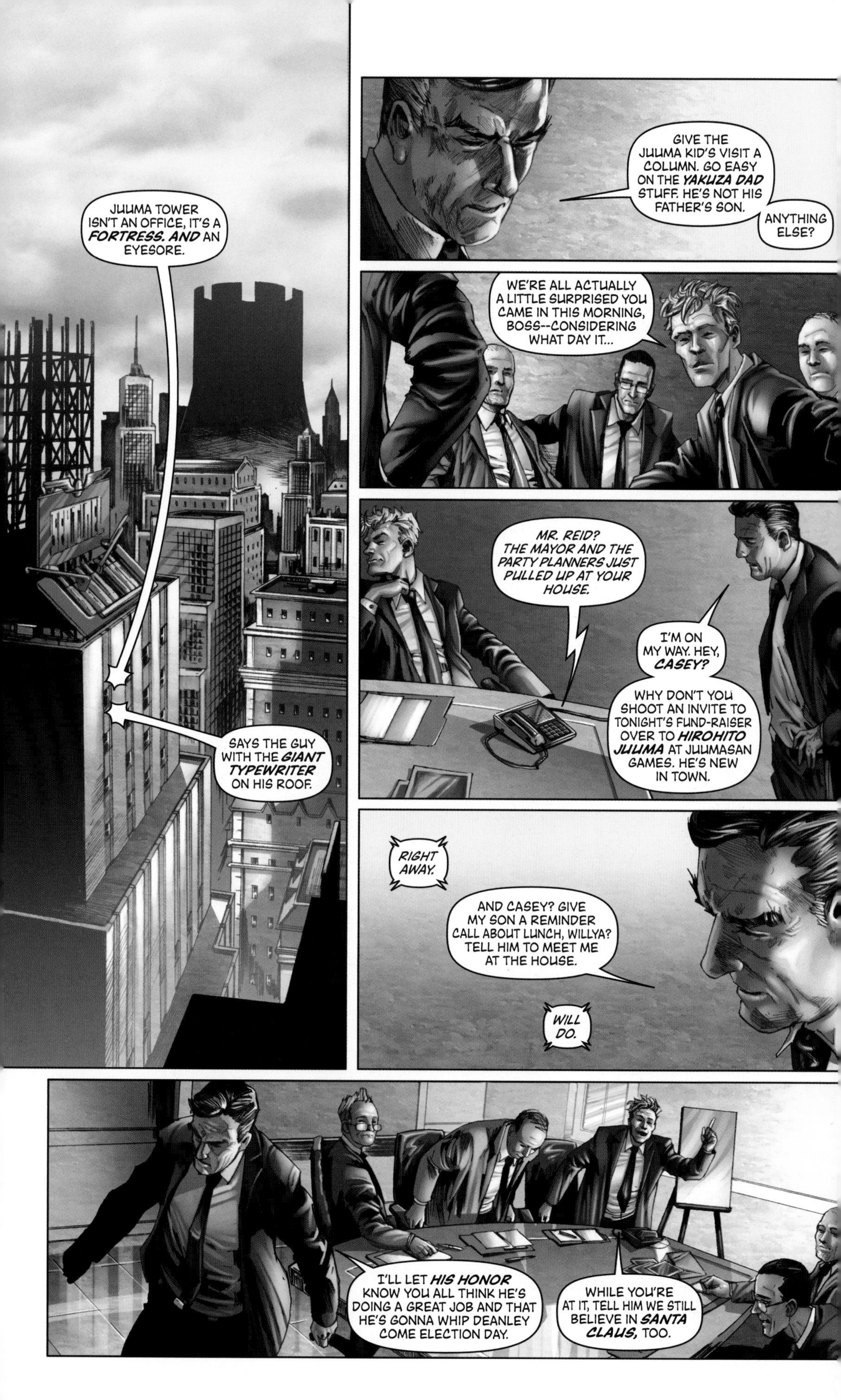
JUUMA TOWER ISN'T AN OFFICE, IT'S A FORTRESS. AND AN EYESORE.
SAYS THE GUY WITH THE GIANT TYPEWRITER ON HIS ROOF.
GIVE THE JUUMA KID'S VISIT A COLUMN. GO EASY ON THE YAKUZA DAD STUFF. HE'S NOT HIS FATHER'S SON.
ANYTHING ELSE?
WE'RE ALL ACTUALLY A LITTLE SURPRISED YOU CAME IN THIS MORNING, BOSS--CONSIDERING WHAT DAY IT...
MR. REID? THE MAYOR AND THE PARTY PLANNERS JUST PULLED UP AT YOUR HOUSE.
I'M ON MY WAY. HEY, CASEY?
WHY DON'T YOU SHOOT AN INVITE TO TONIGHT'S FUND-RAISER OVER TO HIROHITO JUUMA AT JUUMASAN GAMES. HE'S NEW IN TOWN.
RIGHT AWAY.
AND CASEY? GIVE MY SON A REMINDER CALL ABOUT LUNCH, WILLYA? TELL HIM TO MEET ME AT THE HOUSE.
WILL DO.
I'LL LET HIS HONOR KNOW YOU ALL THINK HE'S DOING A GREAT JOB AND THAT HE'S GONNA WHIP DEANLEY COME ELECTION DAY.
WHILE YOU'RE AT IT, TELL HIM WE STILL BELIEVE IN SANTA CLAUS, TOO.

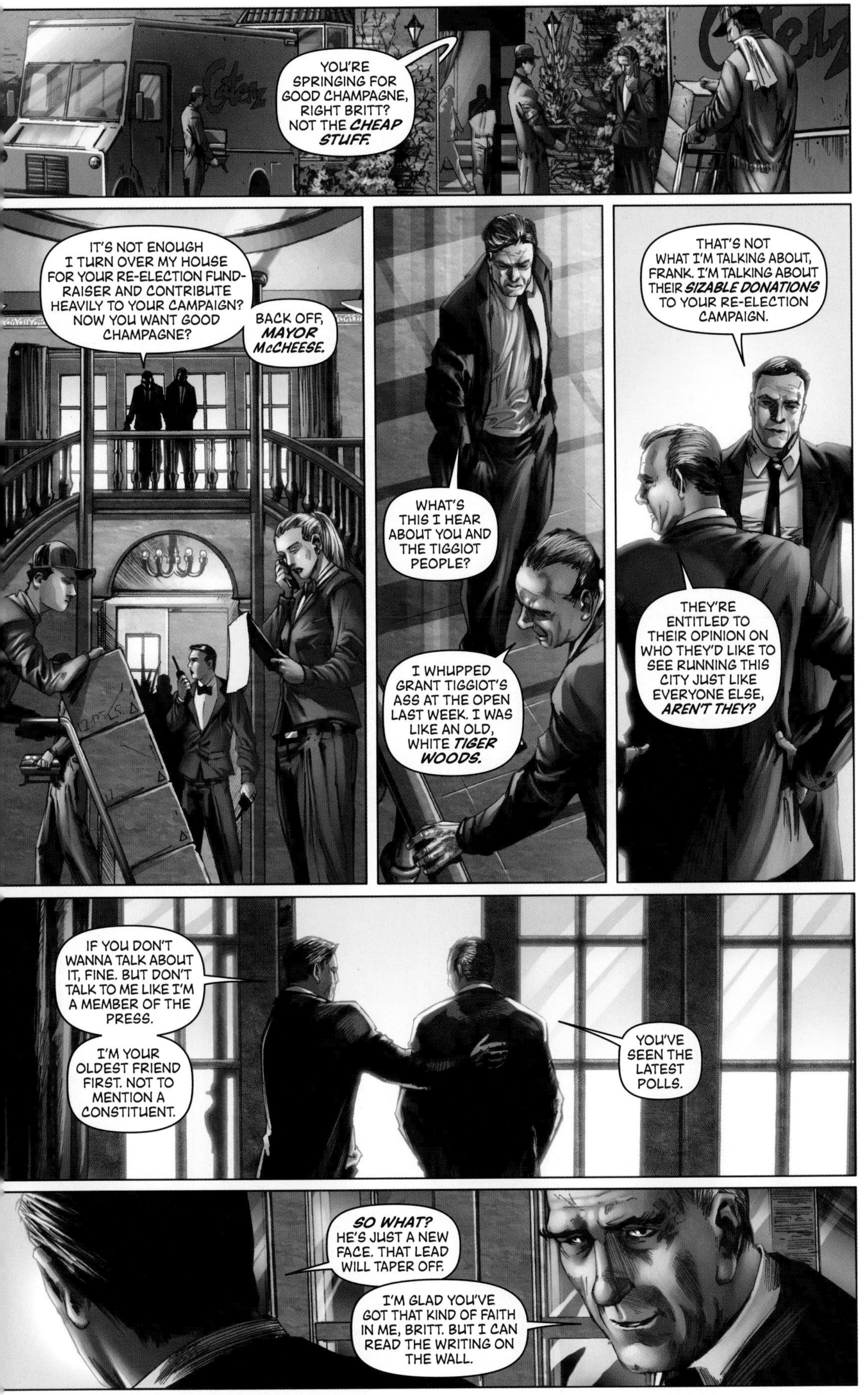

YOU'RE SPRINGING FOR GOOD CHAMPAGNE, RIGHT BRITT? NOT THE CHEAP STUFF.
IT'S NOT ENOUGH I TURN OVER MY HOUSE FOR YOUR RE-ELECTION FUND-RAISER AND CONTRIBUTE HEAVILY TO YOUR CAMPAIGN? NOW YOU WANT GOOD CHAMPAGNE?
BACK OFF, MAYOR McCHEESE.
WHAT'S THIS I HEAR ABOUT YOU AND THE TIGGIOT PEOPLE?
I WHUPPED GRANT TIGGIOT'S ASS AT THE OPEN LAST WEEK. I WAS LIKE AN OLD, WHITE TIGER WOODS.
THAT'S NOT WHAT I'M TALKING ABOUT, FRANK. I'M TALKING ABOUT THEIR SIZABLE DONATIONS TO YOUR RE-ELECTION CAMPAIGN.
THEY'RE ENTITLED TO THEIR OPINION ON WHO THEY'D LIKE TO SEE RUNNING THIS CITY JUST LIKE EVERYONE ELSE, AREN'T THEY?
IF YOU DON'T WANNA TALK ABOUT IT, FINE. BUT DON'T TALK TO ME LIKE I'M A MEMBER OF THE PRESS.
I'M YOUR OLDEST FRIEND FIRST. NOT TO MENTION A CONSTITUENT.
YOU'VE SEEN THE LATEST POLLS.
SO WHAT? HE'S JUST A NEW FACE. THAT LEAD WILL TAPER OFF.
I'M GLAD YOU'VE GOT THAT KIND OF FAITH IN ME, BRITT. BUT I CAN READ THE WRITING ON THE WALL.

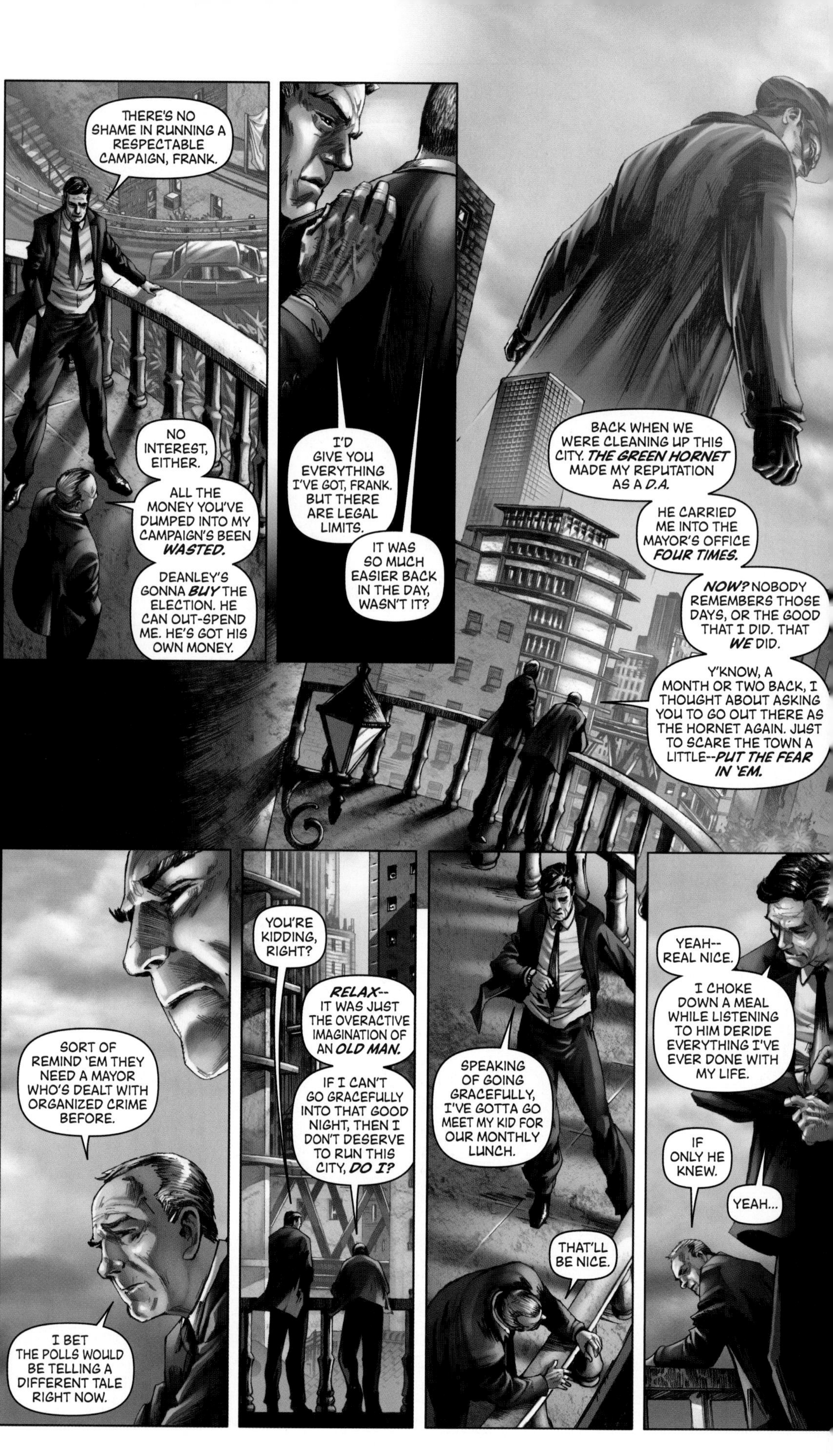
THERE'S NO SHAME IN RUNNING A RESPECTABLE CAMPAIGN, FRANK.
NO INTEREST, EITHER.
ALL THE MONEY YOU'VE DUMPED INTO MY CAMPAIGN'S BEEN WASTED.
DEANLEY'S GONNA BUY THE ELECTION. HE CAN OUT-SPEND ME. HE'S GOT HIS OWN MONEY.
I'D GIVE YOU EVERYTHING I'VE GOT, FRANK. BUT THERE ARE LEGAL LIMITS.
IT WAS SO MUCH EASIER BACK IN THE DAY, WASN'T IT?
BACK WHEN WE WERE CLEANING UP THIS CITY. THE GREEN HORNET MADE MY REPUTATION AS A D.A.
HE CARRIED ME INTO THE MAYOR'S OFFICE FOUR TIMES.
NOW? NOBODY REMEMBERS THOSE DAYS, OR THE GOOD THAT I DID. THAT WE DID.
Y'KNOW, A MONTH OR TWO BACK, I THOUGHT ABOUT ASKING YOU TO GO OUT THERE AS THE HORNET AGAIN. JUST TO SCARE THE TOWN A LITTLE--PUT THE FEAR IN 'EM.
SORT OF REMIND 'EM THEY NEED A MAYOR WHO'S DEALT WITH ORGANIZED CRIME BEFORE.
I BET THE POLLS WOULD BE TELLING A DIFFERENT TALE RIGHT NOW.
YOU'RE KIDDING, RIGHT?
RELAX-- IT WAS JUST THE OVERACTIVE IMAGINATION OF AN OLD MAN.
IF I CAN'T GO GRACEFULLY INTO THAT GOOD NIGHT, THEN I DON'T DESERVE TO RUN THIS CITY, DO I?
SPEAKING OF GOING GRACEFULLY, I'VE GOTTA GO MEET MY KID FOR OUR MONTHLY LUNCH.
THAT'LL BE NICE.
YEAH-- REAL NICE.
I CHOKE DOWN A MEAL WHILE LISTENING TO HIM DERIDE EVERYTHING I'VE EVER DONE WITH MY LIFE.
IF ONLY HE KNEW.
YEAH...

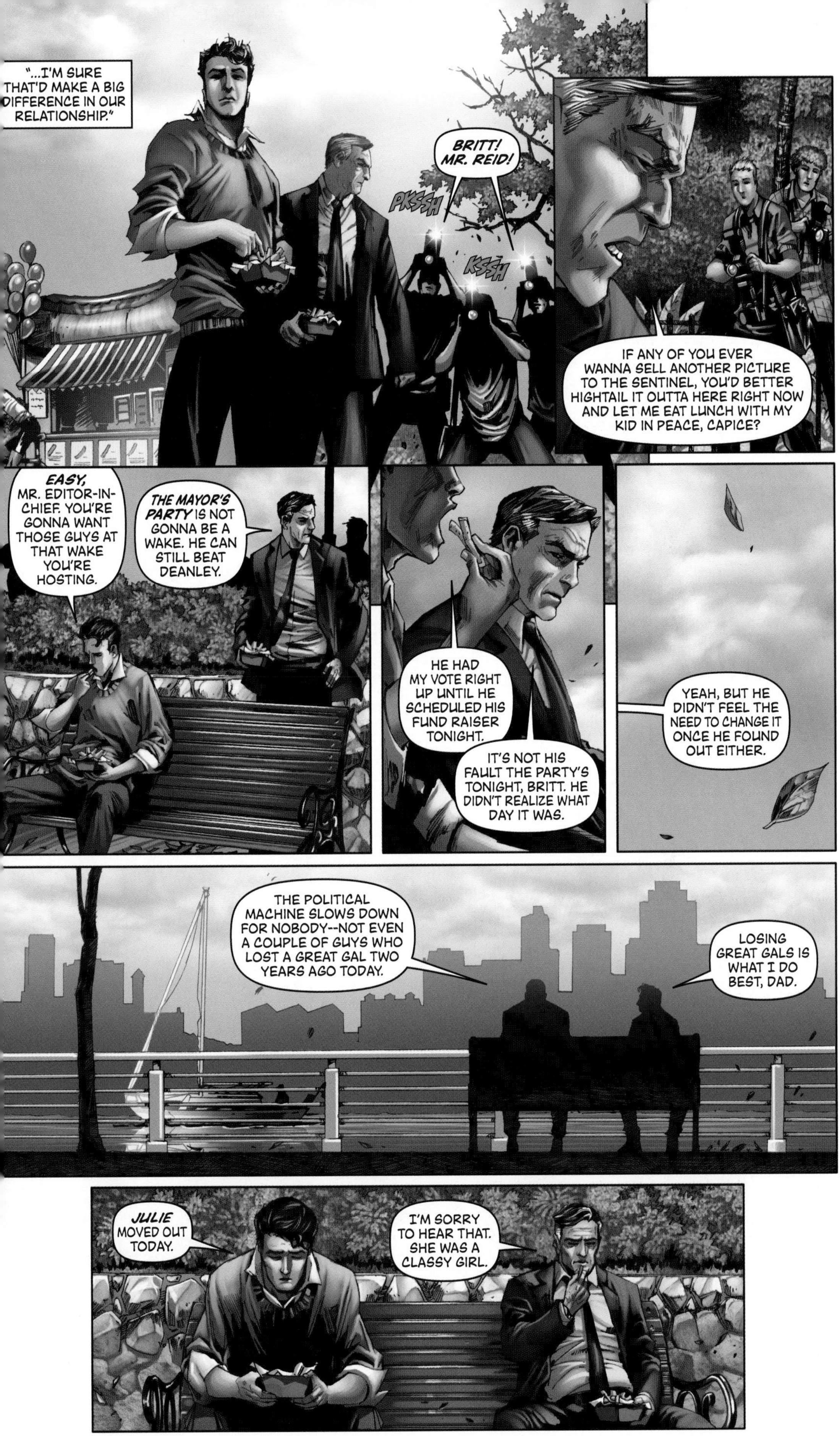
"...I'M SURE THAT'D MAKE A BIG DIFFERENCE IN OUR RELATIONSHIP."
BRITT! MR. REID!
PKSSH
KSSH
IF ANY OF YOU EVER WANNA SELL ANOTHER PICTURE TO THE SENTINEL, YOU'D BETTER HIGHTAIL IT OUTTA HERE RIGHT NOW AND LET ME EAT LUNCH WITH MY KID IN PEACE, CAPICE?
EASY, MR. EDITOR-IN-CHIEF. YOU'RE GONNA WANT THOSE GUYS AT THAT WAKE YOU'RE HOSTING.
THE MAYOR'S PARTY IS NOT GONNA BE A WAKE. HE CAN STILL BEAT DEANLEY.
HE HAD MY VOTE RIGHT UP UNTIL HE SCHEDULED HIS FUND RAISER TONIGHT.
IT'S NOT HIS FAULT THE PARTY'S TONIGHT, BRITT. HE DIDN'T REALIZE WHAT DAY IT WAS.
YEAH, BUT HE DIDN'T FEEL THE NEED TO CHANGE IT ONCE HE FOUND OUT EITHER.
THE POLITICAL MACHINE SLOWS DOWN FOR NOBODY--NOT EVEN A COUPLE OF GUYS WHO LOST A GREAT GAL TWO YEARS AGO TODAY.
LOSING GREAT GALS IS WHAT I DO BEST, DAD.
JULIE MOVED OUT TODAY.
I'M SORRY TO HEAR THAT. SHE WAS A CLASSY GIRL.

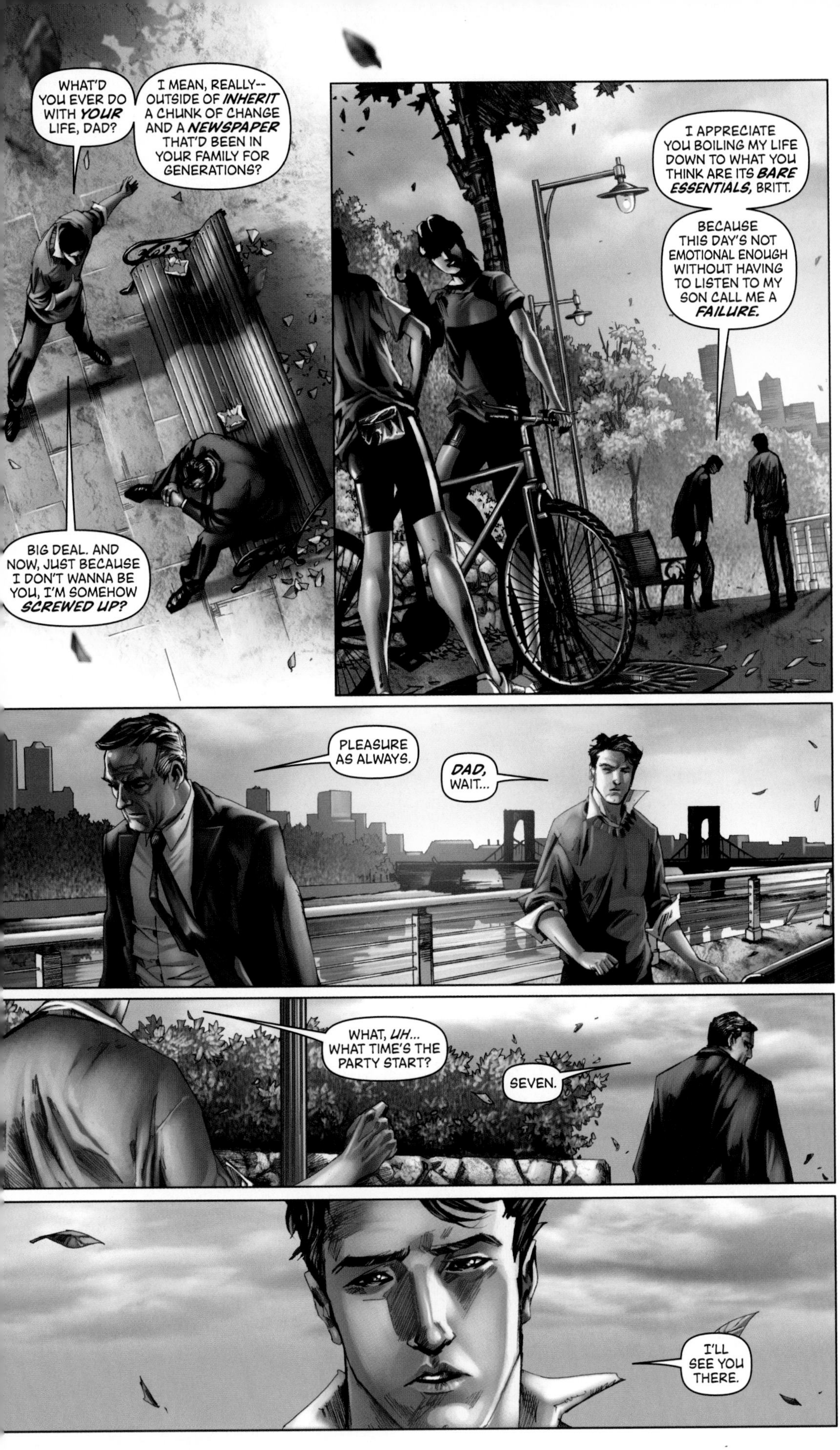
WHAT'D YOU EVER DO WITH *YOUR* LIFE, DAD?
I MEAN, REALLY-- OUTSIDE OF *INHERIT* A CHUNK OF CHANGE AND A *NEWSPAPER* THAT'D BEEN IN YOUR FAMILY FOR GENERATIONS?
BIG DEAL. AND NOW, JUST BECAUSE I DON'T WANNA BE YOU, I'M SOMEHOW *SCREWED UP?*
I APPRECIATE YOU BOILING MY LIFE DOWN TO WHAT YOU THINK ARE ITS *BARE ESSENTIALS,* BRITT.
BECAUSE THIS DAY'S NOT EMOTIONAL ENOUGH WITHOUT HAVING TO LISTEN TO MY SON CALL ME A *FAILURE.*
PLEASURE AS ALWAYS.
DAD, WAIT...
WHAT, *UH*... WHAT TIME'S THE PARTY START?
SEVEN.
I'LL SEE YOU THERE.

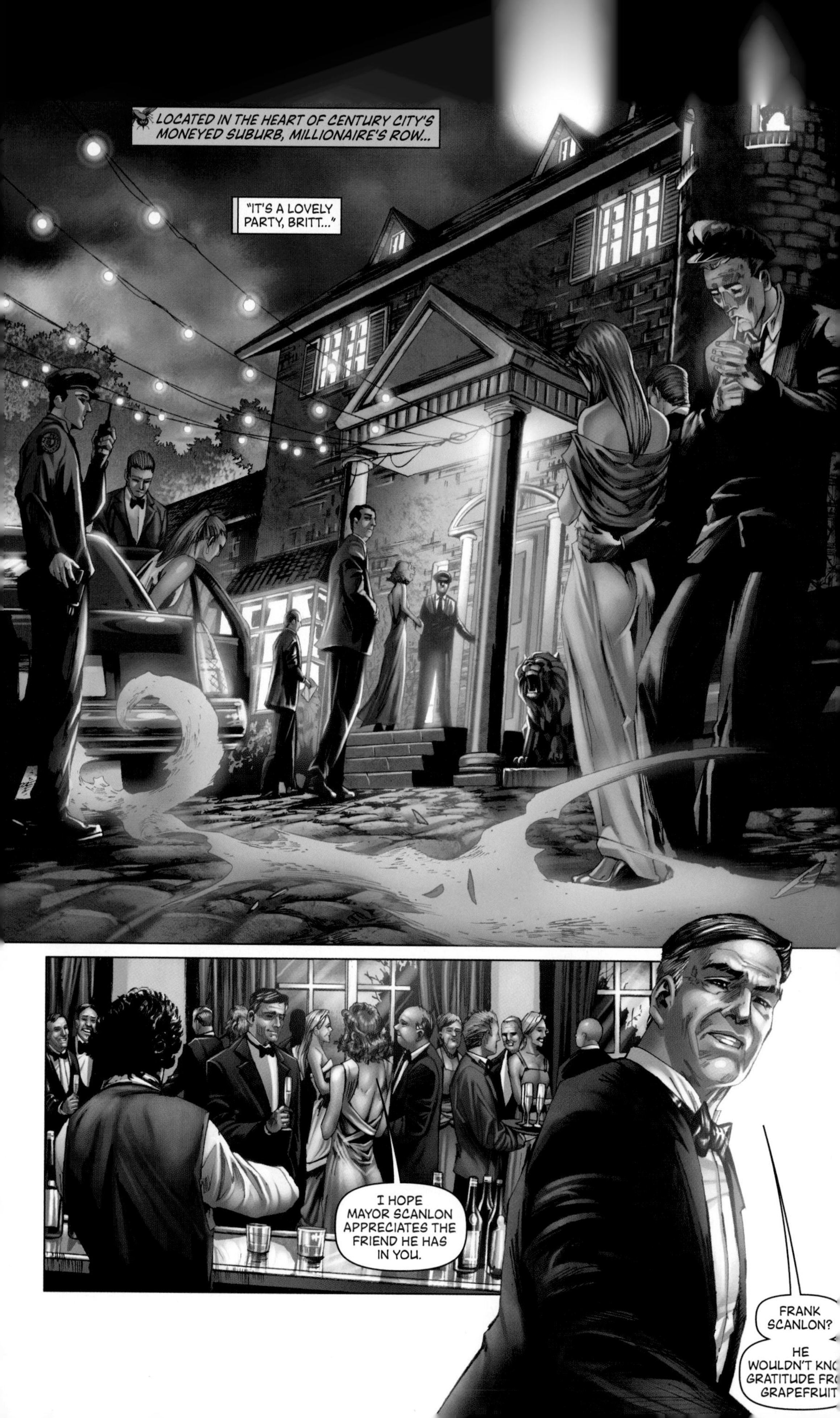
LOCATED IN THE HEART OF CENTURY CITY'S MONEYED SUBURB, MILLIONAIRE'S ROW...
"IT'S A LOVELY PARTY, BRITT..."
I HOPE MAYOR SCANLON APPRECIATES THE FRIEND HE HAS IN YOU.
FRANK SCANLON?
HE WOULDN'T KNO GRATITUDE FR GRAPEFRUIT

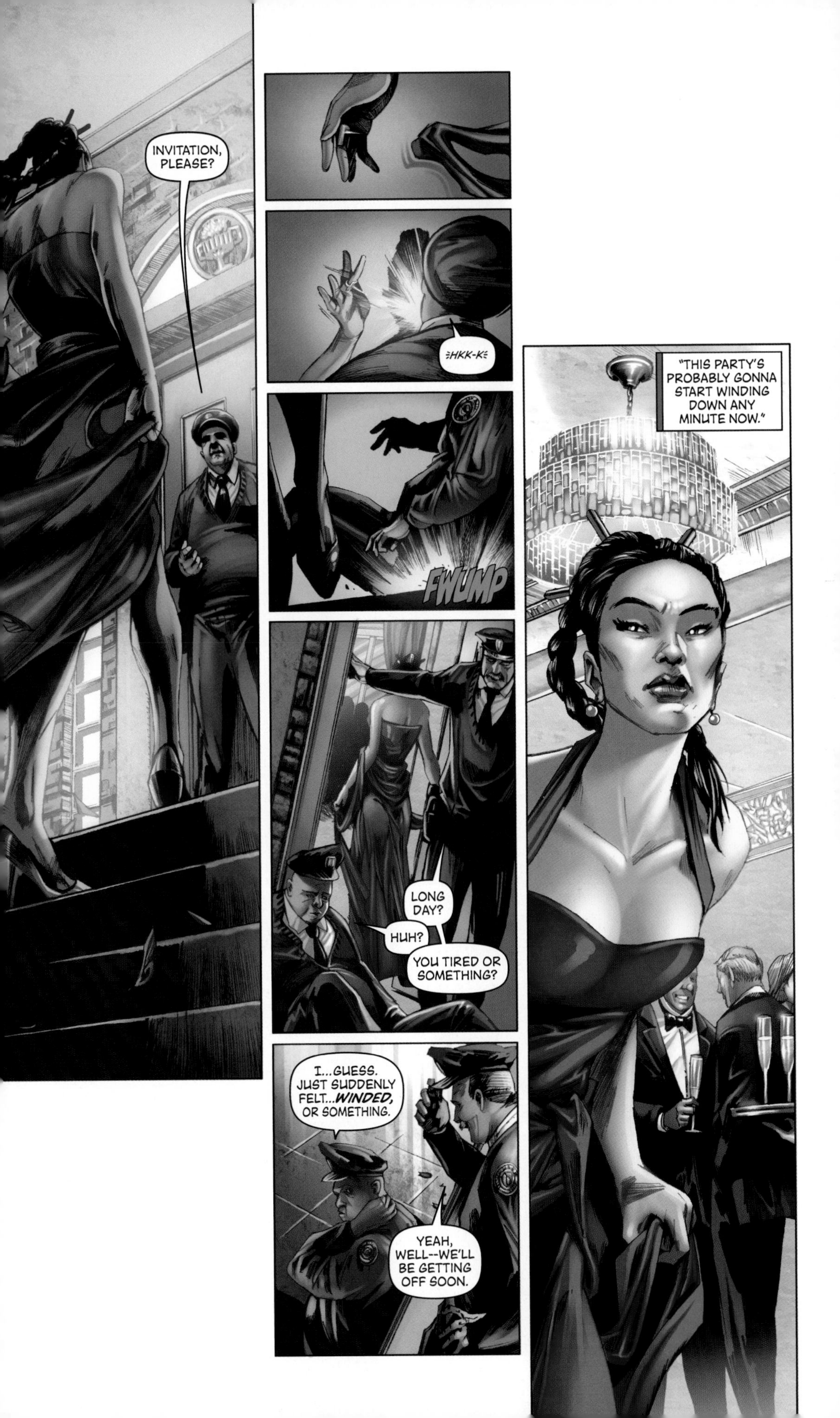

INVITATION, PLEASE?
HKK-K
FWUMP
LONG DAY?
HUH?
YOU TIRED OR SOMETHING?
I...GUESS. JUST SUDDENLY FELT...*WINDED,* OR SOMETHING.
YEAH, WELL--WE'LL BE GETTING OFF SOON.
"THIS PARTY'S PROBABLY GONNA START WINDING DOWN ANY MINUTE NOW."

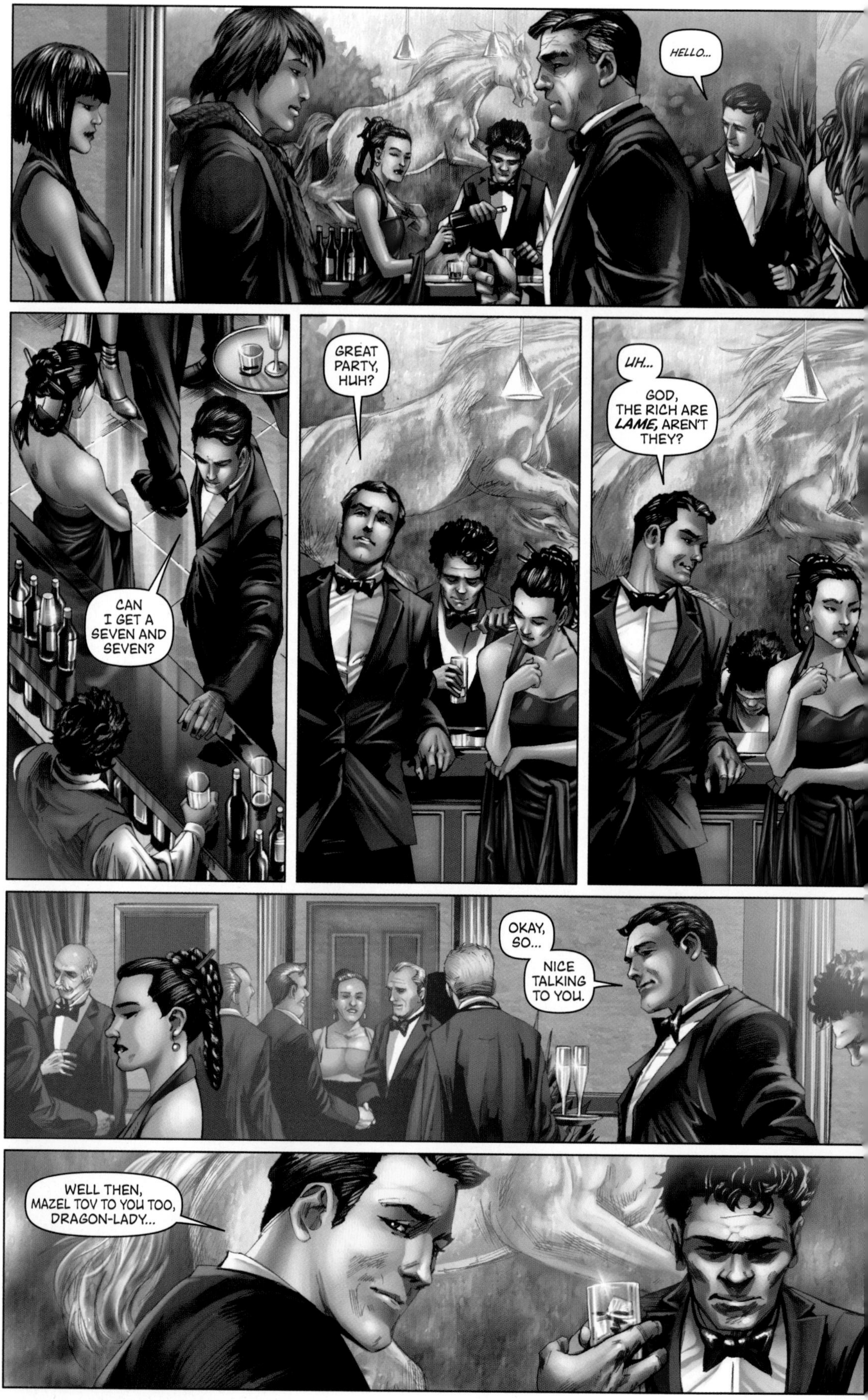
HELLO...
CAN I GET A SEVEN AND SEVEN?
GREAT PARTY, HUH?
UH...
GOD, THE RICH ARE LAME, AREN'T THEY?
OKAY, SO...
NICE TALKING TO YOU.
WELL THEN, MAZEL TOV TO YOU TOO, DRAGON-LADY...

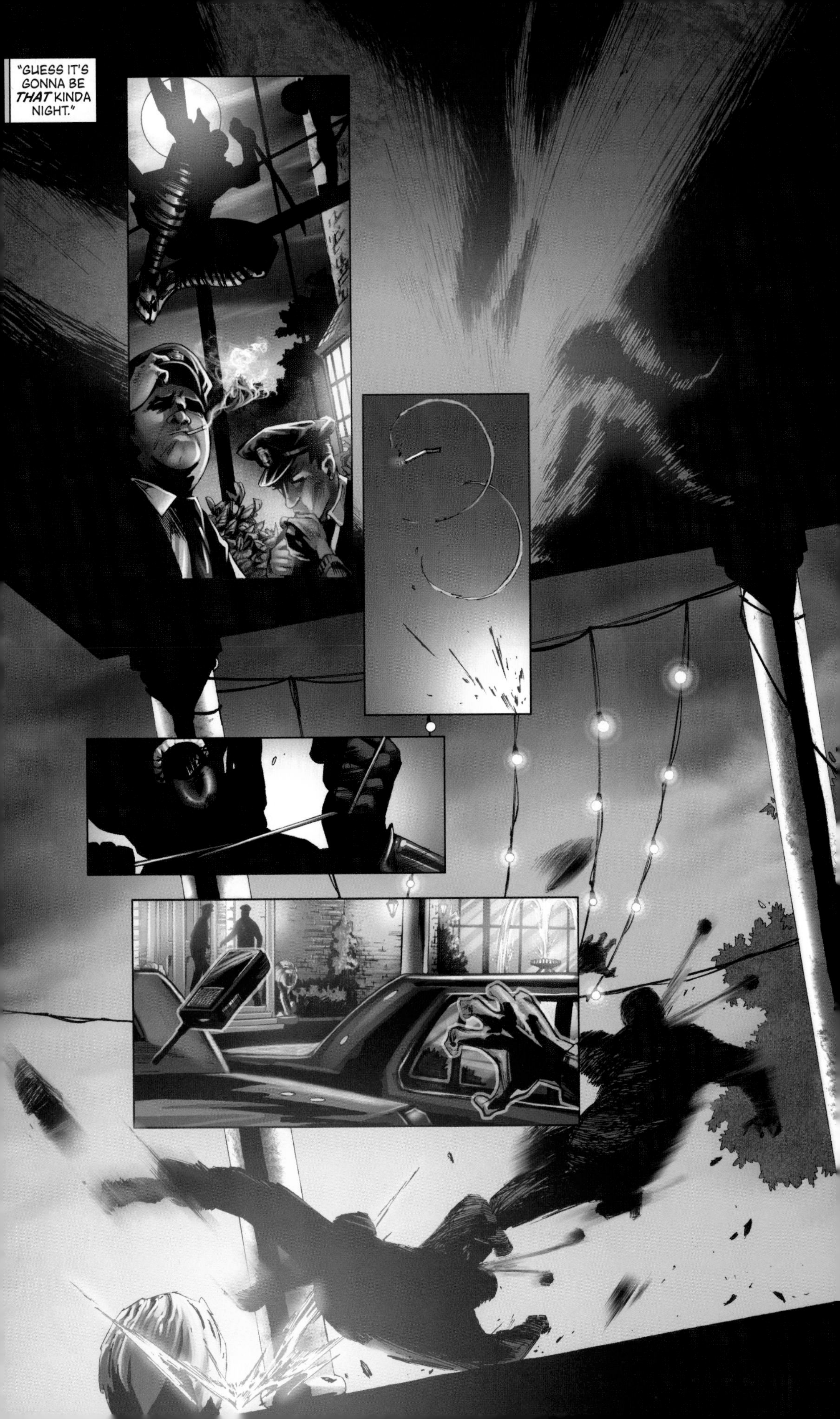

"GUESS IT'S GONNA BE *THAT* KINDA NIGHT."

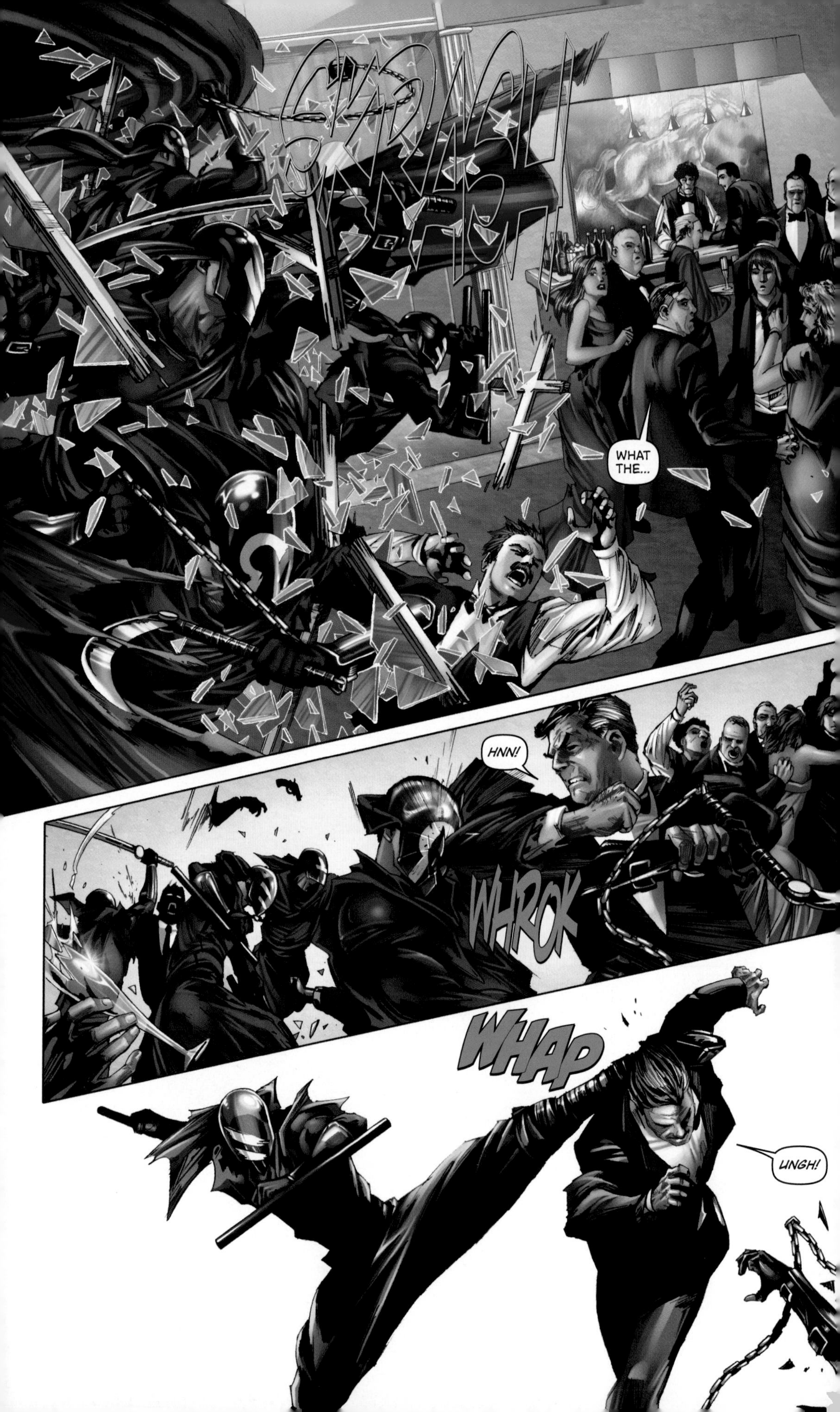
WHAT THE...
HNN!
WHROK
WHAP
UNGH!

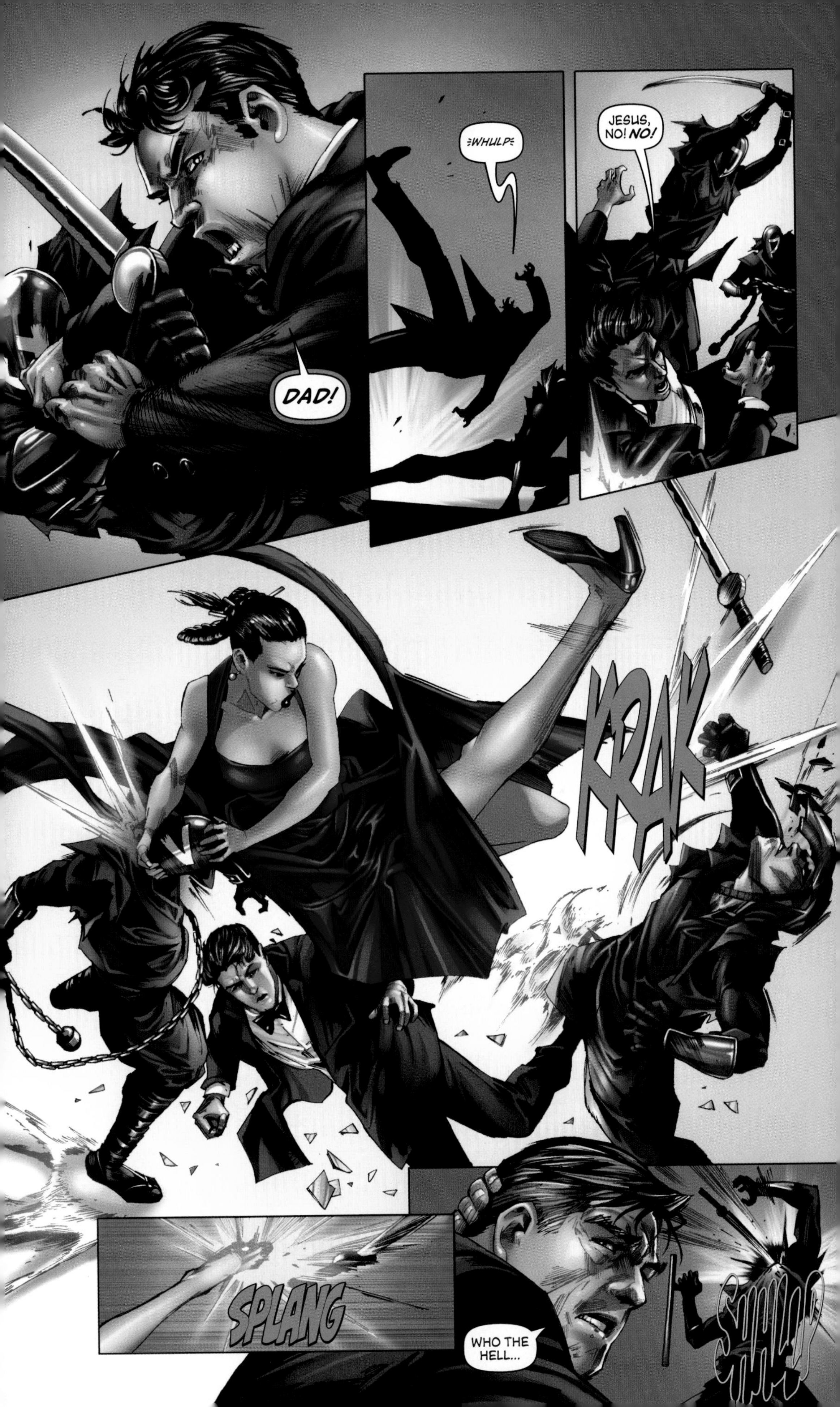
DAD!
WHULP
JESUS, NO! NO!
KRAK
SPLANG
WHO THE HELL...

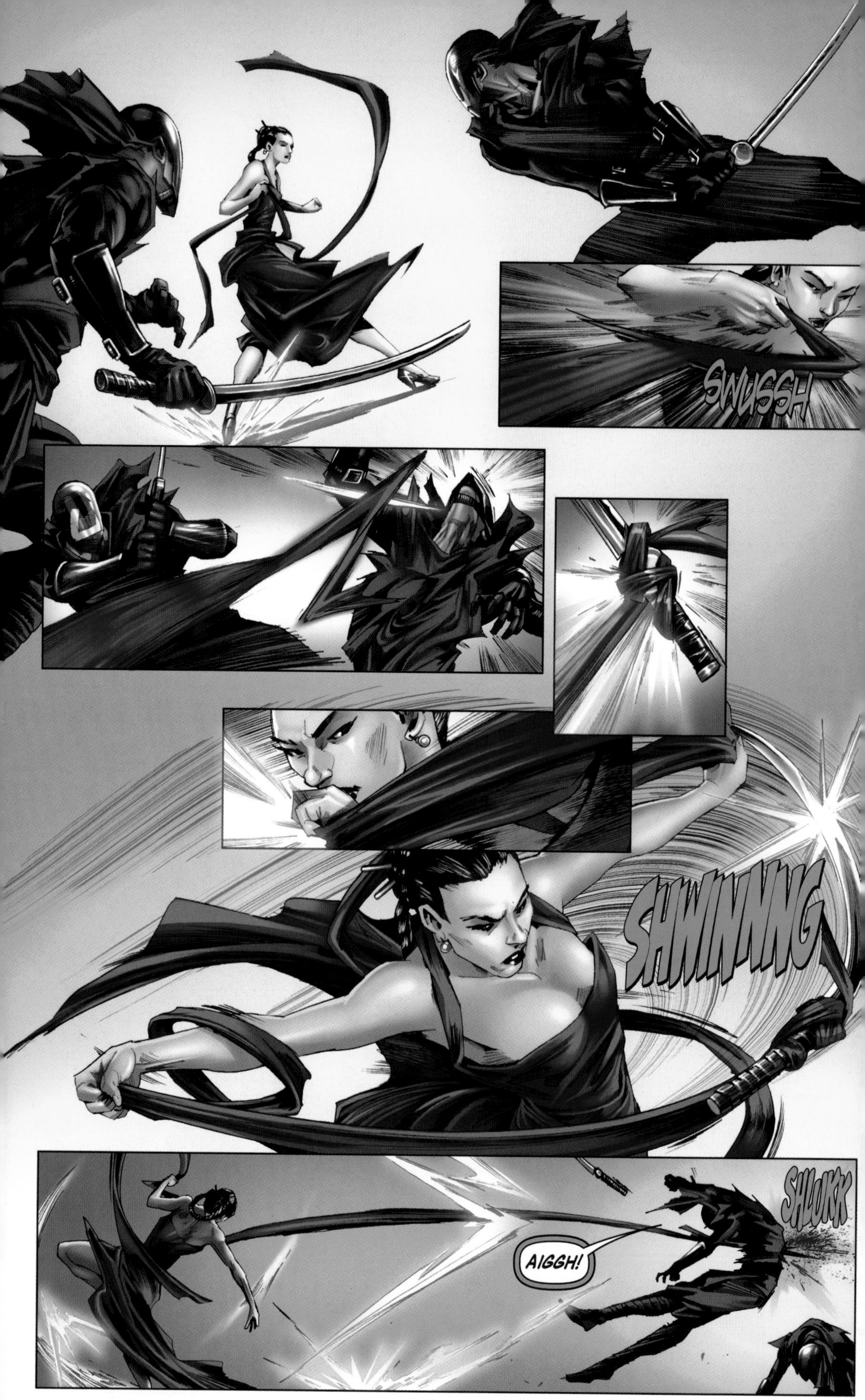
SWUSSH
SHWINNNG
SHLUKK
AIGGH!

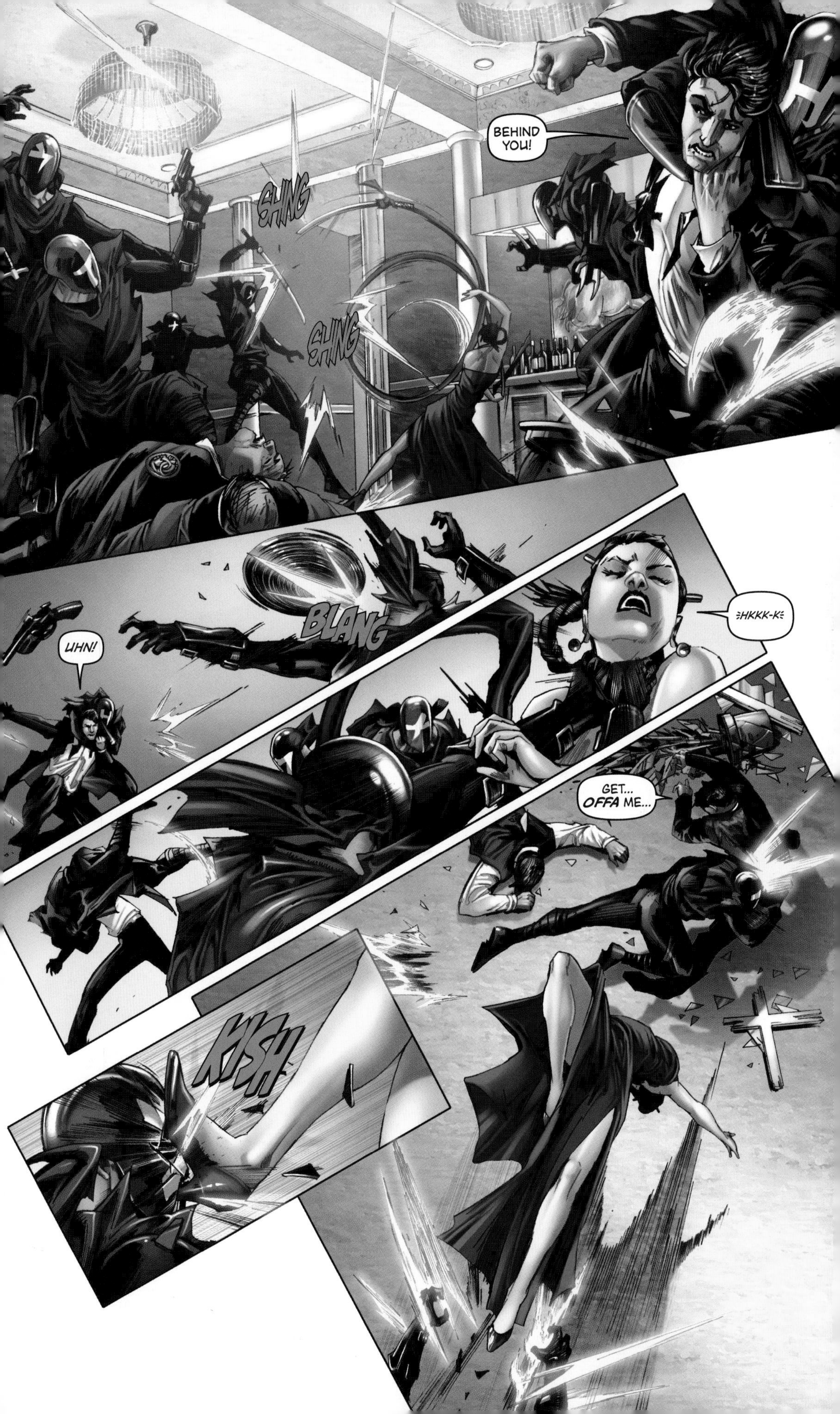
BEHIND YOU!
SHING
SHING
BLANG
UHN!
HKKK-K
GET... OFFA ME...
KISH

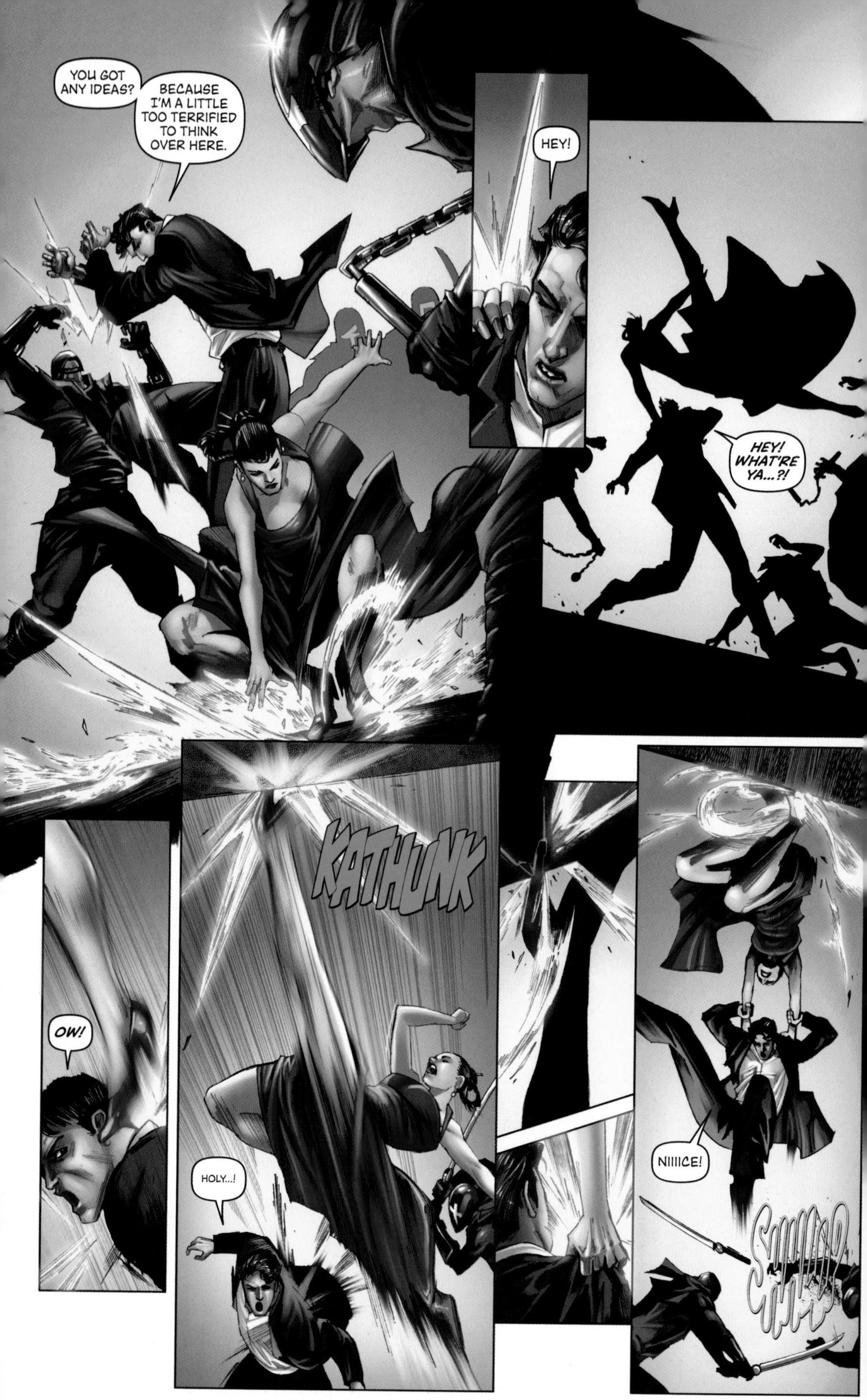
YOU GOT ANY IDEAS?
BECAUSE I'M A LITTLE TOO TERRIFIED TO THINK OVER HERE.
HEY!
HEY! WHAT'RE YA...?!
OW!
KATHUNK
HOLY...!
NIIIICE!

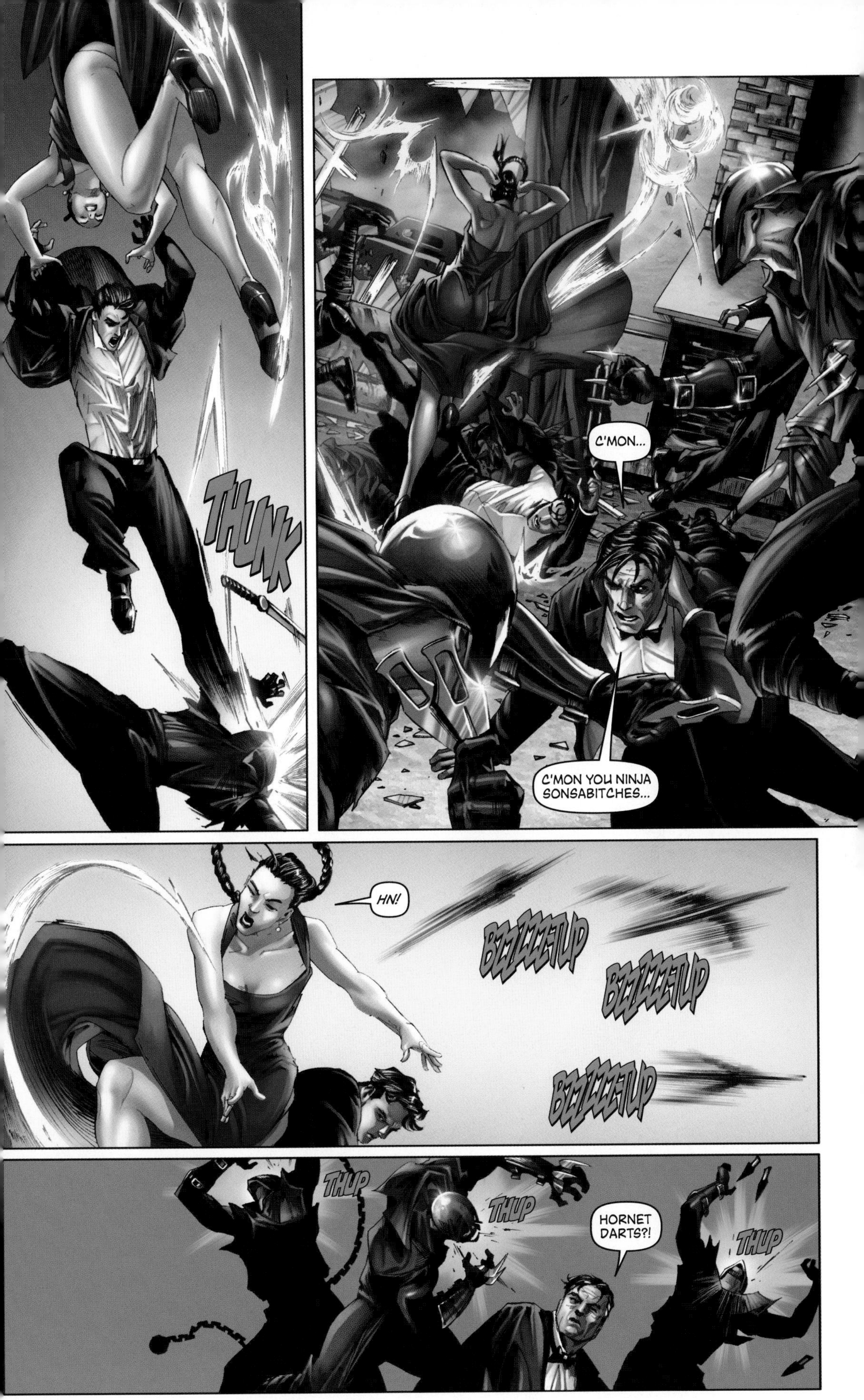
THUNK
C'MON...
C'MON YOU NINJA SONSABITCHES...
HN!
BZZZZZTUP
BZZZZZTUP
BZZZZZTUP
THUP
THUP
HORNET DARTS?!
THUP

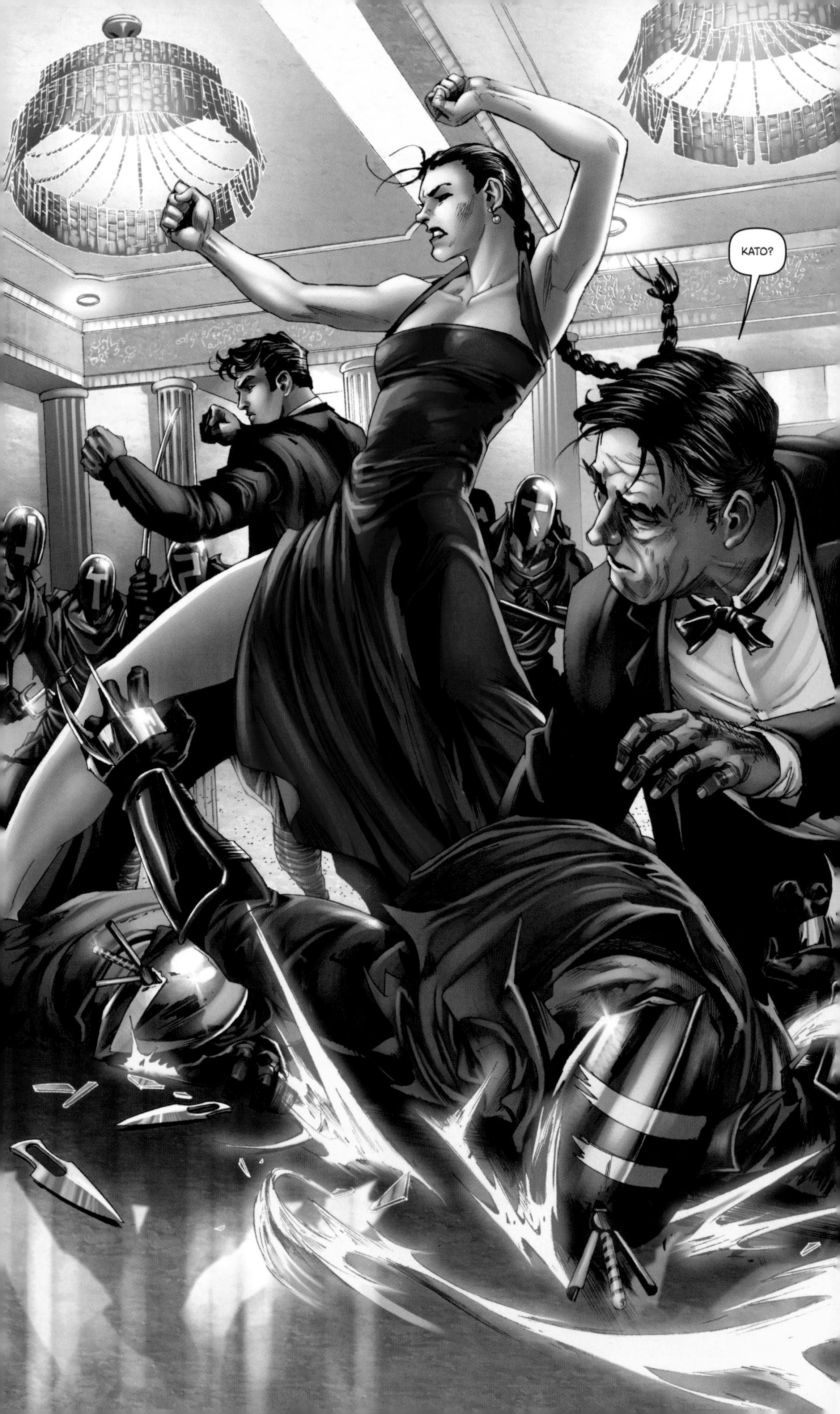
KATO?

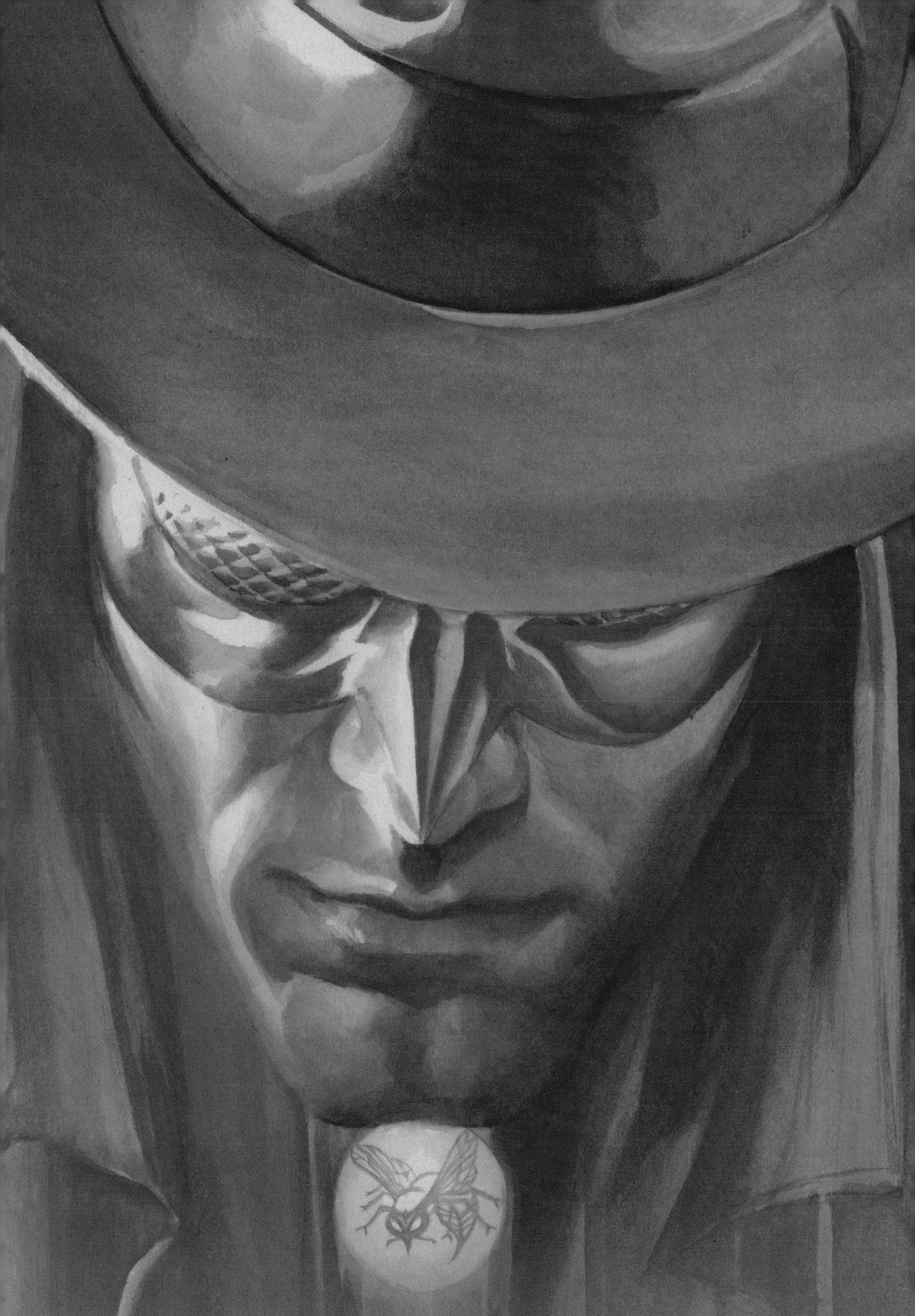

EPISODE THREE: SINS OF THE FATHER

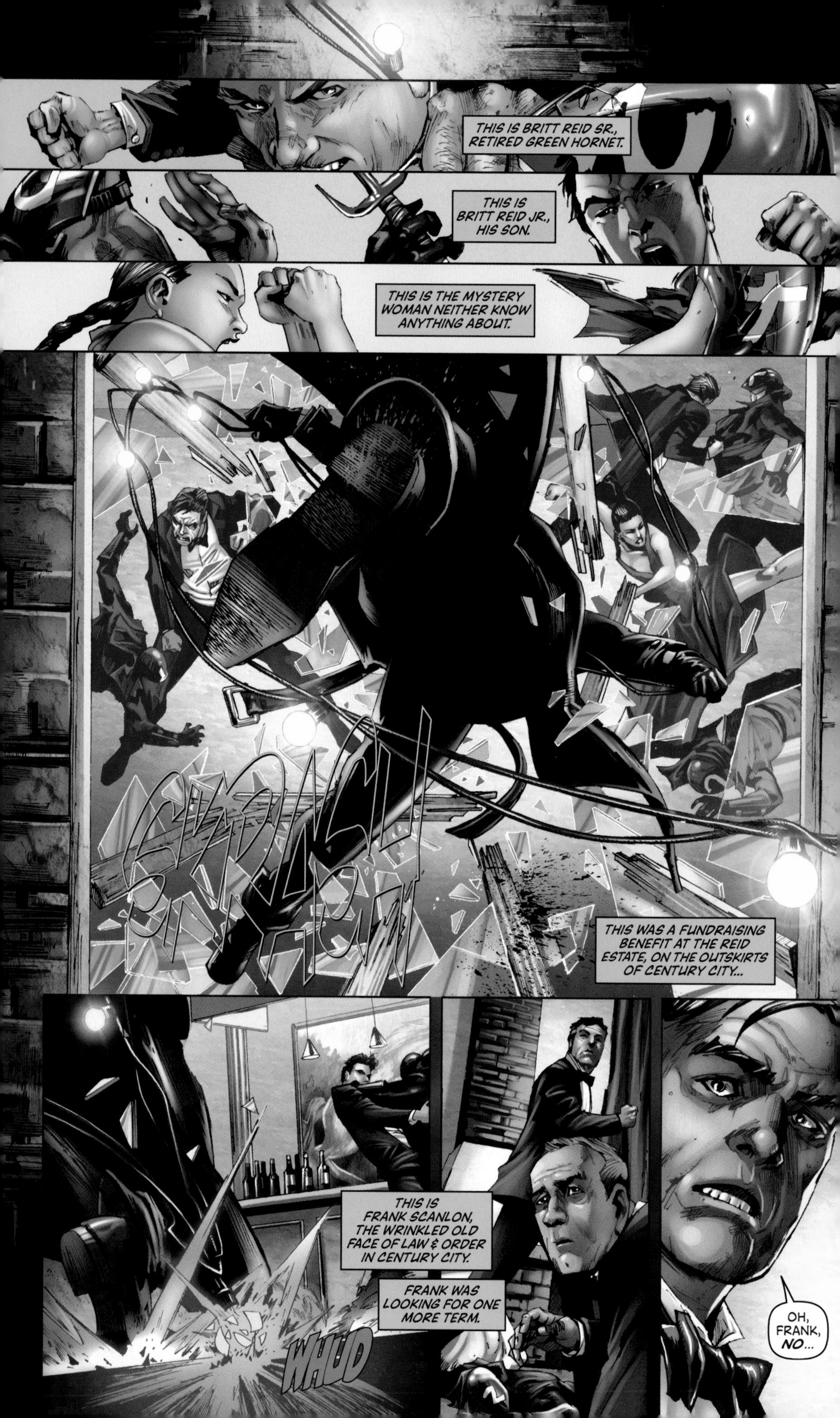
THIS IS BRITT REID SR., RETIRED GREEN HORNET.
THIS IS BRITT REID JR., HIS SON.
THIS IS THE MYSTERY WOMAN NEITHER KNOW ANYTHING ABOUT.
THIS WAS A FUNDRAISING BENEFIT AT THE REID ESTATE, ON THE OUTSKIRTS OF CENTURY CITY...
THIS IS FRANK SCANLON, THE WRINKLED OLD FACE OF LAW & ORDER IN CENTURY CITY.
FRANK WAS LOOKING FOR ONE MORE TERM.
WHUD
OH, FRANK, NO...

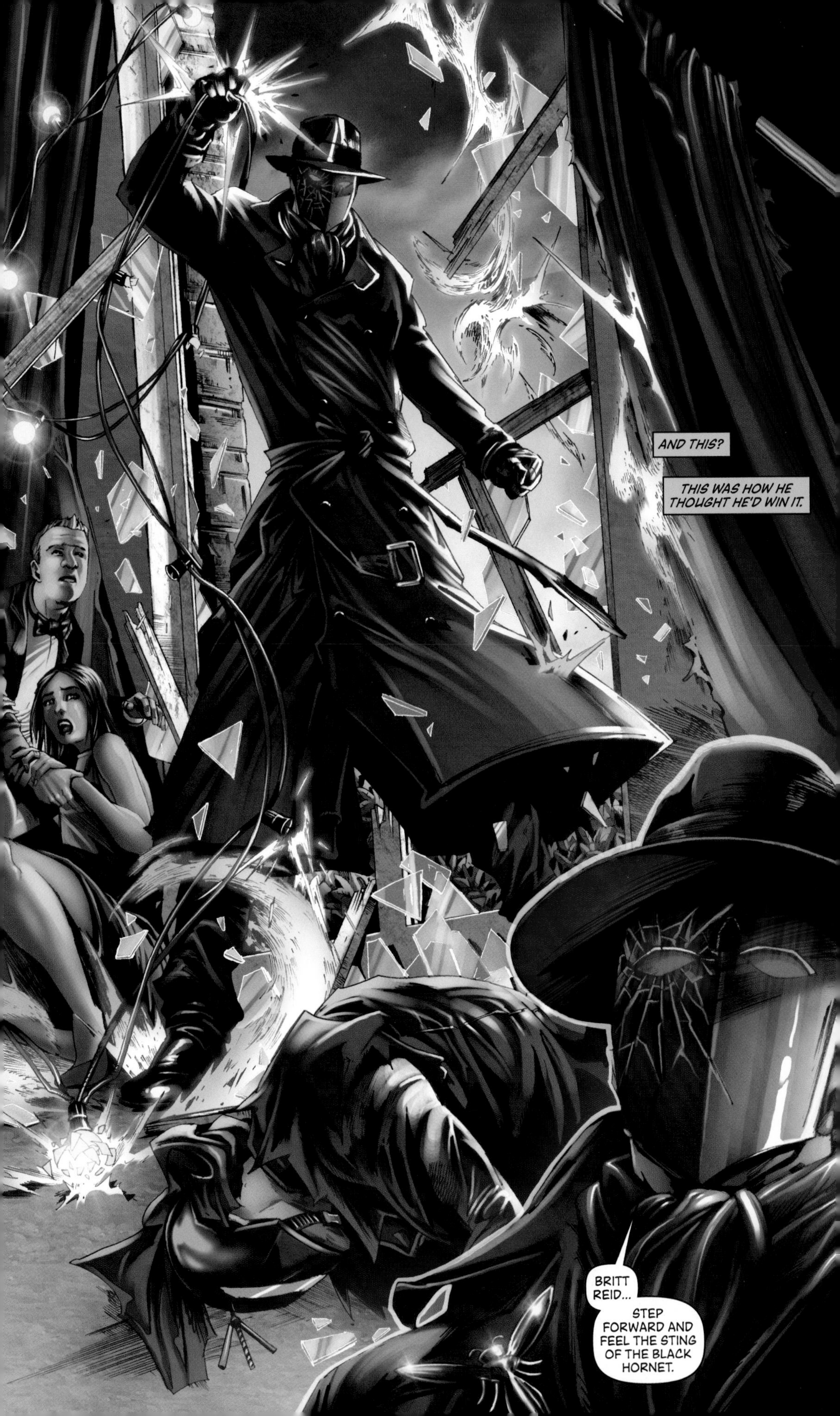
AND THIS?
THIS WAS HOW HE THOUGHT HE'D WIN IT.
BRITT REID... STEP FORWARD AND FEEL THE STING OF THE BLACK HORNET.

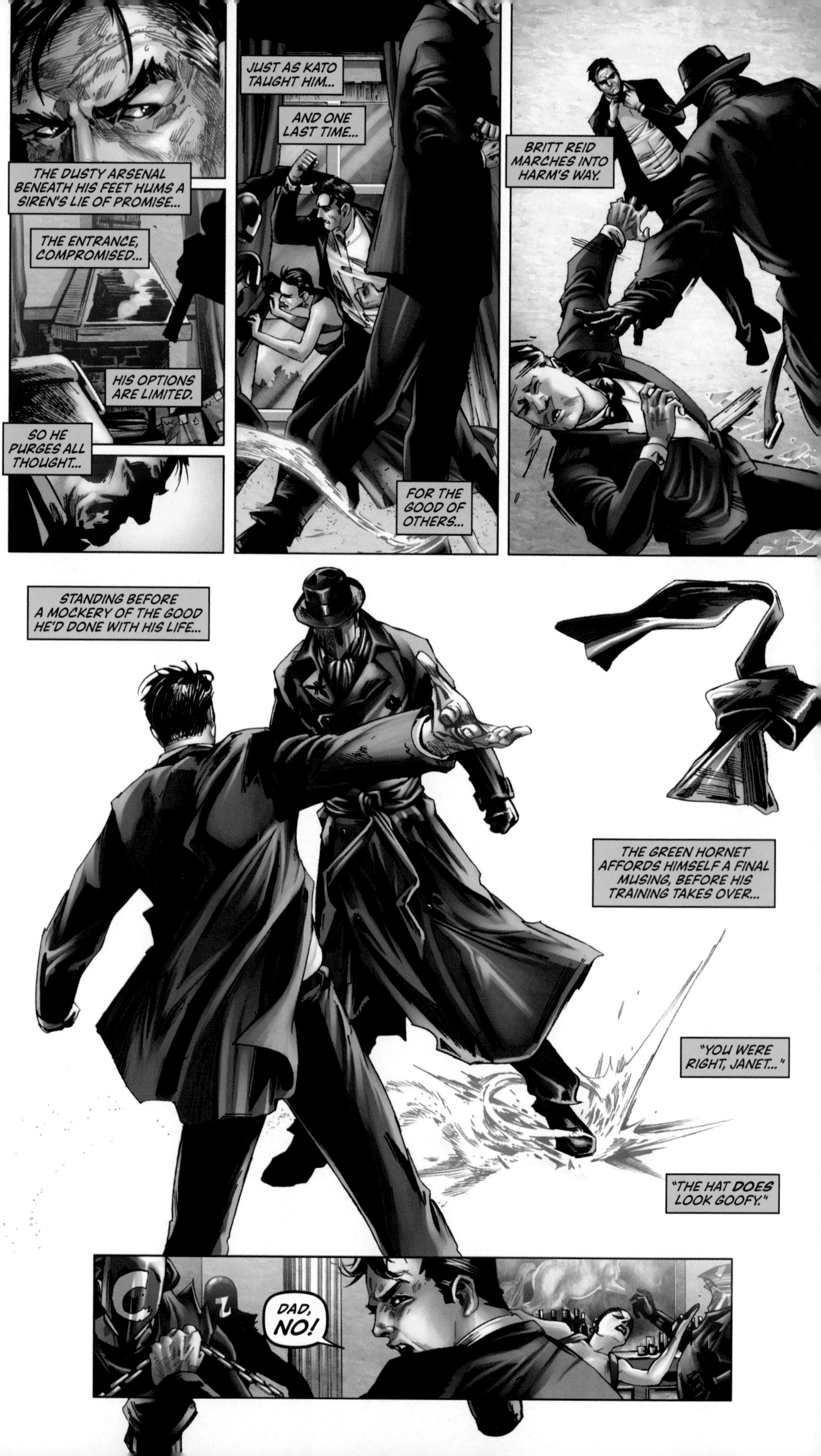
THE DUSTY ARSENAL BENEATH HIS FEET HUMS A SIREN'S LIE OF PROMISE...
THE ENTRANCE, COMPROMISED...
HIS OPTIONS ARE LIMITED.
SO HE PURGES ALL THOUGHT...
JUST AS KATO TAUGHT HIM...
AND ONE LAST TIME...
FOR THE GOOD OF OTHERS...
BRITT REID MARCHES INTO HARM'S WAY.
STANDING BEFORE A MOCKERY OF THE GOOD HE'D DONE WITH HIS LIFE...
THE GREEN HORNET AFFORDS HIMSELF A FINAL MUSING, BEFORE HIS TRAINING TAKES OVER...
"YOU WERE RIGHT, JANET..."
"THE HAT DOES LOOK GOOFY."
DAD, NO!

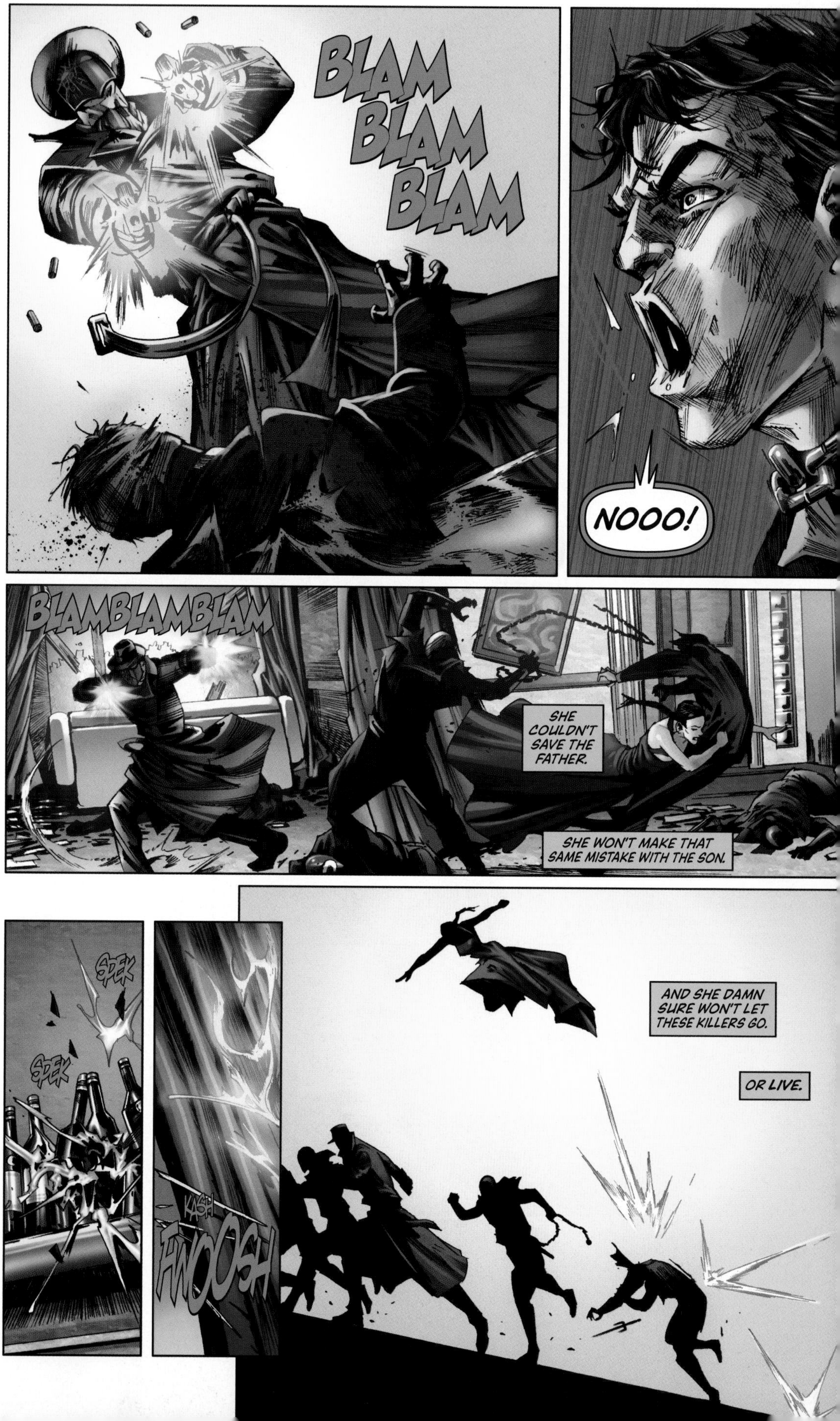
BLAM
BLAM
BLAM
NOOO!
BLAMBLAMBLAM
SHE COULDN'T SAVE THE FATHER.
SHE WON'T MAKE THAT SAME MISTAKE WITH THE SON.
SPEK
SPEK
KASH
FWOOSH
AND SHE DAMN SURE WON'T LET THESE KILLERS GO.
OR LIVE.

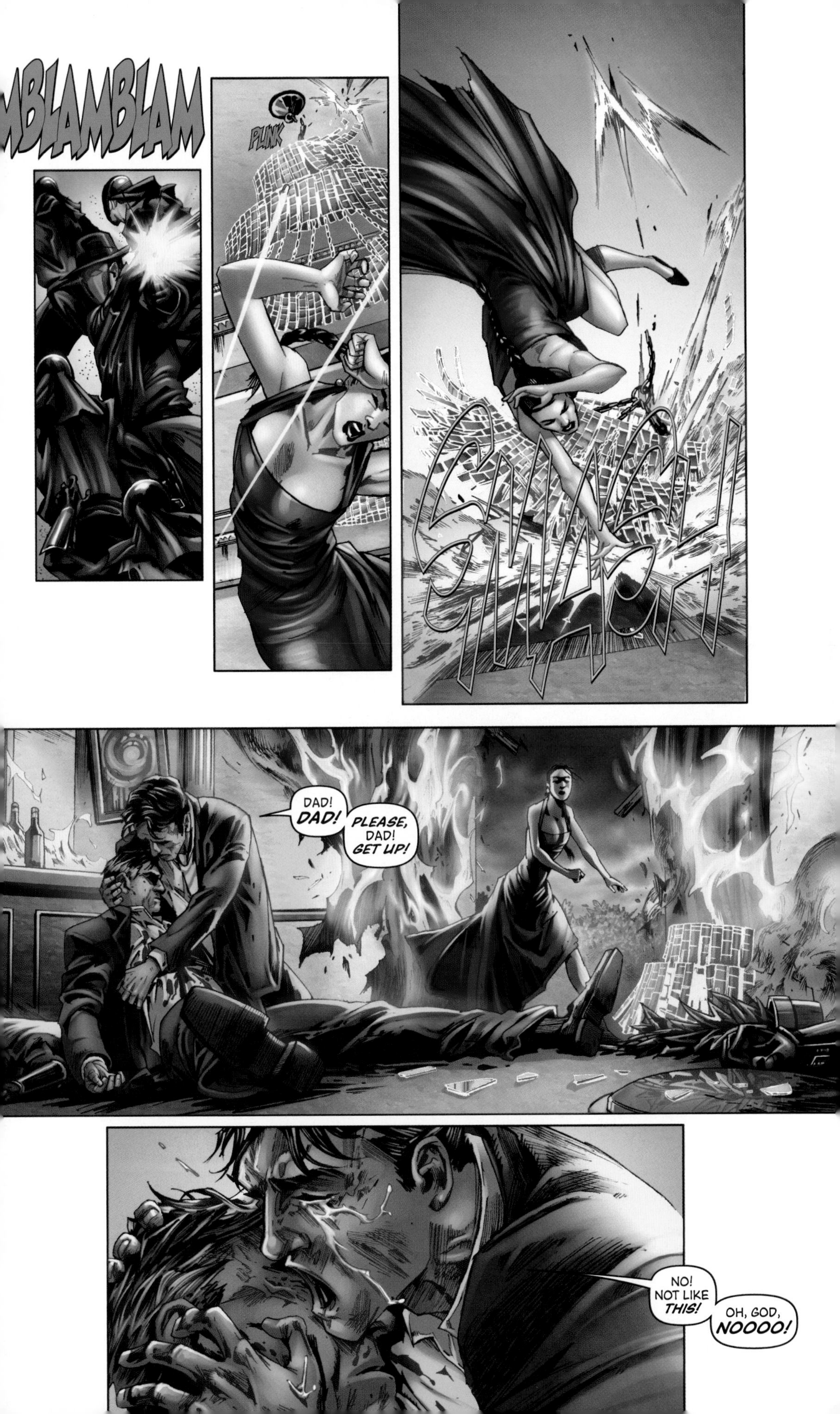

MBLAMBLAM
PLINK
DAD! DAD!
PLEASE, DAD! GET UP!
NO! NOT LIKE THIS!
OH, GOD, NOOOO!

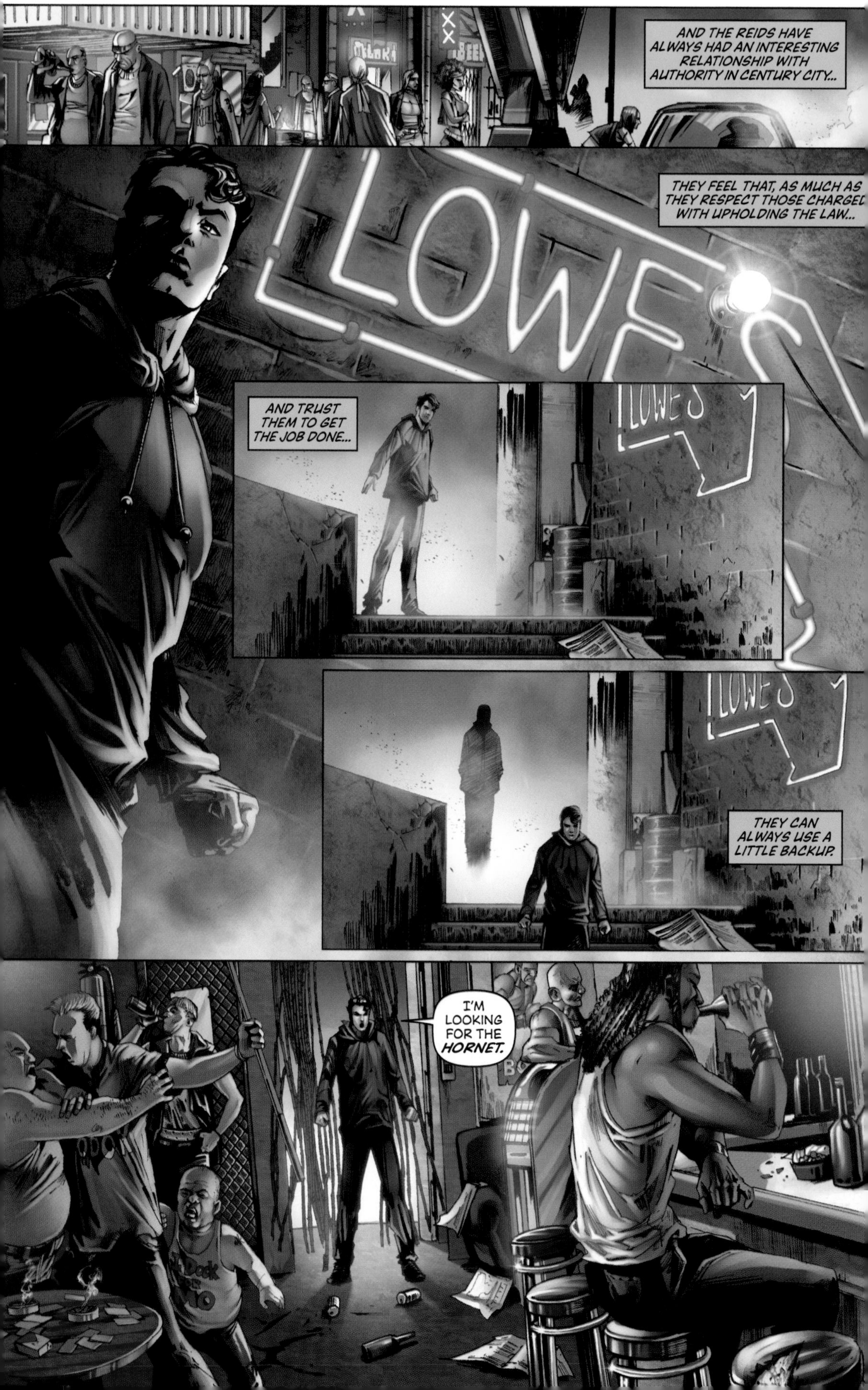
AND THE REIDS HAVE ALWAYS HAD AN INTERESTING RELATIONSHIP WITH AUTHORITY IN CENTURY CITY...
LOWE'S
THEY FEEL THAT, AS MUCH AS THEY RESPECT THOSE CHARGED WITH UPHOLDING THE LAW...
AND TRUST THEM TO GET THE JOB DONE...
LOWE'S
LOWE'S
THEY CAN ALWAYS USE A LITTLE BACKUP.
I'M LOOKING FOR THE *HORNET.*

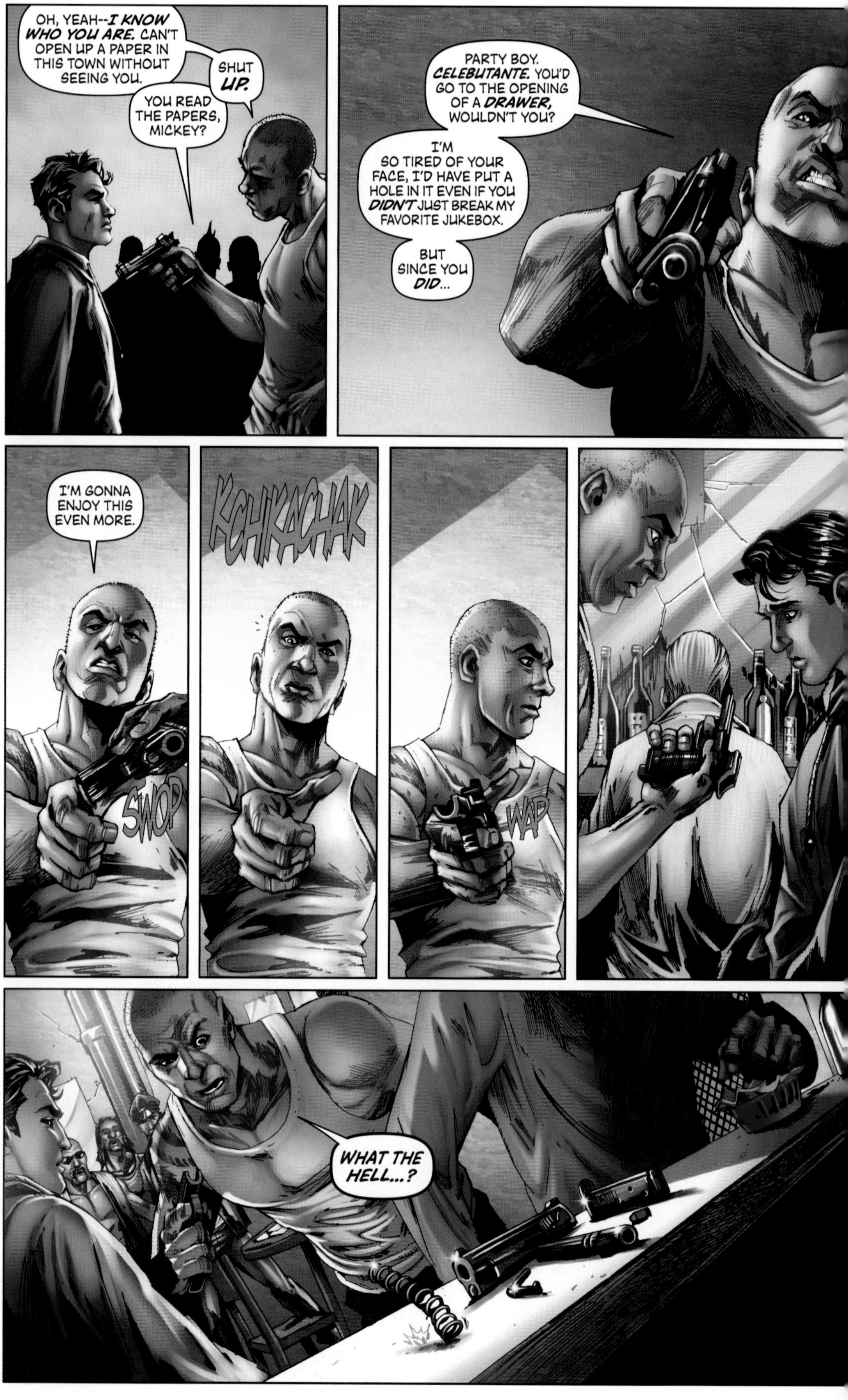
OH, YEAH--I KNOW WHO YOU ARE. CAN'T OPEN UP A PAPER IN THIS TOWN WITHOUT SEEING YOU.
SHUT UP.
YOU READ THE PAPERS, MICKEY?
PARTY BOY. CELEBUTANTE. YOU'D GO TO THE OPENING OF A DRAWER, WOULDN'T YOU?
I'M SO TIRED OF YOUR FACE, I'D HAVE PUT A HOLE IN IT EVEN IF YOU DIDN'T JUST BREAK MY FAVORITE JUKEBOX.
BUT SINCE YOU DID...
I'M GONNA ENJOY THIS EVEN MORE.
SWOP
KCHIKACHAK
WAP
WHAT THE HELL...?

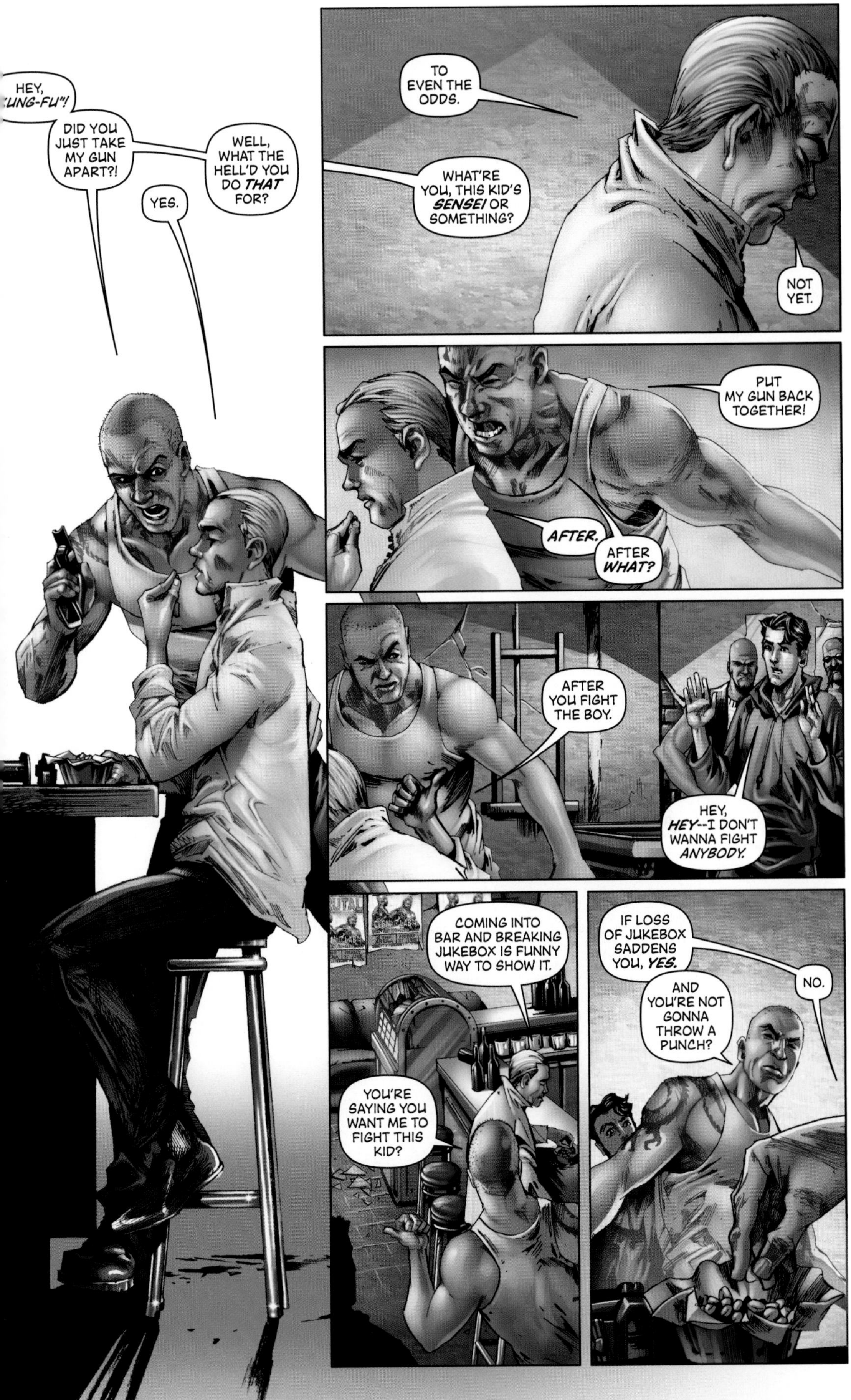

HEY, "KUNG-FU"!
DID YOU JUST TAKE MY GUN APART?!
YES.
WELL, WHAT THE HELL'D YOU DO *THAT* FOR?
TO EVEN THE ODDS.
WHAT'RE YOU, THIS KID'S *SENSEI* OR SOMETHING?
NOT YET.
PUT MY GUN BACK TOGETHER!
AFTER.
AFTER *WHAT?*
AFTER YOU FIGHT THE BOY.
HEY, *HEY*--I DON'T WANNA FIGHT *ANYBODY.*
COMING INTO BAR AND BREAKING JUKEBOX IS FUNNY WAY TO SHOW IT.
YOU'RE SAYING YOU WANT ME TO FIGHT THIS KID?
IF LOSS OF JUKEBOX SADDENS YOU, *YES.*
NO.
AND YOU'RE NOT GONNA THROW A PUNCH?

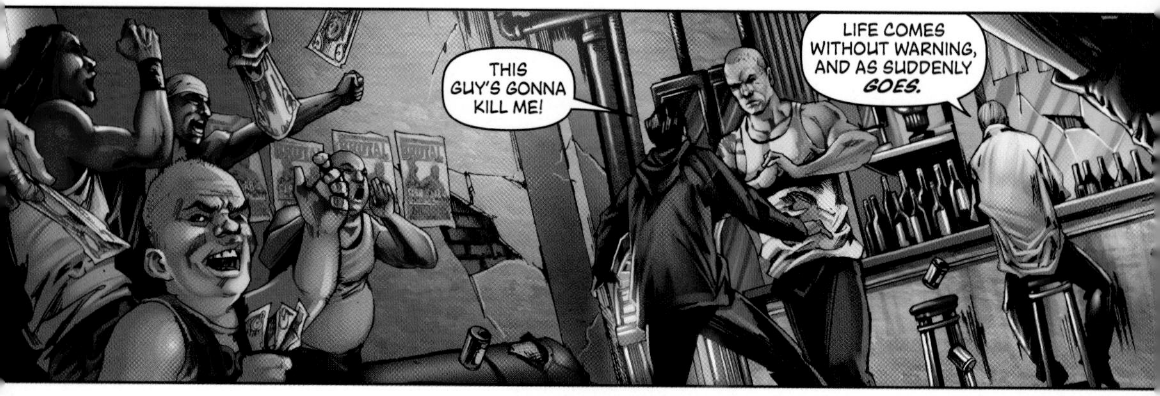
THIS GUY'S GONNA KILL ME!
LIFE COMES WITHOUT WARNING, AND AS SUDDENLY *GOES.*

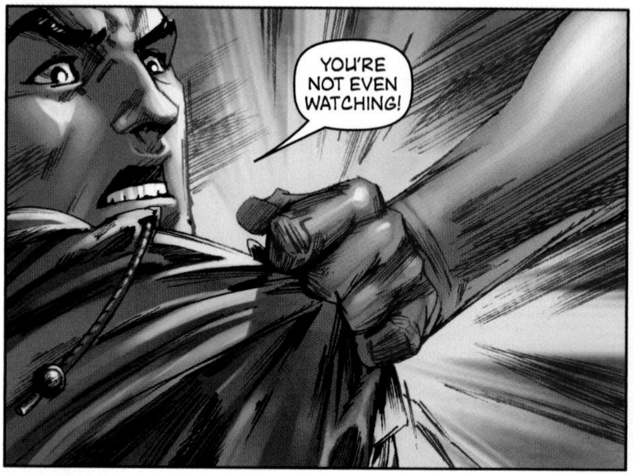
YOU'RE NOT EVEN WATCHING!

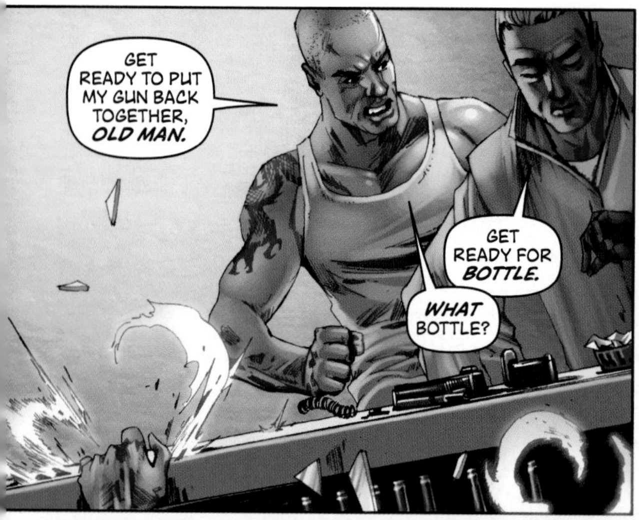
GET READY TO PUT MY GUN BACK TOGETHER, *OLD MAN.*
GET READY FOR *BOTTLE.*
WHAT BOTTLE?

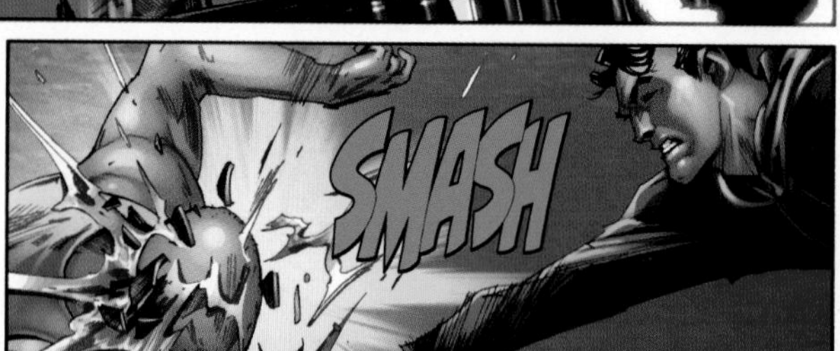
SMASH

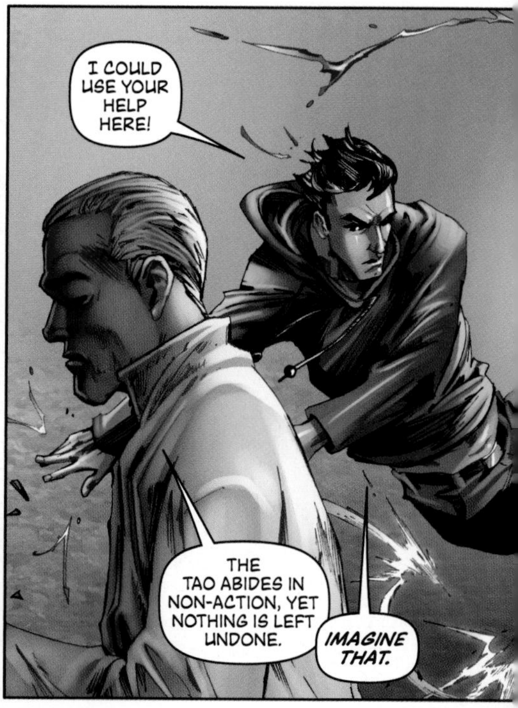
I COULD USE YOUR HELP HERE!
THE TAO ABIDES IN NON-ACTION, YET NOTHING IS LEFT UNDONE.
IMAGINE THAT.

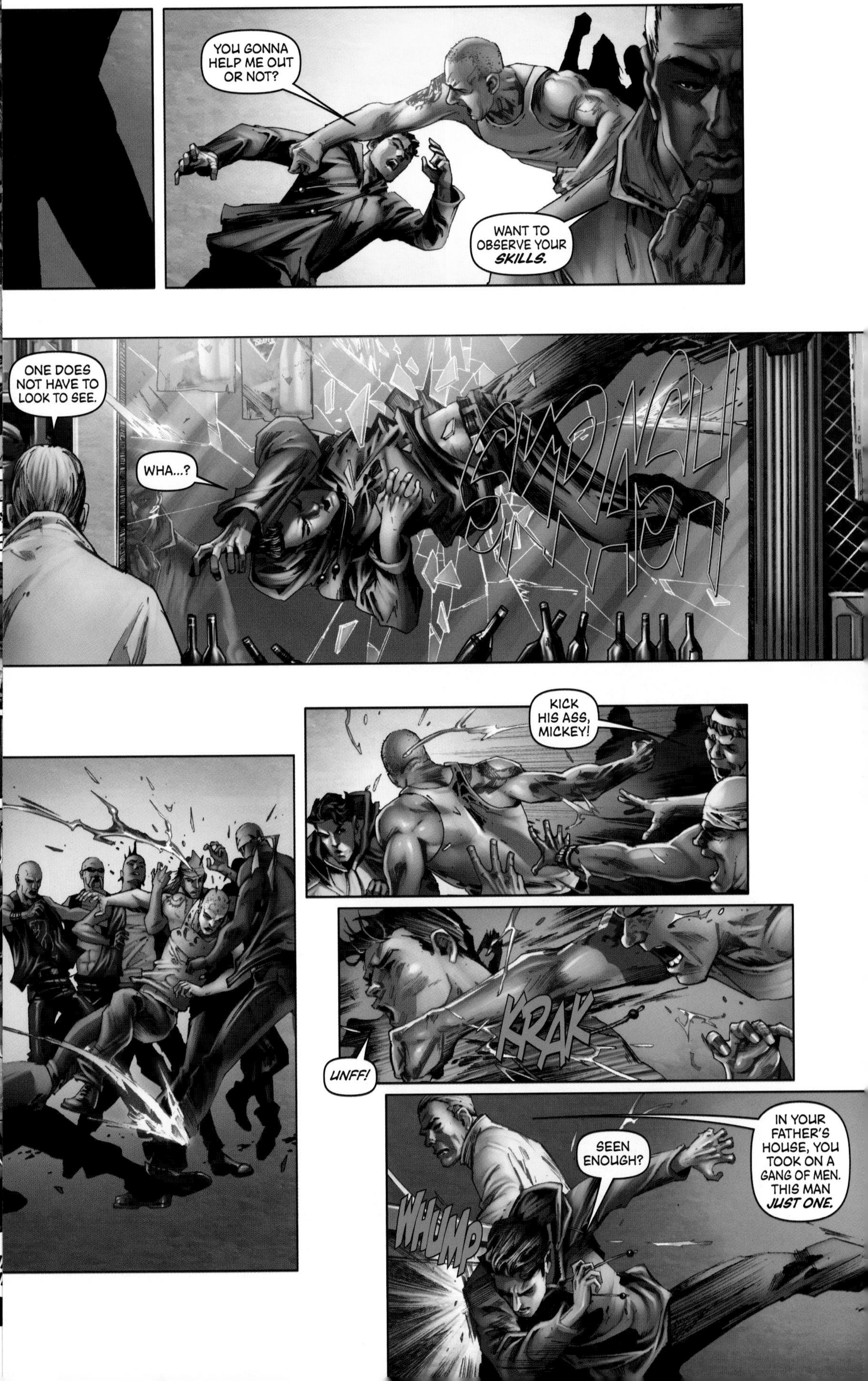

YOU GONNA HELP ME OUT OR NOT?
WANT TO OBSERVE YOUR *SKILLS.*
ONE DOES NOT HAVE TO LOOK TO SEE.
WHA...?
KICK HIS ASS, MICKEY!
KRAK
UNFF!
SEEN ENOUGH?
IN YOUR FATHER'S HOUSE, YOU TOOK ON A GANG OF MEN. THIS MAN *JUST ONE.*
WHUMP

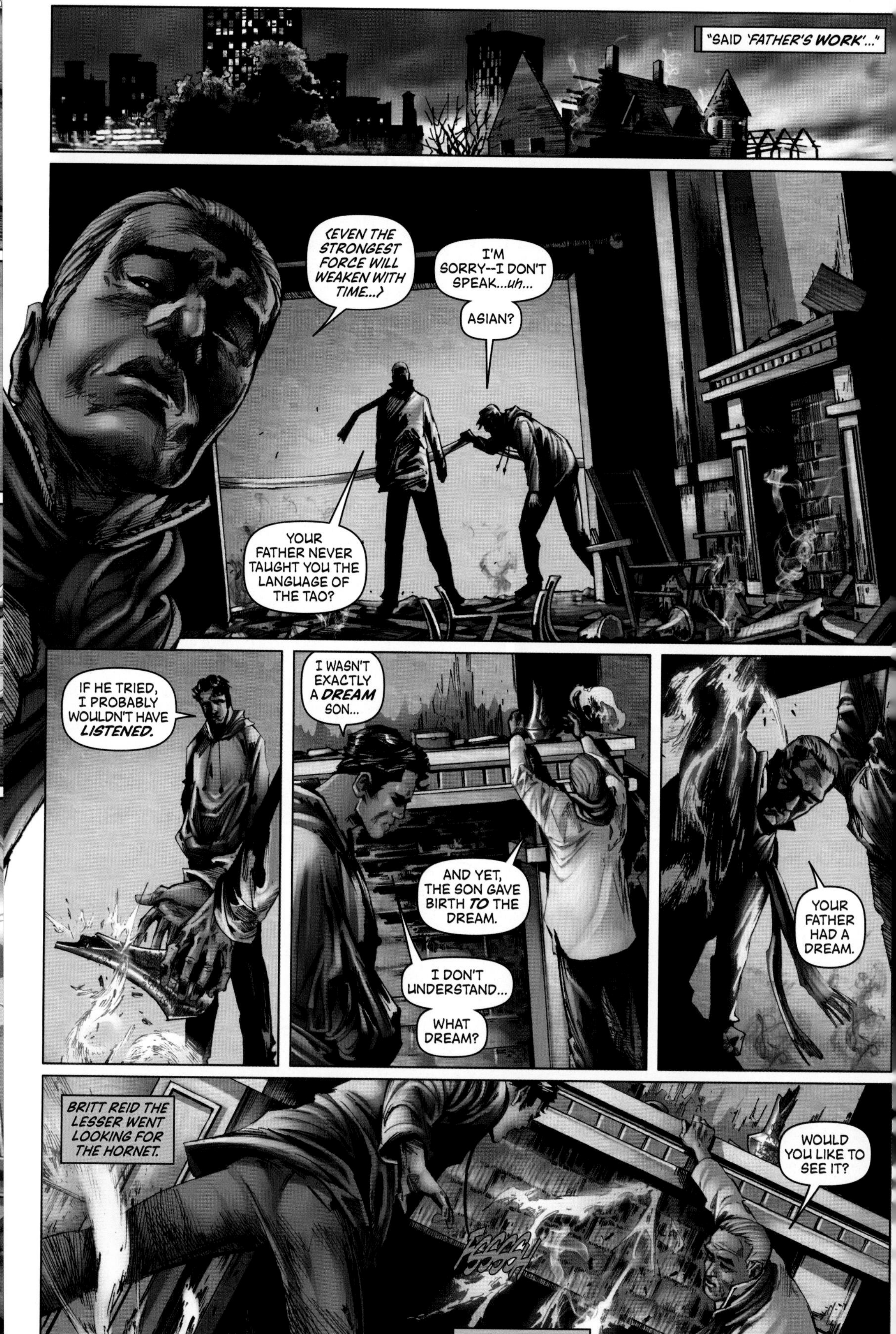
"SAID 'FATHER'S WORK'..."
<EVEN THE STRONGEST FORCE WILL WEAKEN WITH TIME...>
I'M SORRY--I DON'T SPEAK...uh...
ASIAN?
YOUR FATHER NEVER TAUGHT YOU THE LANGUAGE OF THE TAO?
IF HE TRIED, I PROBABLY WOULDN'T HAVE LISTENED.
I WASN'T EXACTLY A DREAM SON...
AND YET, THE SON GAVE BIRTH TO THE DREAM.
I DON'T UNDERSTAND...
WHAT DREAM?
YOUR FATHER HAD A DREAM.
BRITT REID THE LESSER WENT LOOKING FOR THE HORNET.
WOULD YOU LIKE TO SEE IT?
AND IN DOING SO...

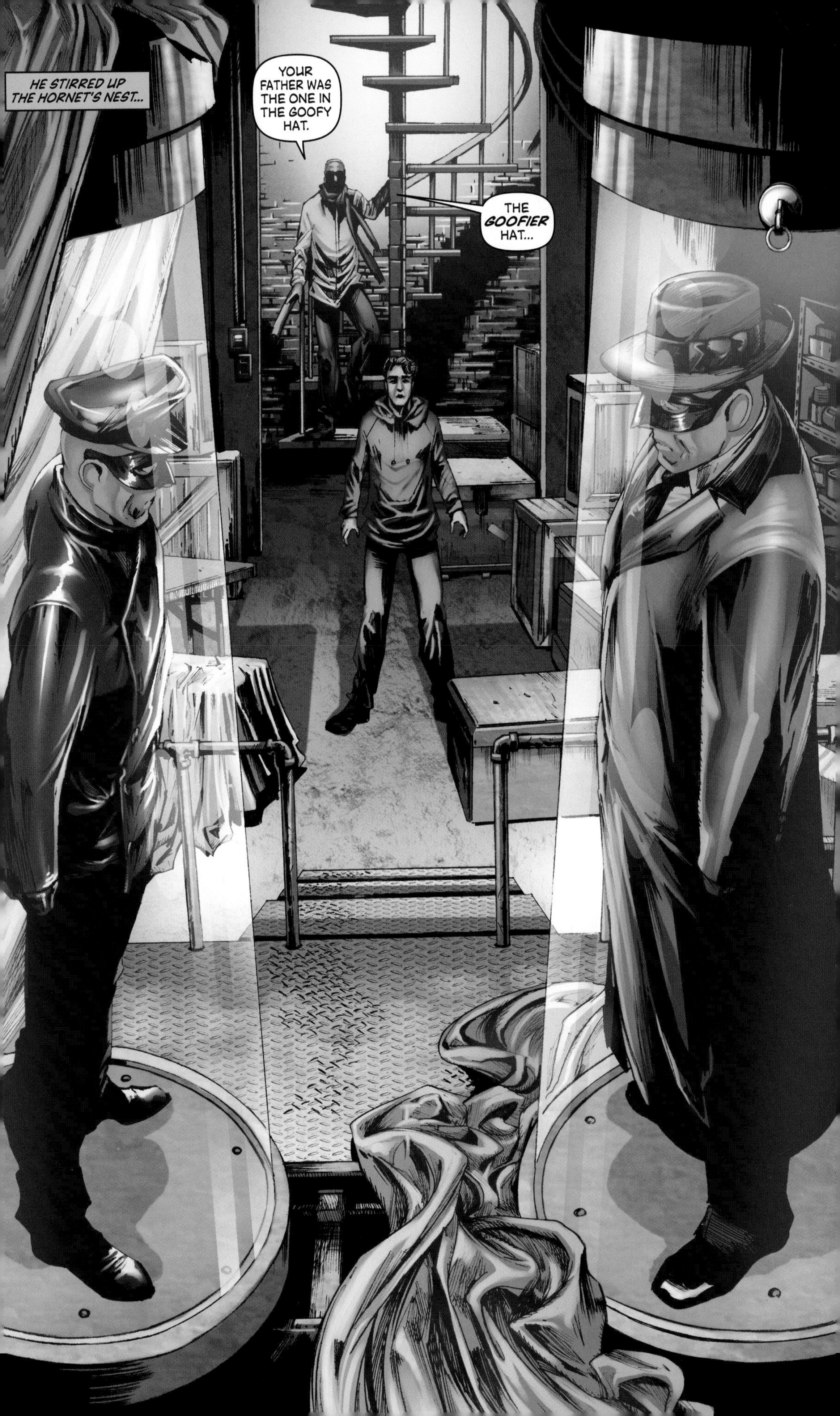
HE STIRRED UP THE HORNET'S NEST...
YOUR FATHER WAS THE ONE IN THE GOOFY HAT.
THE *GOOFIER* HAT...

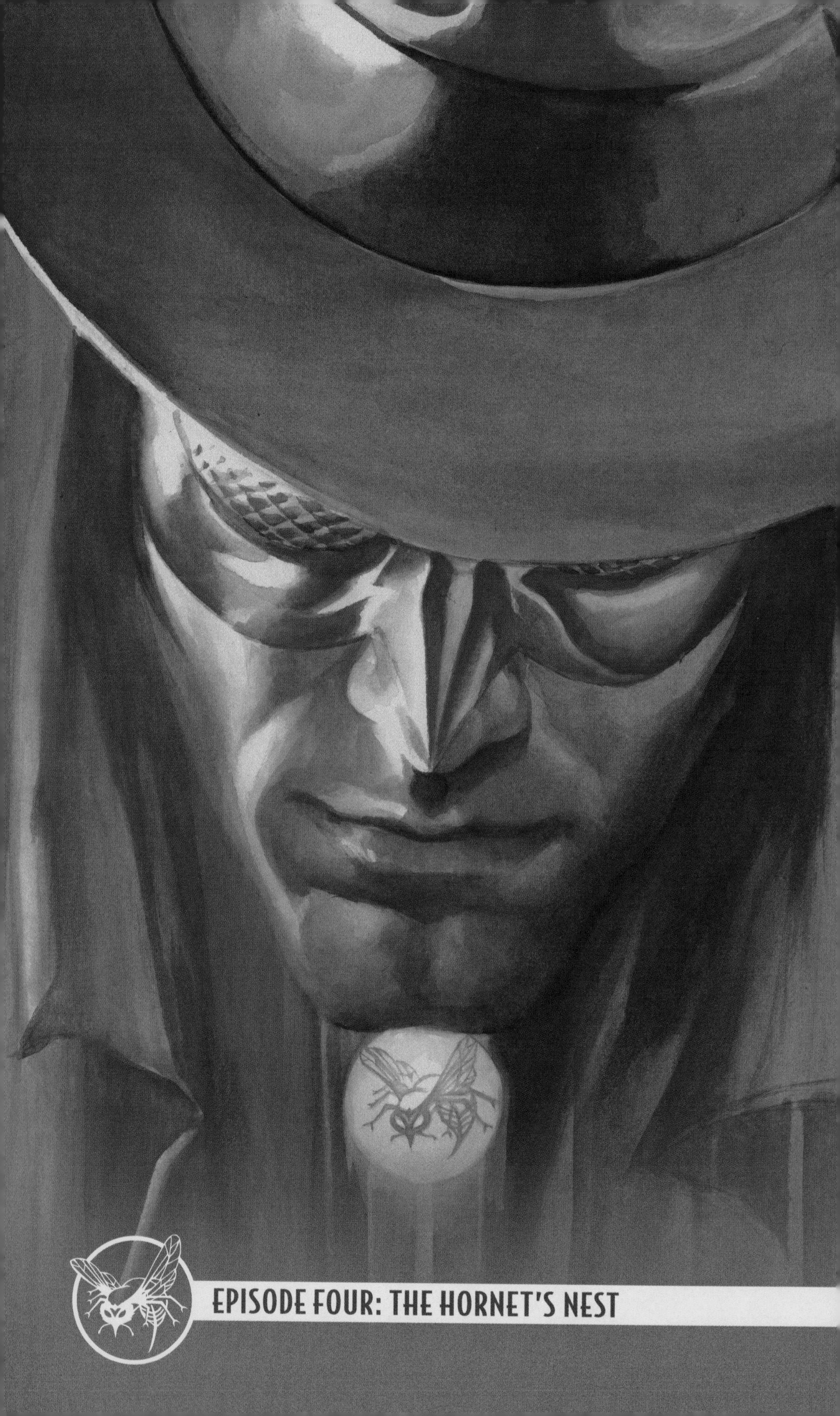

EPISODE FOUR: THE HORNET'S NEST

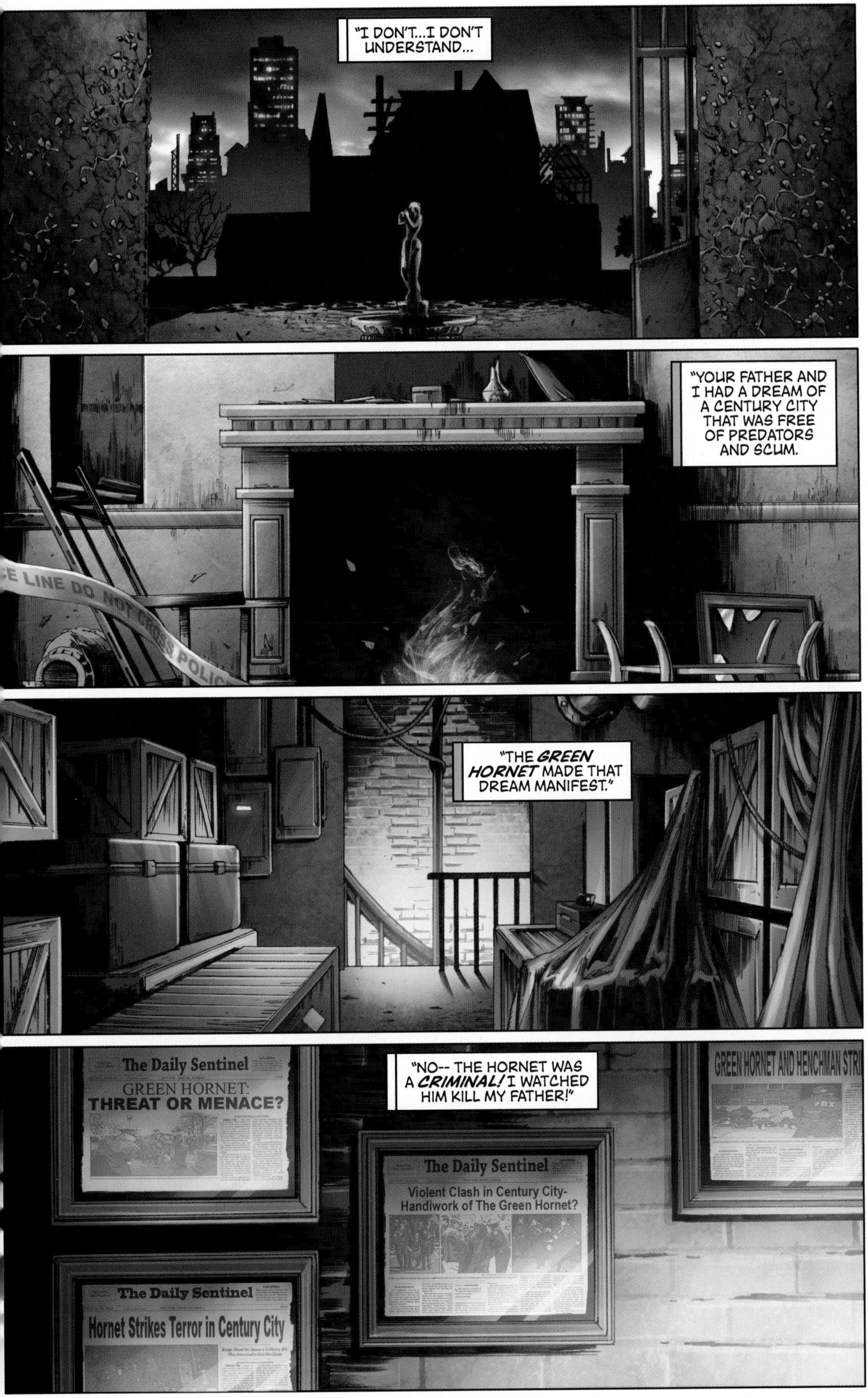
"I DON'T...I DON'T UNDERSTAND...
"YOUR FATHER AND I HAD A DREAM OF A CENTURY CITY THAT WAS FREE OF PREDATORS AND SCUM.
"THE *GREEN HORNET* MADE THAT DREAM MANIFEST."
"NO-- THE HORNET WAS A *CRIMINAL!* I WATCHED HIM KILL MY FATHER!"
The Daily Sentinel
GREEN HORNET: THREAT OR MENACE?
The Daily Sentinel
Violent Clash in Century City- Handiwork of The Green Hornet?
The Daily Sentinel
Hornet Strikes Terror in Century City

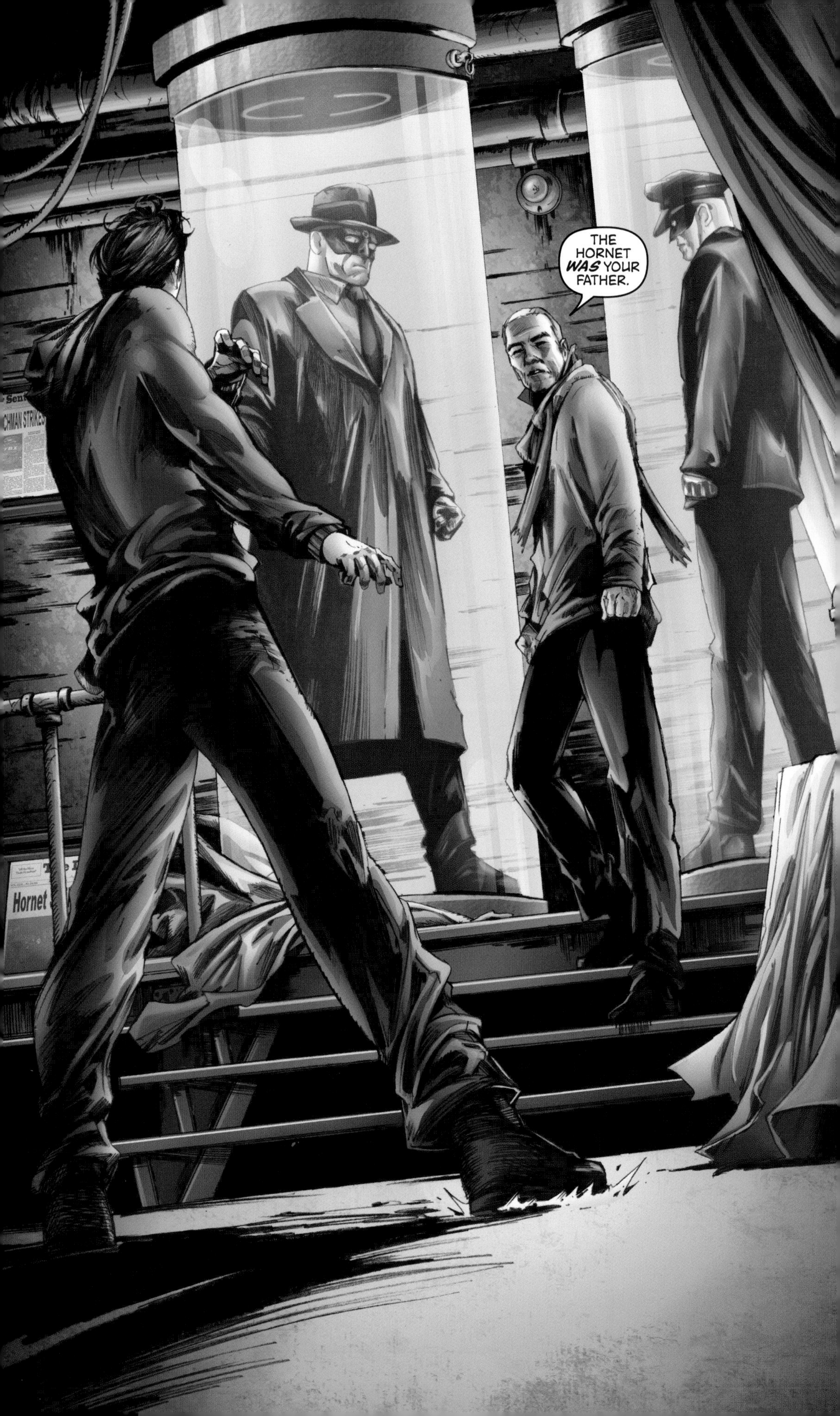
THE HORNET **WAS** YOUR FATHER.

WHEN YOU WERE TWO, YOUR FATHER AND I TOOK ON THE HABADASHERS-- A PARTICULARLY VICIOUS WEST SIDE GANG KNOWN FOR SCALPING THEIR ENEMIES ALIVE.

AFTER YOUR FATHER WAS NEARLY DECAPITATED BY A FIFTEEN YEAR OLD HAB LOOKING TO MAKE HIS BONES, HE DREW UP A PAIR OF LIVING WILLS: ONE FOR BRITT REID...

AND ONE FOR THE HORNET.

THE SECRET WILL STIPULATES THAT IF HE WERE TO BE KILLED AS BRITT REID BY AN ENEMY OF THE GREEN HORNET...

IT MEANT THE HORNET IDENTITY WAS COMPROMISED. WHICH MEANT YOU AND YOUR MOTHER WERE IN GRAVE DANGER.

SO OUR FIRST PRIORITY IS TO GET YOU ON THE REID JET AND OFF TO CHINA.

THERE IS A SAFE-HOUSE WHERE YOU'LL STAY UNTIL THIS CITY IS SECURED AGAIN-- AND YOUR FATHER'S MURDERER IS NEUTRALIZED.

YOU'RE OUT OF YOUR *MIND!* I'M NOT GOING TO CHINA!

CHINA?!

I'M AFRAID YOU HAVE NO CHOICE. YOU CAN GET ON THE PLANE WILLINGLY...

OR WE CAN *ASSIST* YOU.

AND WHAT ARE YOU TWO GONNA DO?

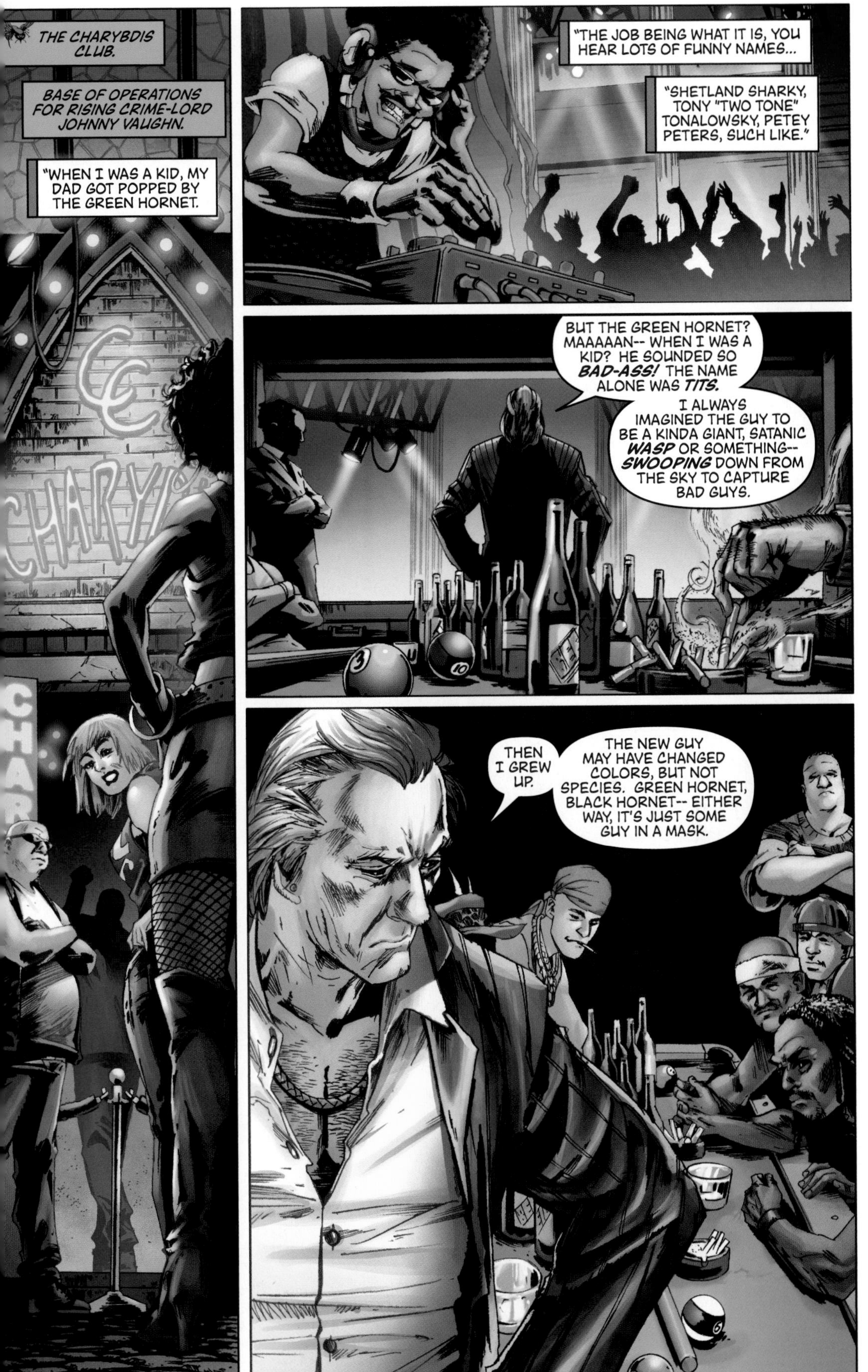
THE CHARYBDIS CLUB.
BASE OF OPERATIONS FOR RISING CRIME-LORD JOHNNY VAUGHN.
"WHEN I WAS A KID, MY DAD GOT POPPED BY THE GREEN HORNET.
"THE JOB BEING WHAT IT IS, YOU HEAR LOTS OF FUNNY NAMES...
"SHETLAND SHARKY, TONY "TWO TONE" TONALOWSKY, PETEY PETERS, SUCH LIKE."
BUT THE GREEN HORNET? MAAAAAN-- WHEN I WAS A KID? HE SOUNDED SO BAD-ASS! THE NAME ALONE WAS TITS.
I ALWAYS IMAGINED THE GUY TO BE A KINDA GIANT, SATANIC WASP OR SOMETHING-- SWOOPING DOWN FROM THE SKY TO CAPTURE BAD GUYS.
THEN I GREW UP.
THE NEW GUY MAY HAVE CHANGED COLORS, BUT NOT SPECIES. GREEN HORNET, BLACK HORNET-- EITHER WAY, IT'S JUST SOME GUY IN A MASK.

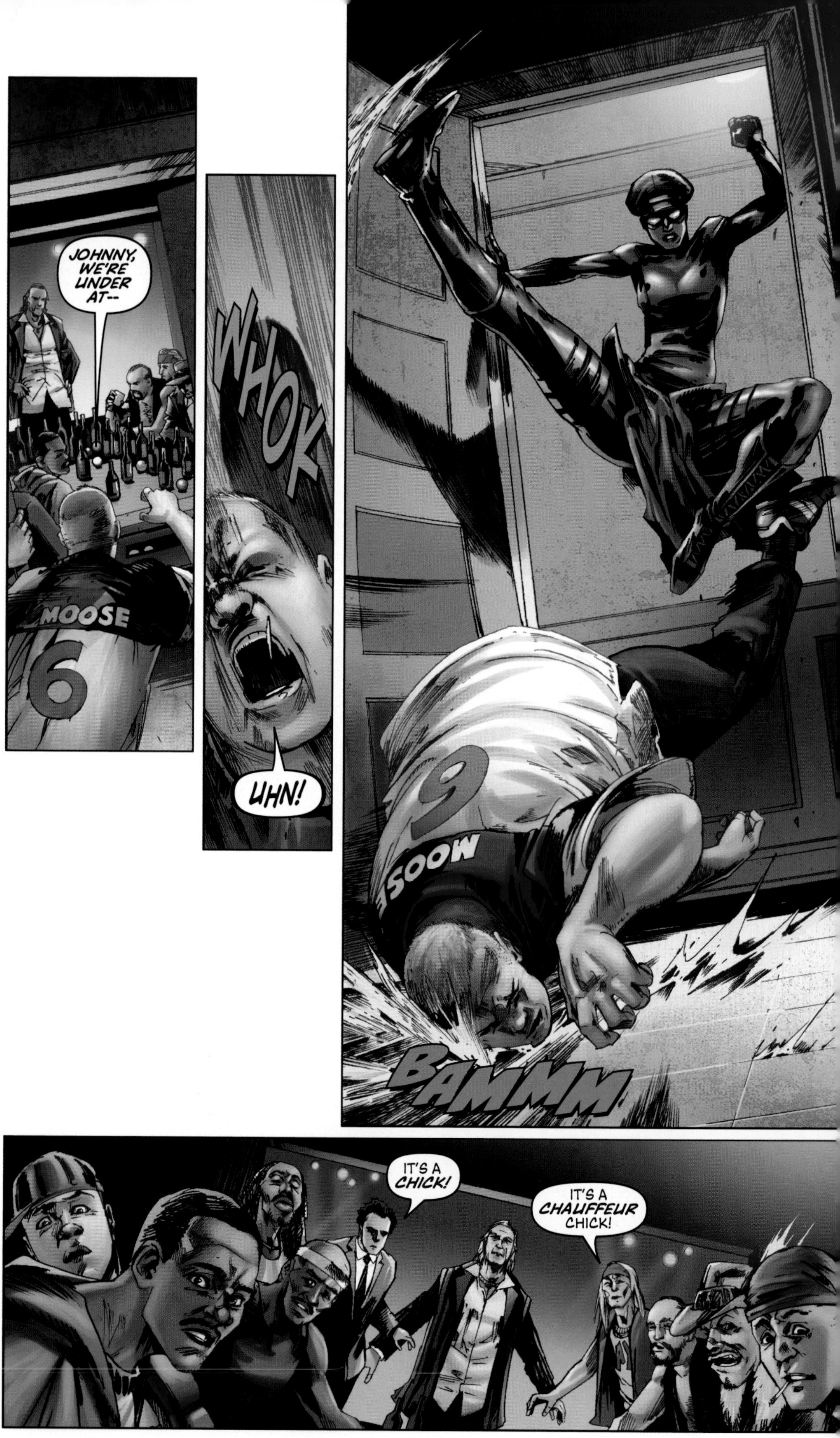
JOHNNY, WE'RE UNDER AT--
MOOSE
6
WHOK
UHN!
MOOSE
6
BAMMM
IT'S A CHICK!
IT'S A CHAUFFEUR CHICK!

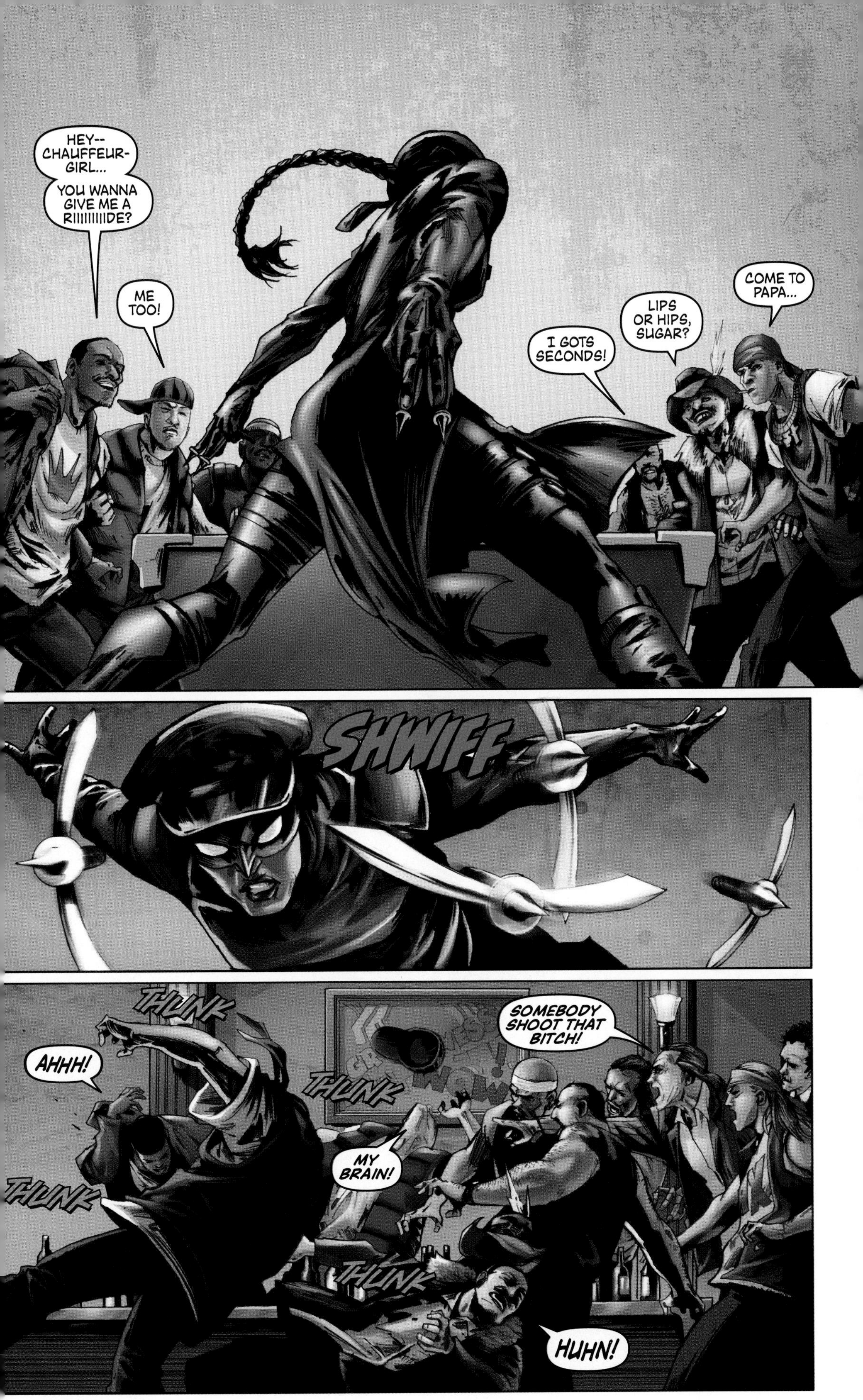
HEY-- CHAUFFEUR-GIRL...
YOU WANNA GIVE ME A RIIIIIIIIIDE?
ME TOO!
I GOTS SECONDS!
LIPS OR HIPS, SUGAR?
COME TO PAPA...
SHWIFF
THUNK
AHHH!
THUNK
THUNK
SOMEBODY SHOOT THAT BITCH!
MY BRAIN!
THUNK
HUHN!

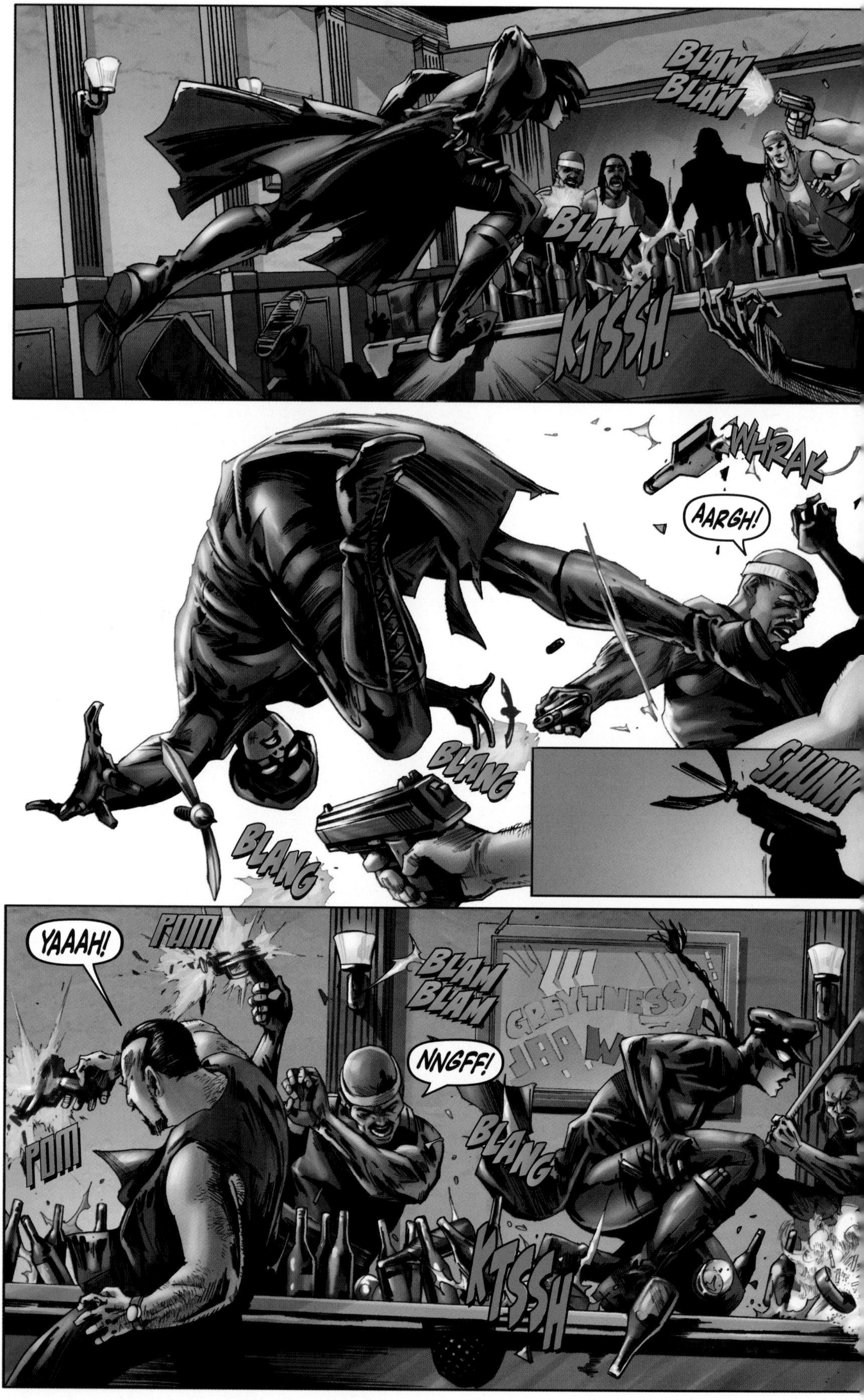
BLAM BLAM
BLAM
KTSSH
WHRAK
AARGH!
BLANG
BLANG
SHUNK
YAAAH!
POM
BLAM BLAM
NNGFF!
POM
GREYTINESS
BLANG
KTSSH

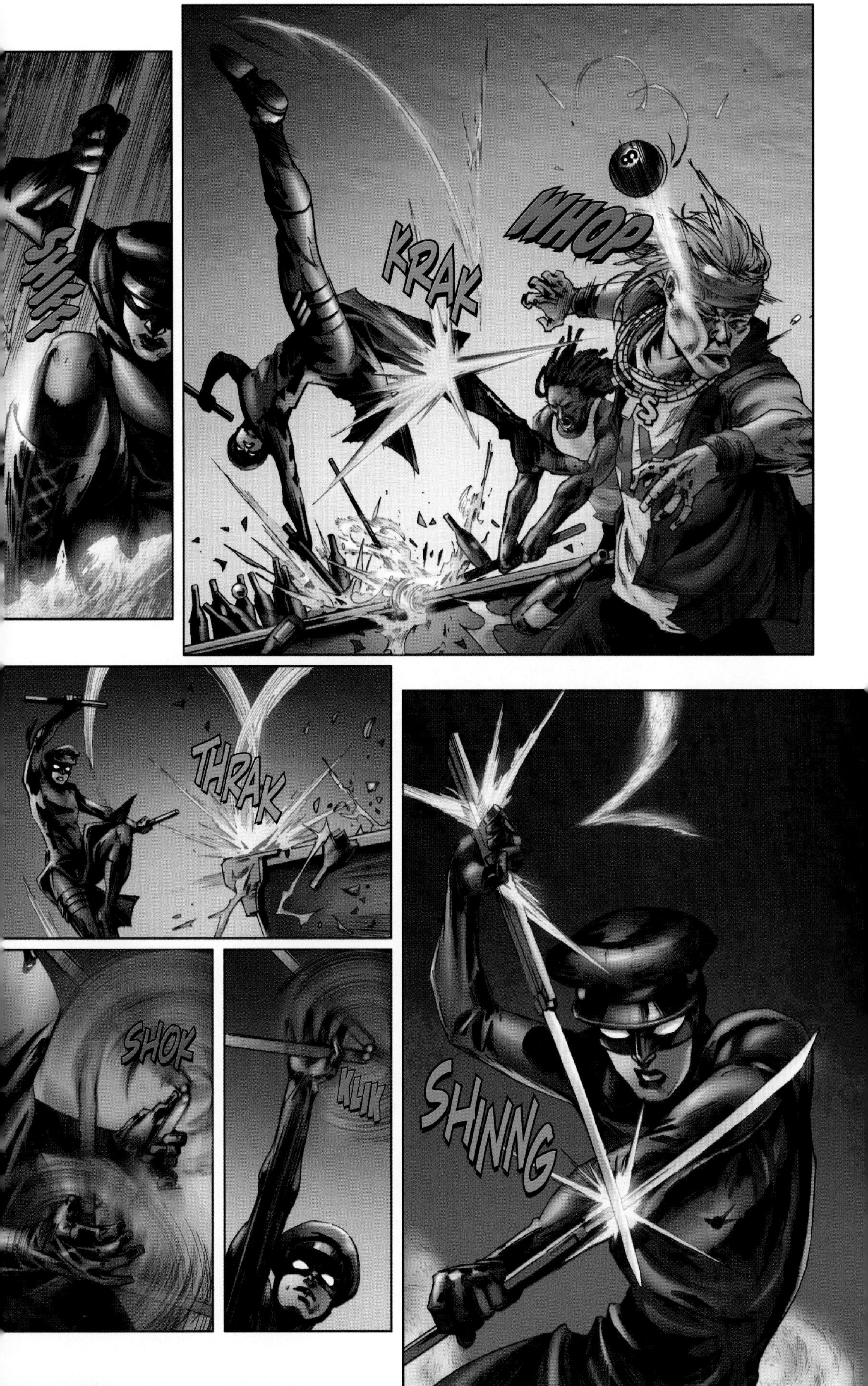
SHIFF
KRAK
WHOP
THRAK
SHOK
KLIK
SHINNG

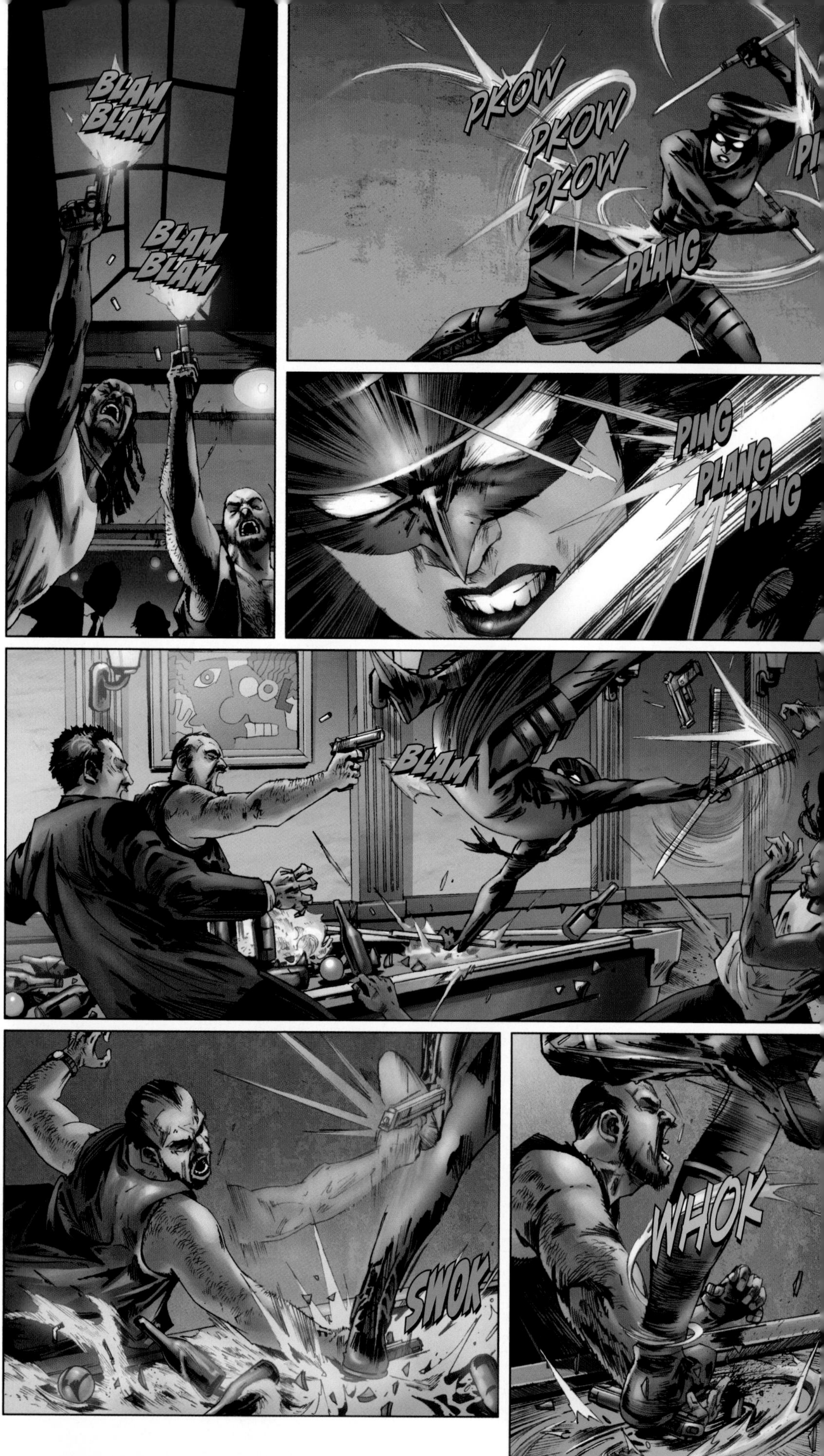
BLAM
BLAM
BLAM
BLAM
PKOW
PKOW
PKOW
PLANG
PING
PLANG
PING
BLAM
SWOK
WHOK

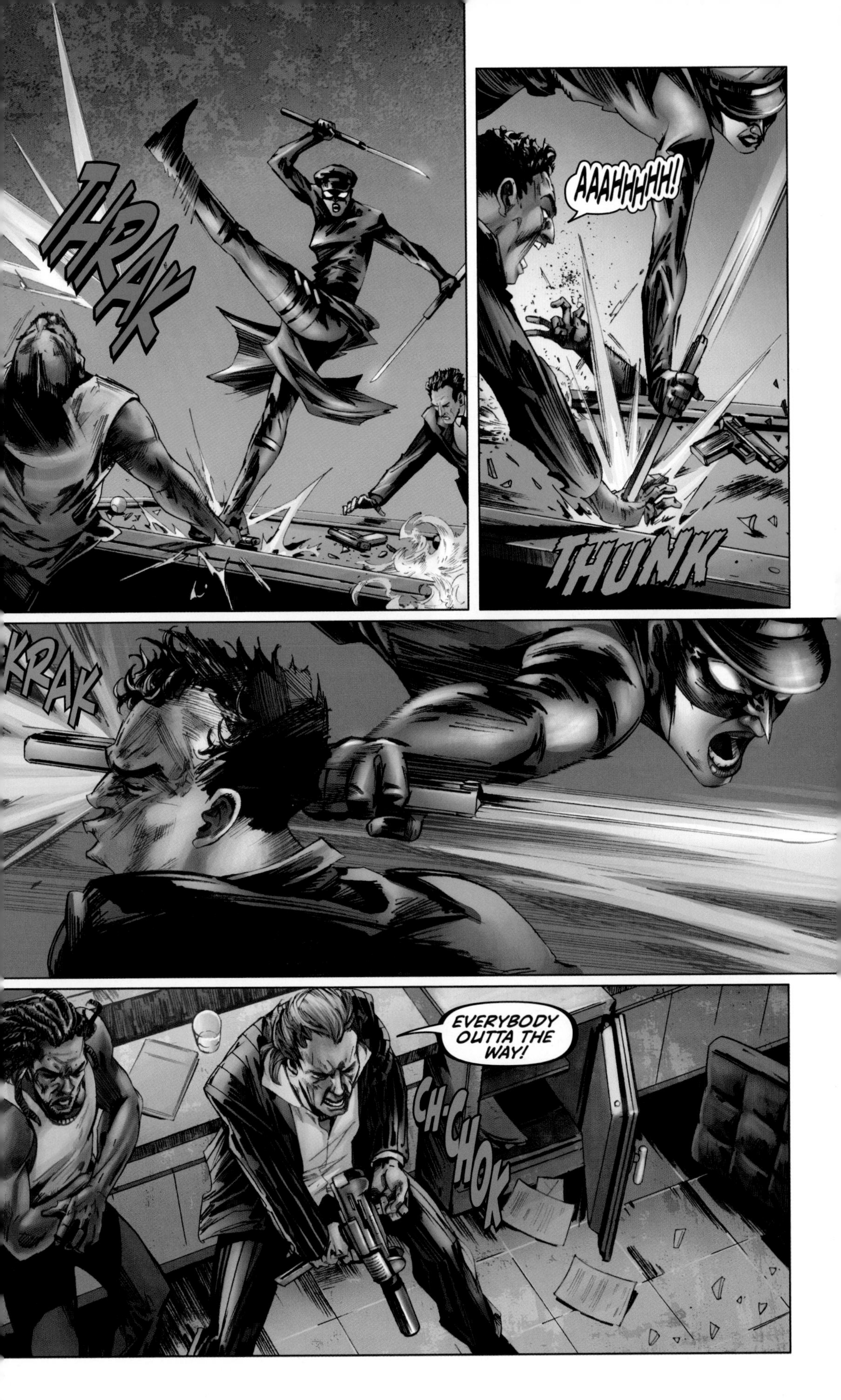
THRAK
AAAHHHHH!
THUNK
KRAK
EVERYBODY OUTTA THE WAY!
CH-CHOK

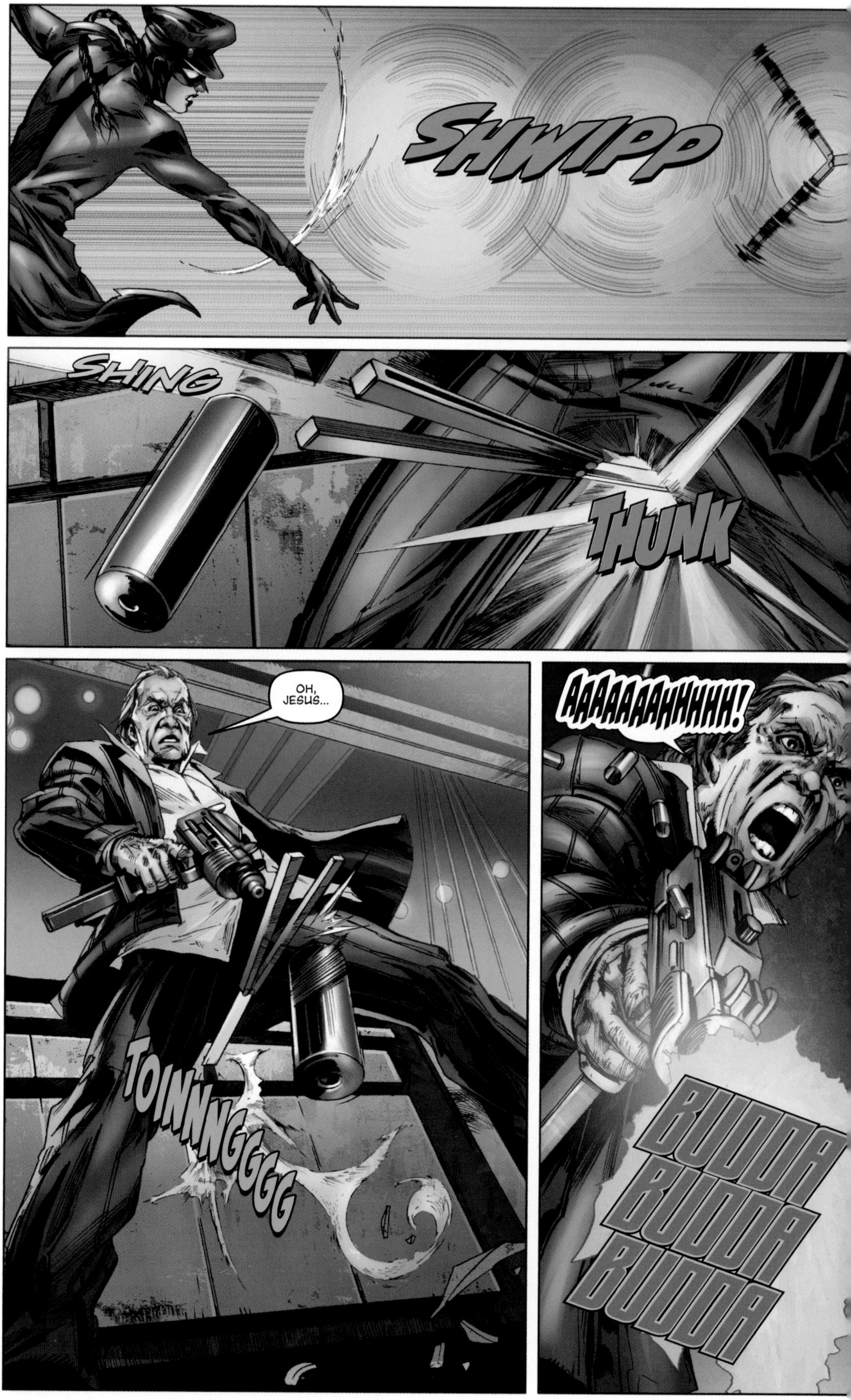
SHWIPP
SHING
THUNK
OH, JESUS...
TOINNNGGGG
AAAAAAAHHHHH!
BUDDA BUDDA BUDDA

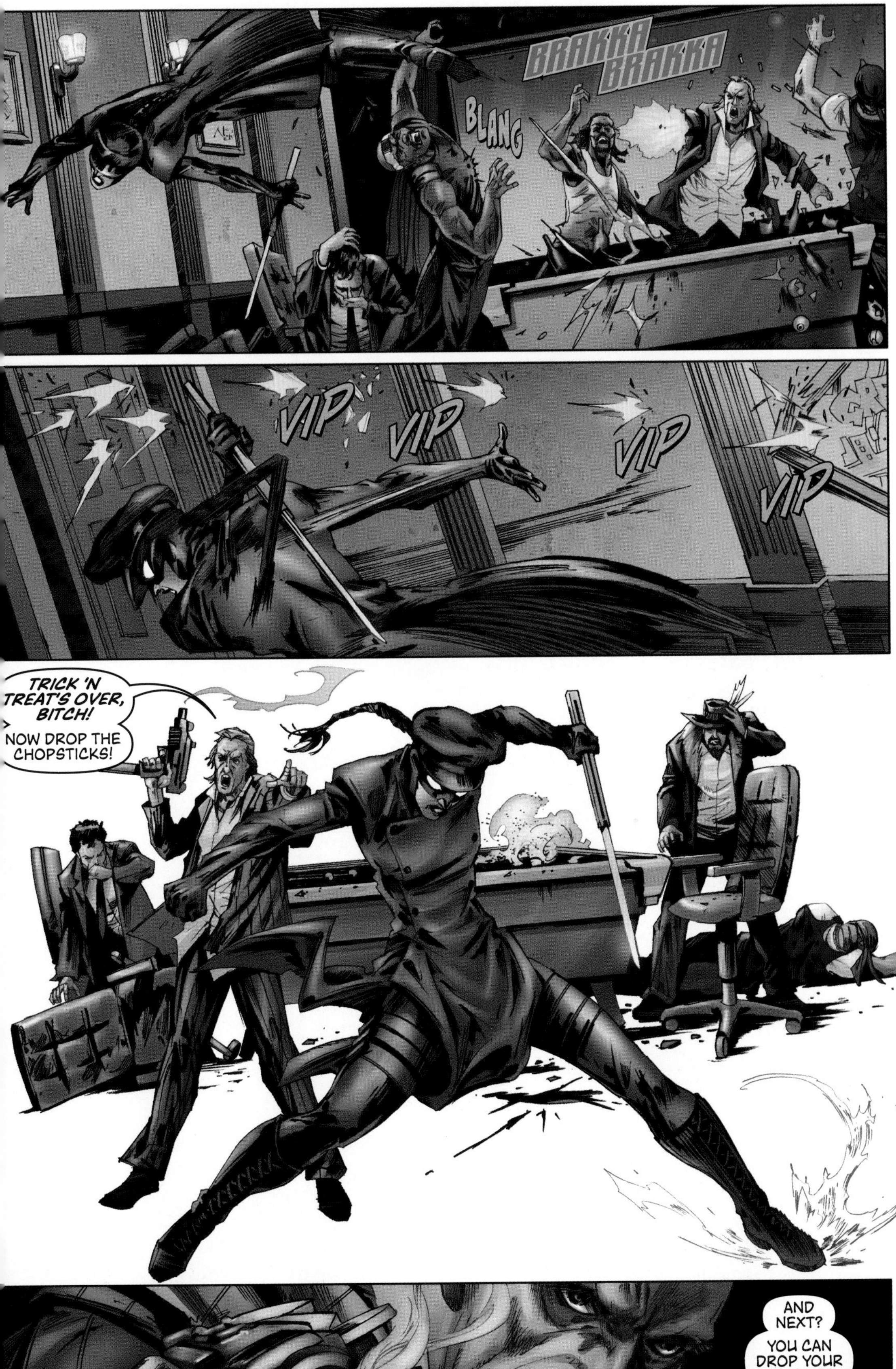
BRAKKA BRAKKA
BLANG
VIP
VIP
VIP
VIP
TRICK 'N TREAT'S OVER, BITCH!
NOW DROP THE CHOPSTICKS!
AND NEXT?
YOU CAN DROP YOUR *PANTIES.*

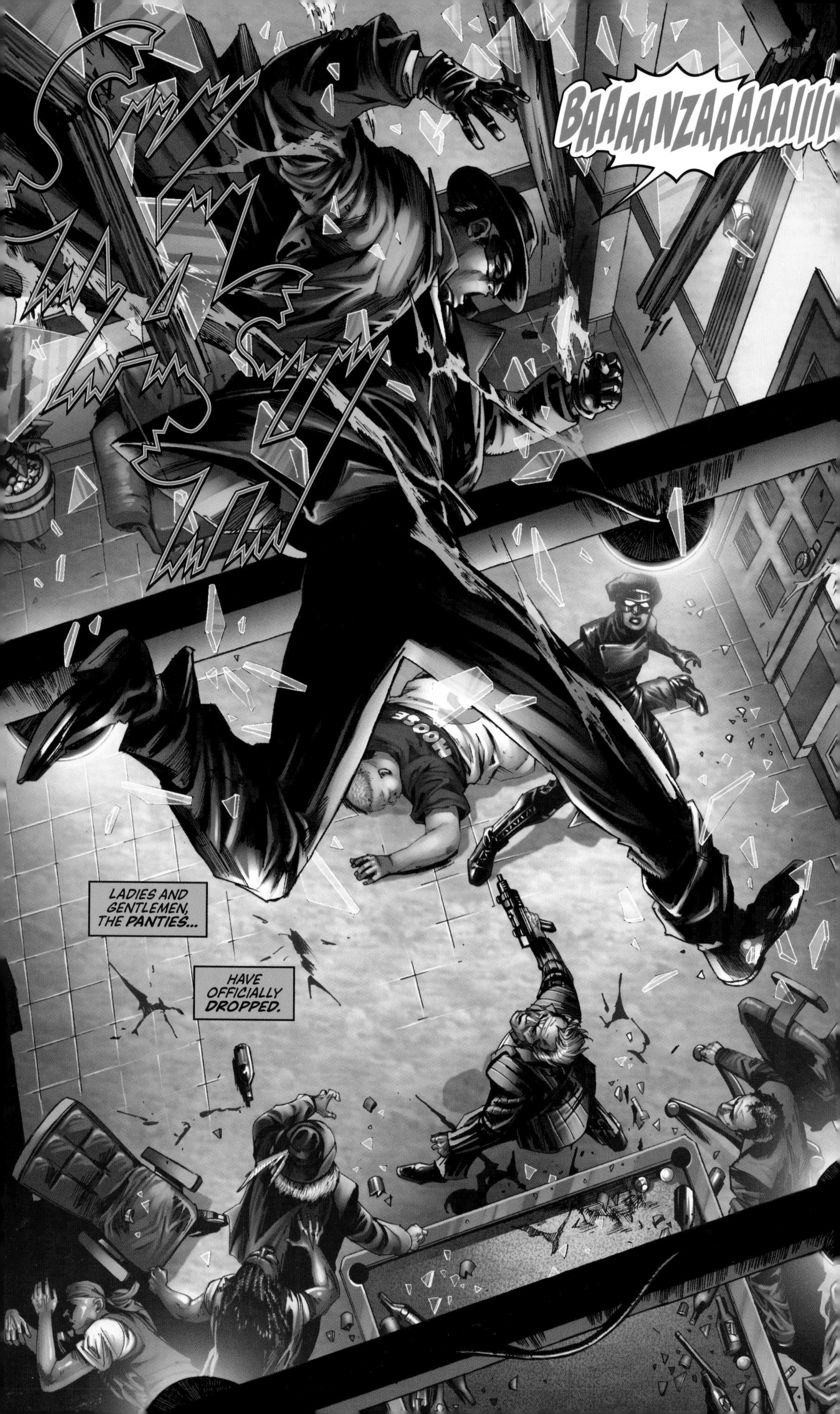
BAAAANZAAAAAIIIII
MOOSE
LADIES AND GENTLEMEN, THE PANTIES...
HAVE OFFICIALLY DROPPED.

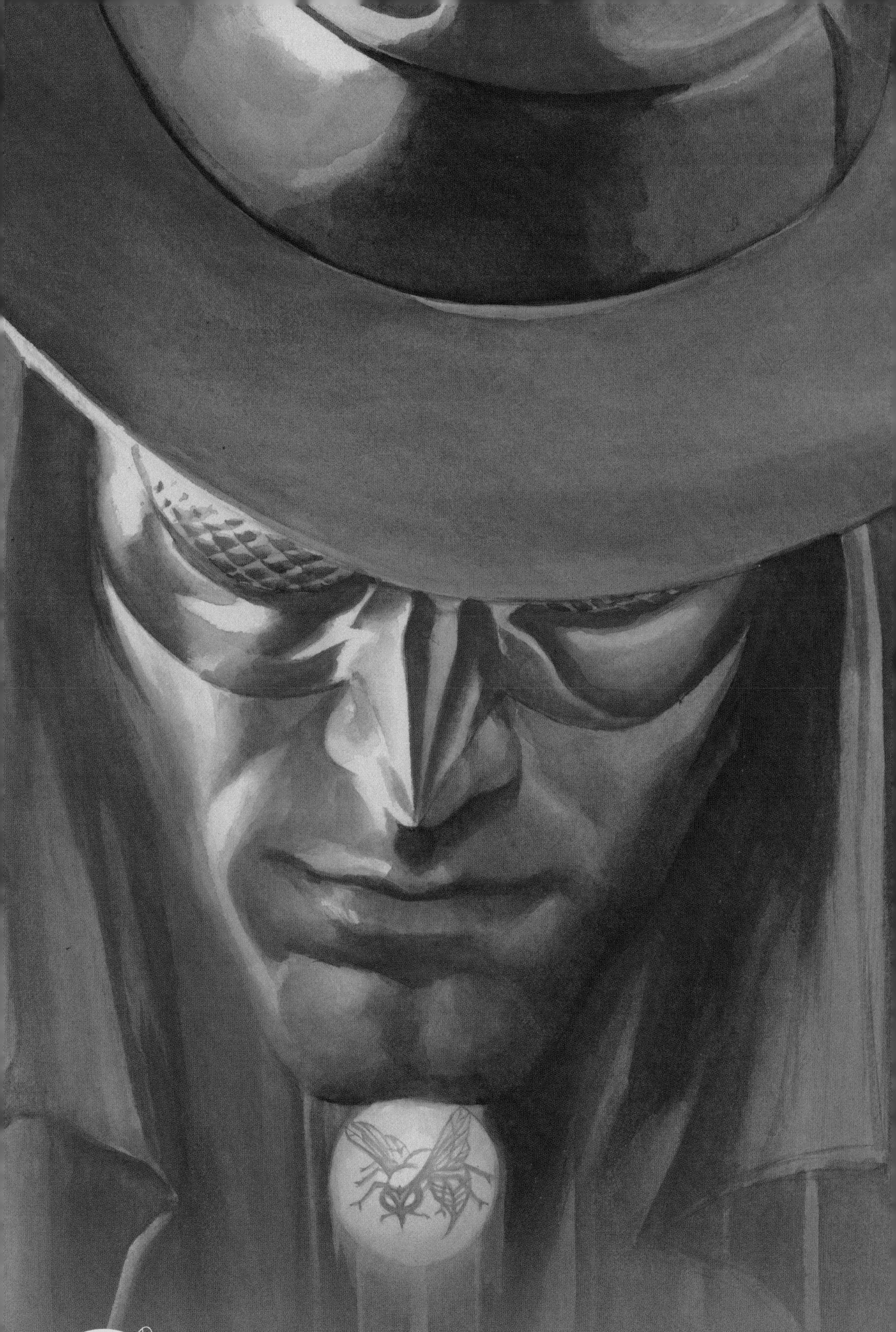

EPISODE FIVE: CRASH COURSE

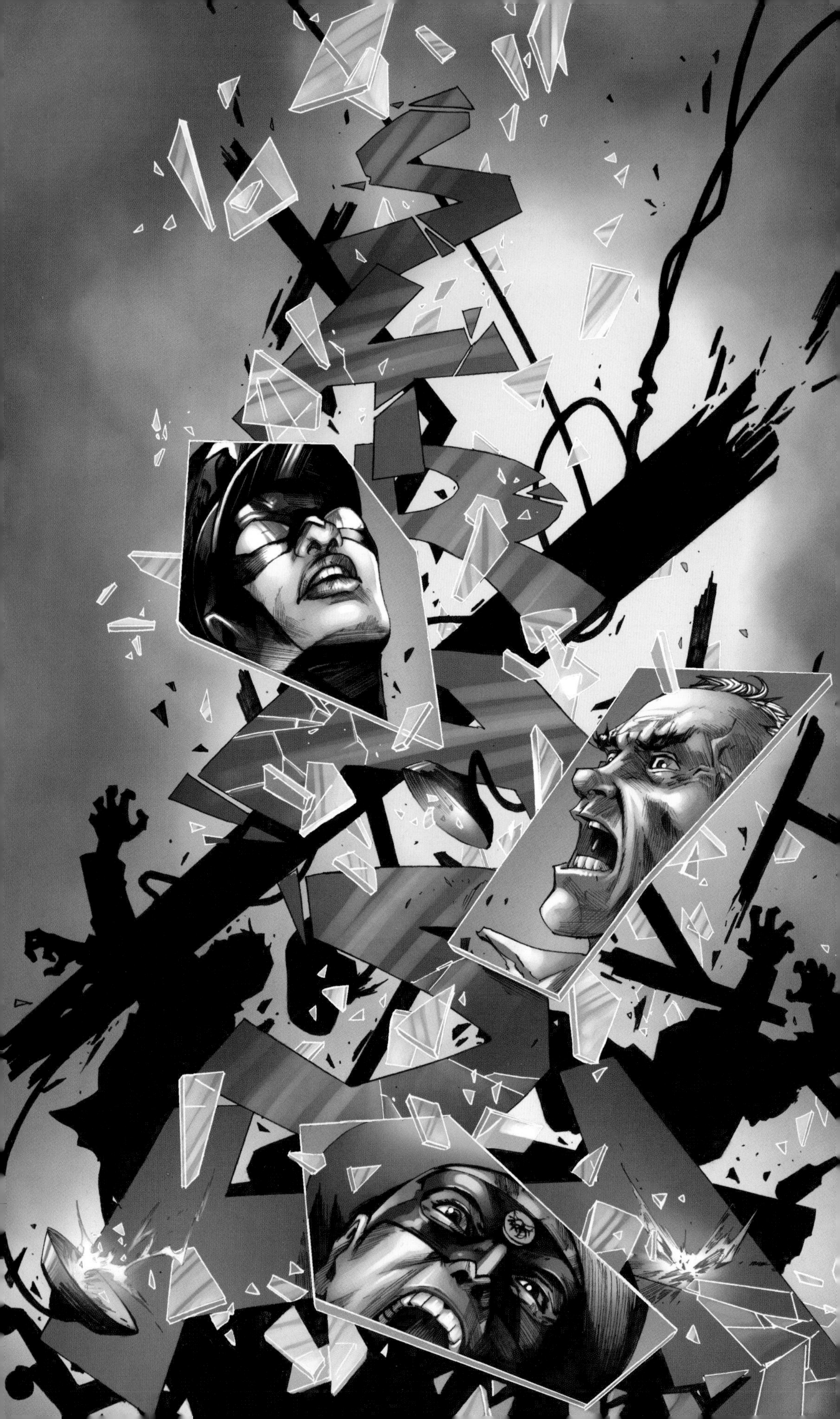

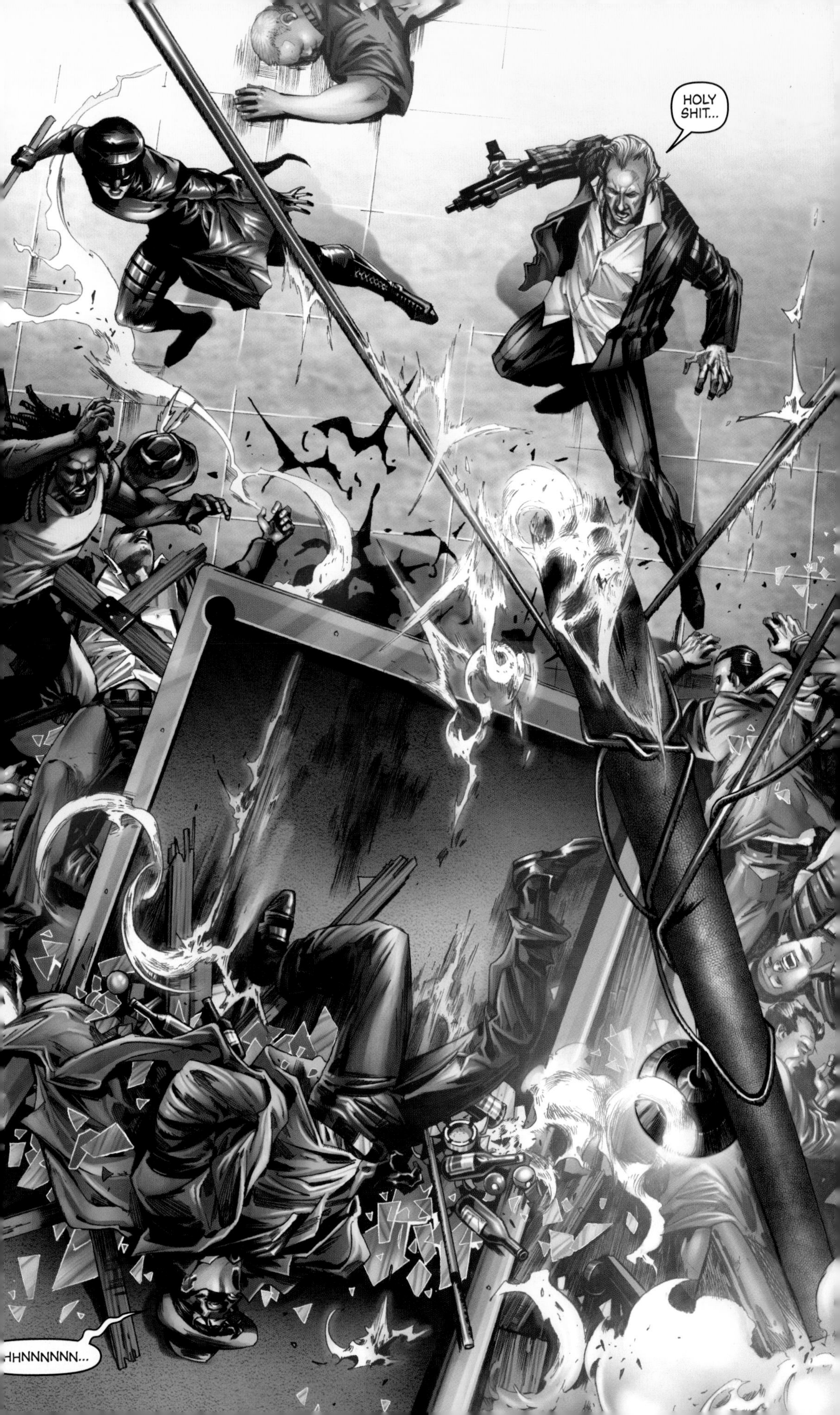
HOLY SHIT...
HHNNNNNNN...

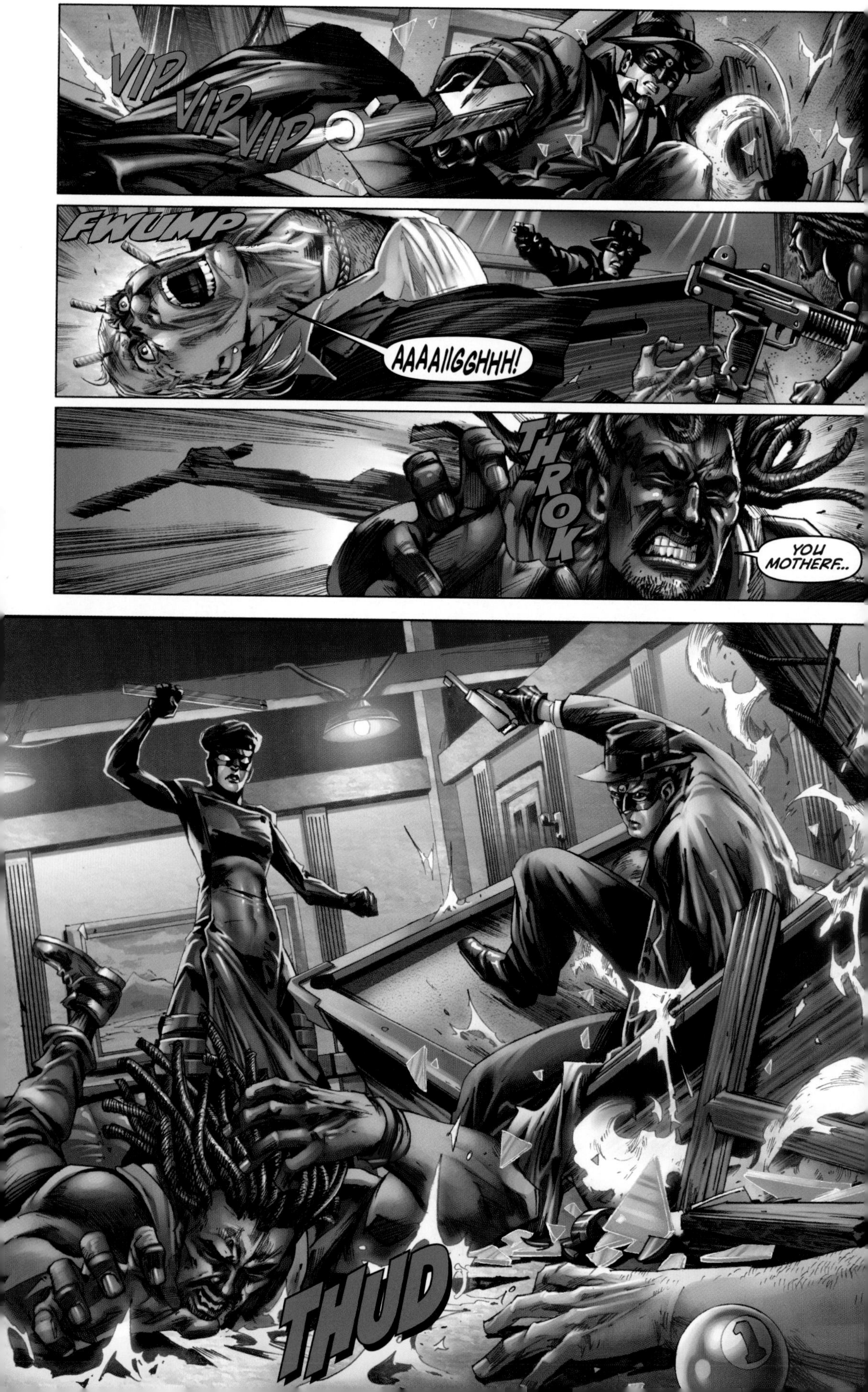
VIP VIP VIP
FWUMP
AAAAIIGGHHH!
THROK
YOU MOTHERF...
THUD

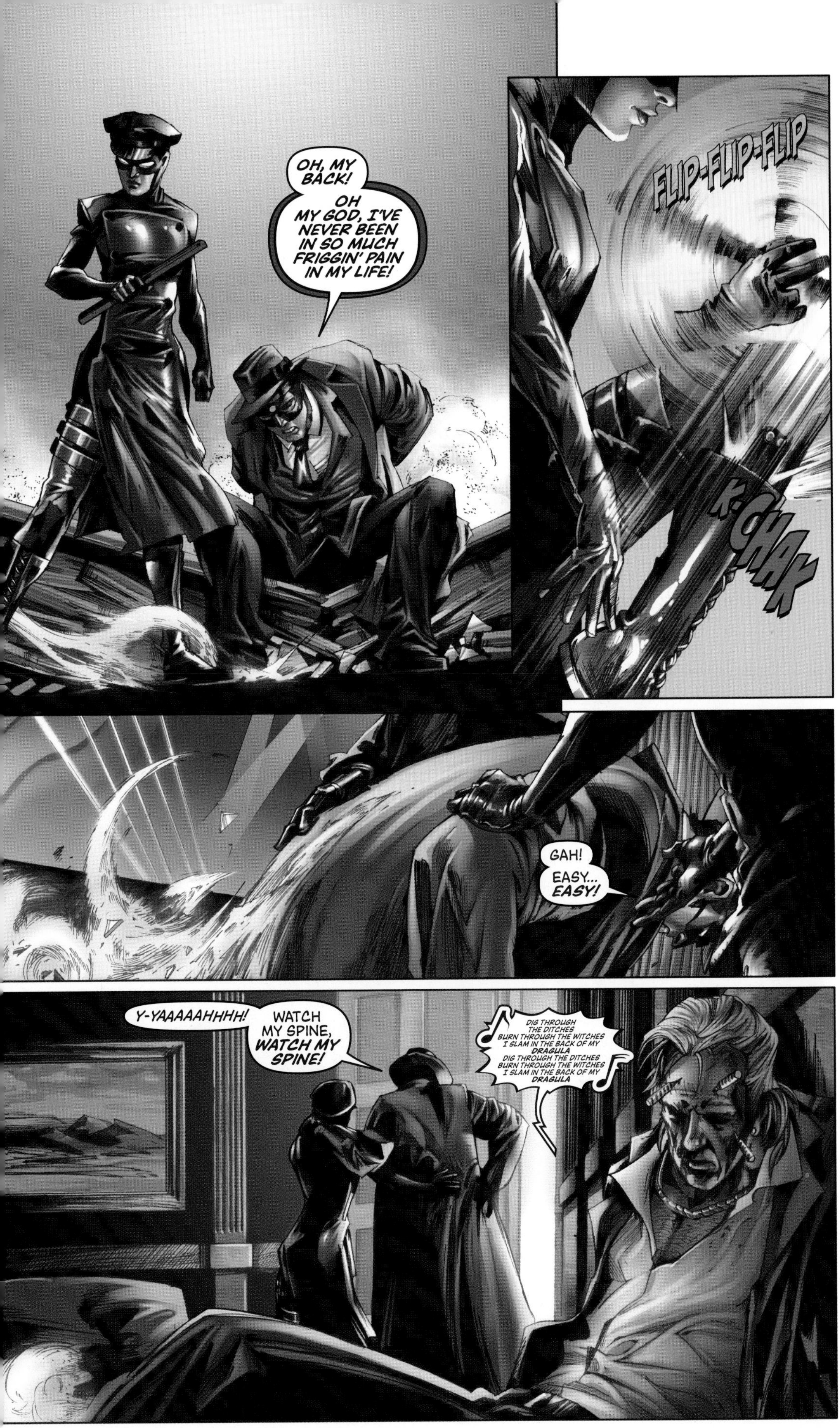
OH, MY BACK!
OH MY GOD, I'VE NEVER BEEN IN SO MUCH FRIGGIN' PAIN IN MY LIFE!
FLIP-FLIP-FLIP
K-CHAK
GAH! EASY... EASY!
Y-YAAAAAHHHH!
WATCH MY SPINE, WATCH MY SPINE!
DIG THROUGH THE DITCHES BURN THROUGH THE WITCHES I SLAM IN THE BACK OF MY DRAGULA DIG THROUGH THE DITCHES BURN THROUGH THE WITCHES I SLAM IN THE BACK OF MY DRAGULA

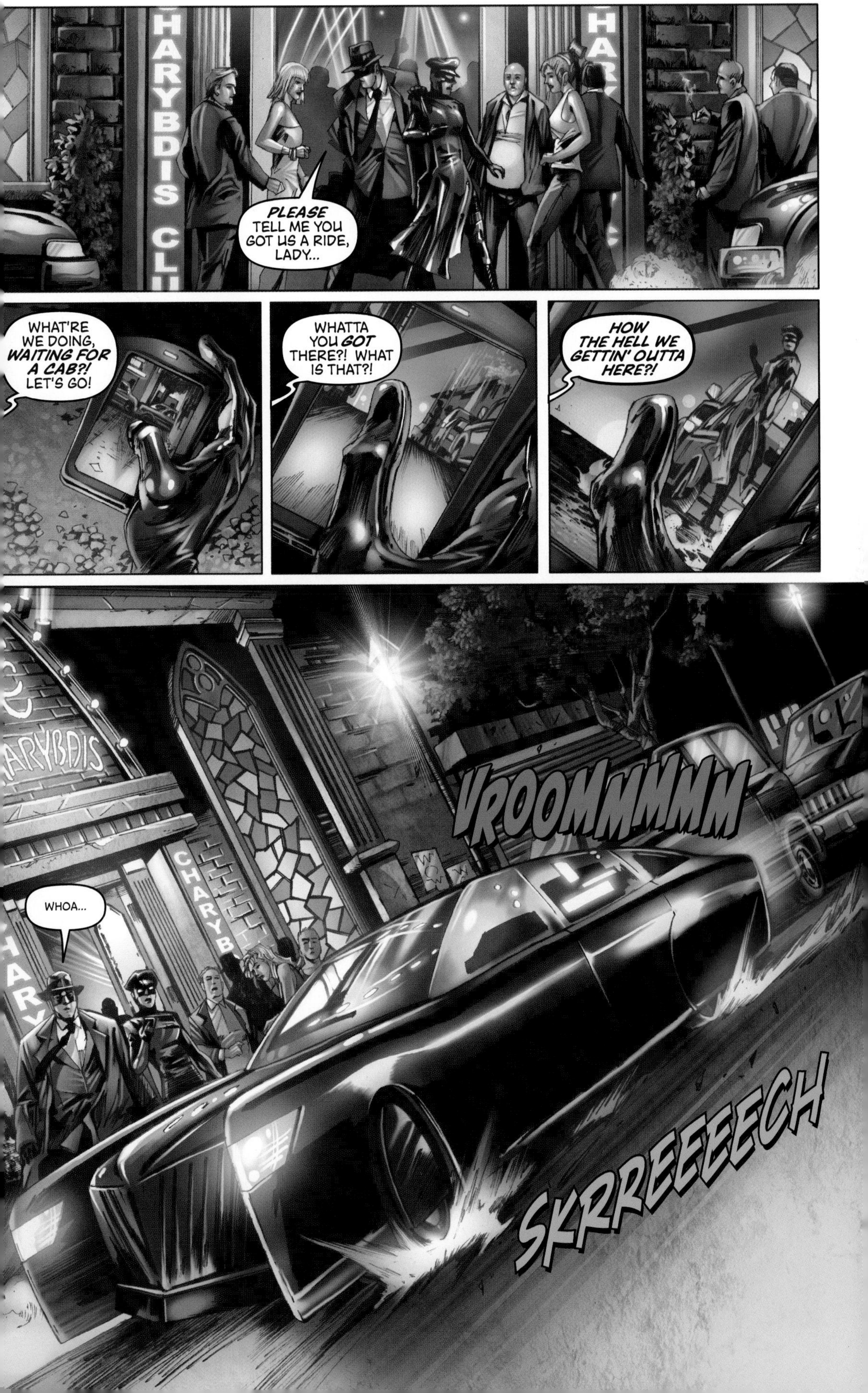
CHARYBDIS CLU
PLEASE TELL ME YOU GOT US A RIDE, LADY...
WHAT'RE WE DOING, WAITING FOR A CAB?! LET'S GO!
WHATTA YOU GOT THERE?! WHAT IS THAT?!
HOW THE HELL WE GETTIN' OUTTA HERE?!
CHARYBDIS
CHARYB
WHOA...
VROOMMMMMM
SKRREEEEECH

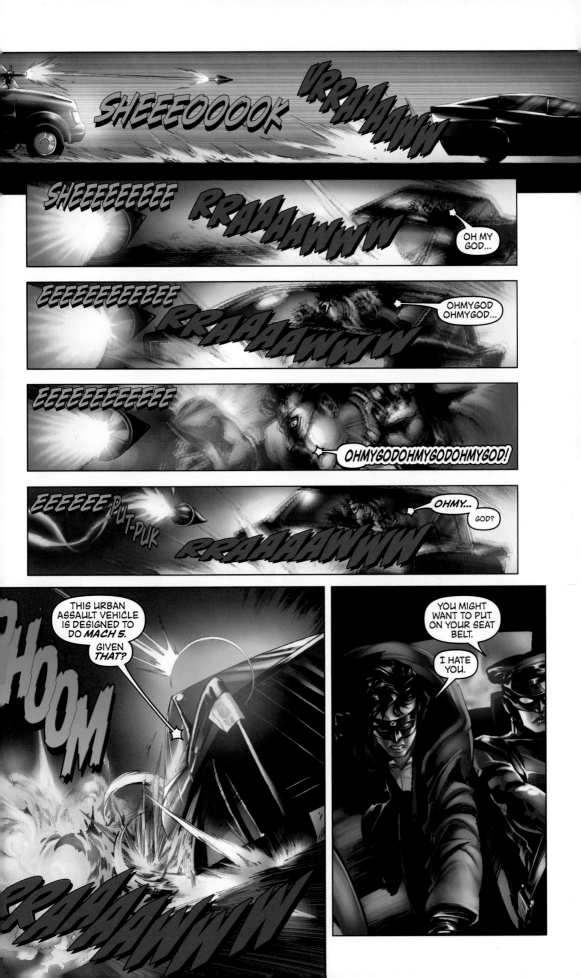

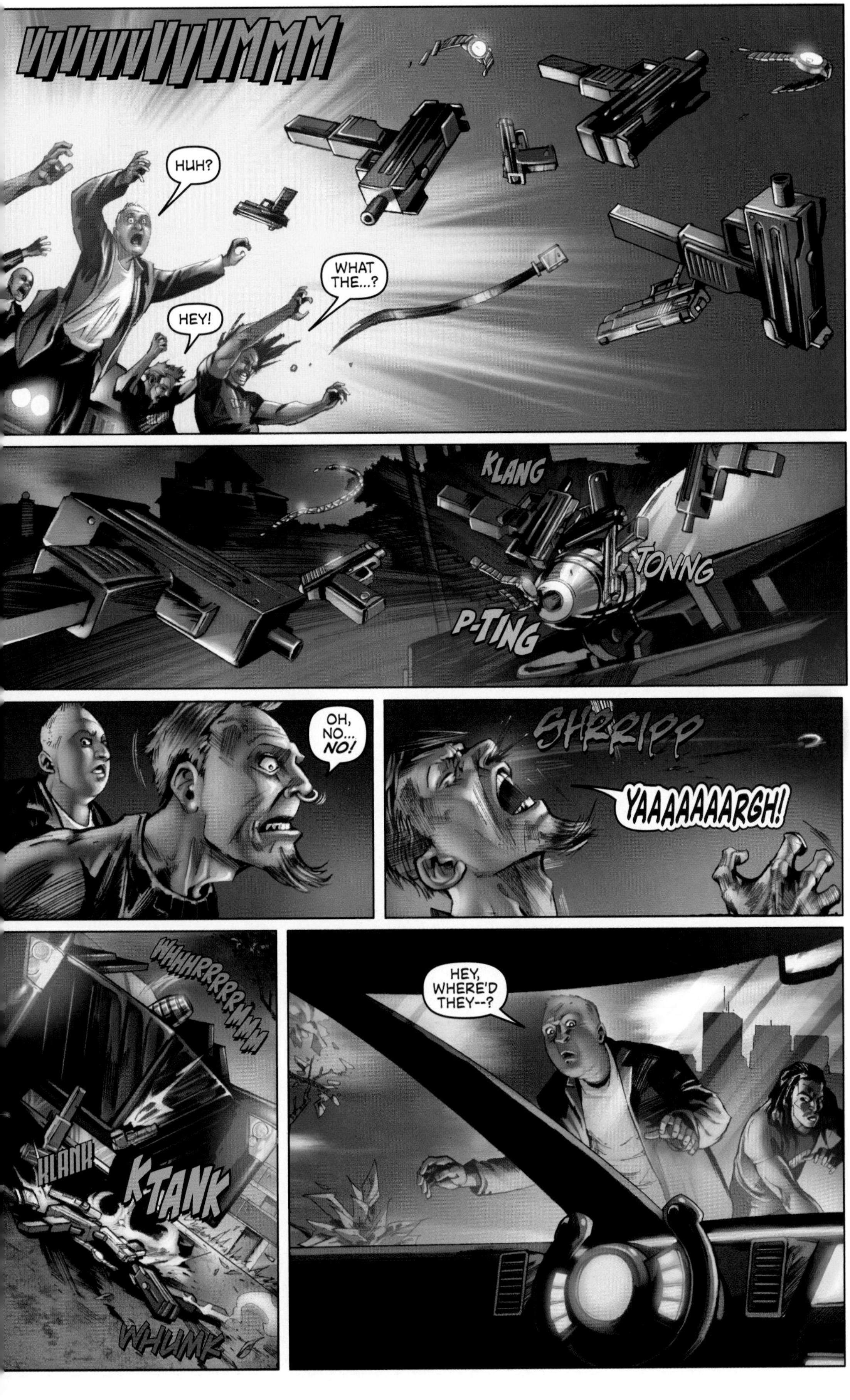
VVVVVVVVVVMMMM
HUH?
WHAT THE...?
HEY!
KLANG
TONNG
P-TING
OH, NO... NO!
SHRRIPP
YAAAAAAARGH!
WHHHRRRRRMMM
KLANK
K-TANK
WHUMK
HEY, WHERE'D THEY--?

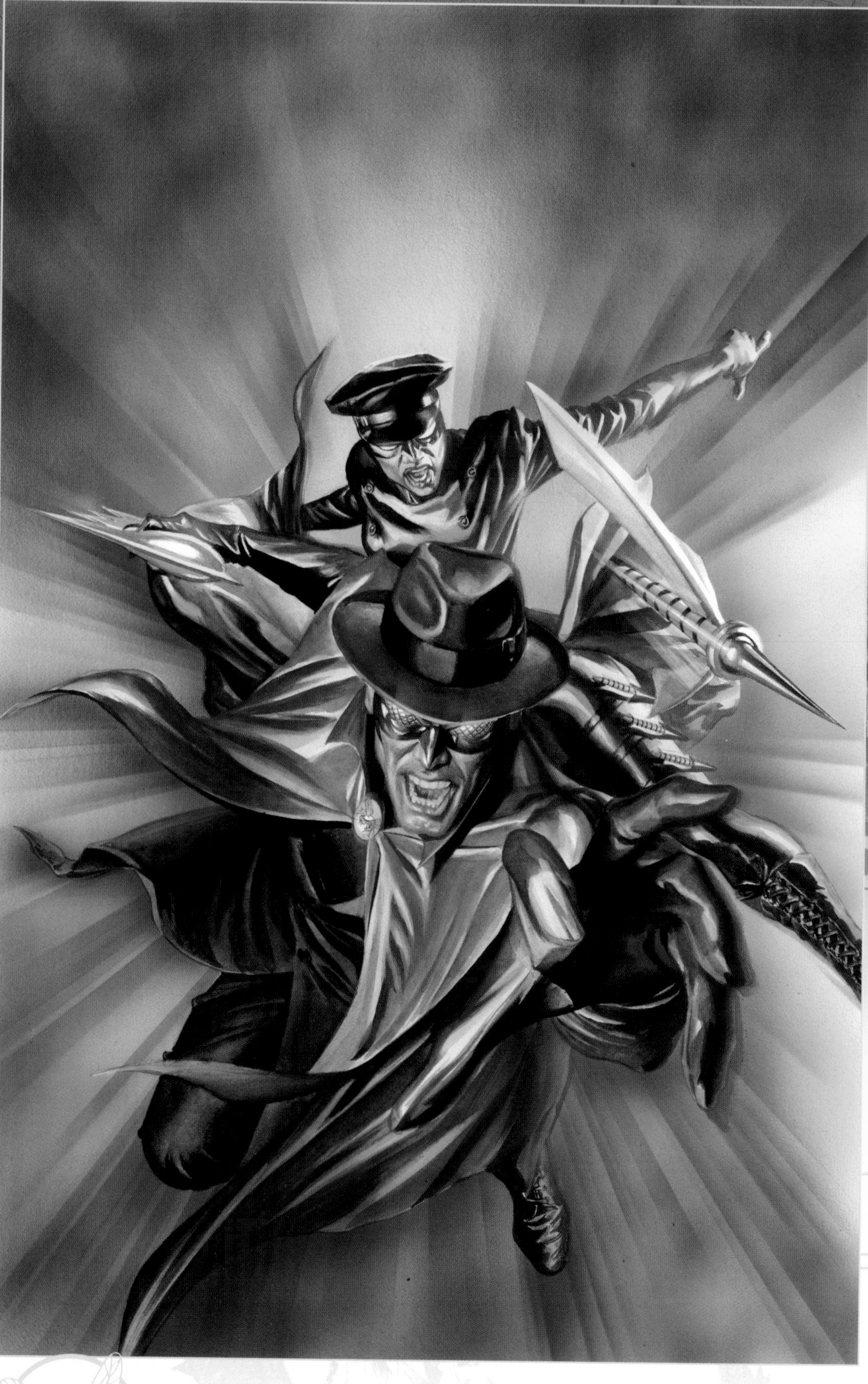

Cover to issue #1 by ALEX ROSS

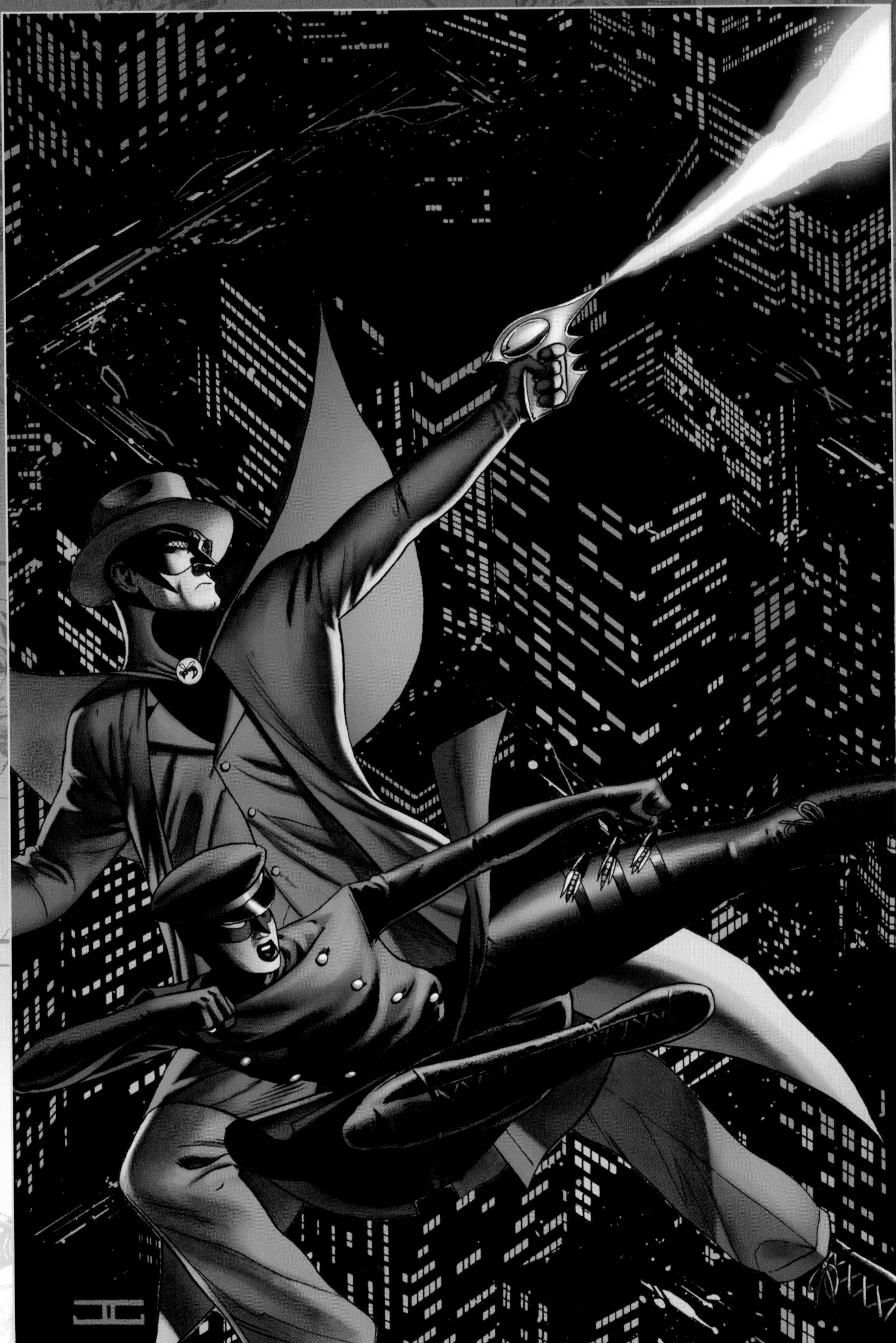

Cover to issue #1 by JOHN CASSADAY

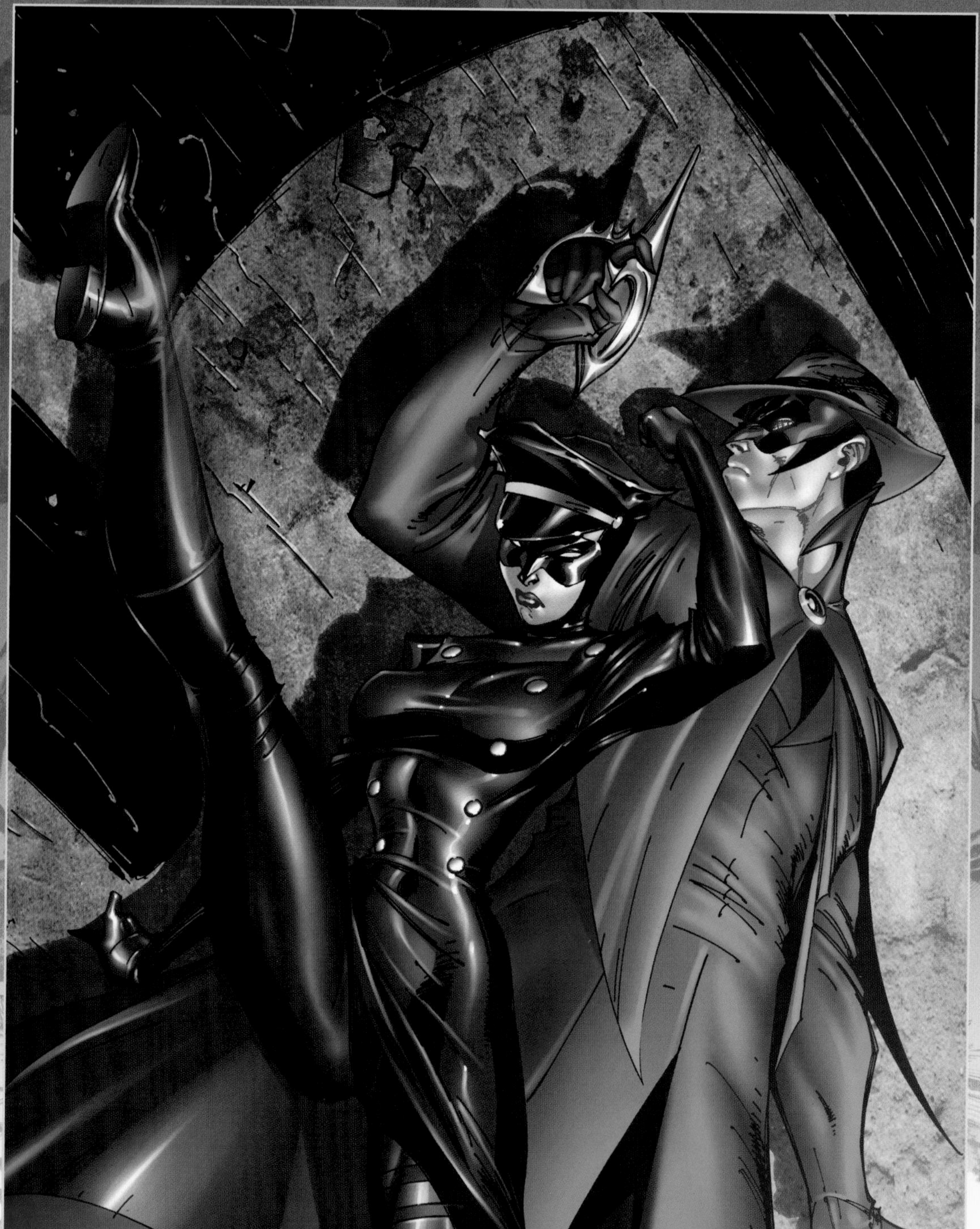

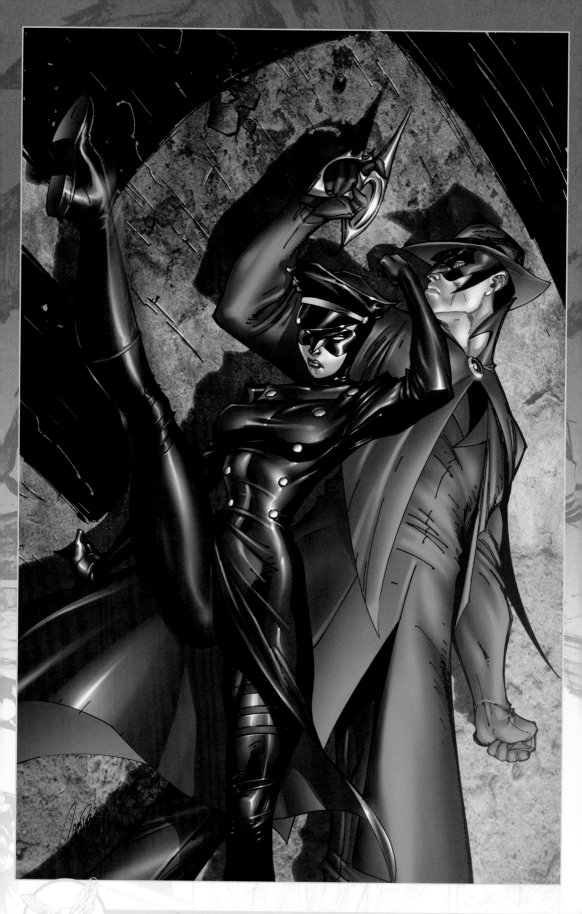

Cover to issue #1 by J. SCOTT CAMPBELL

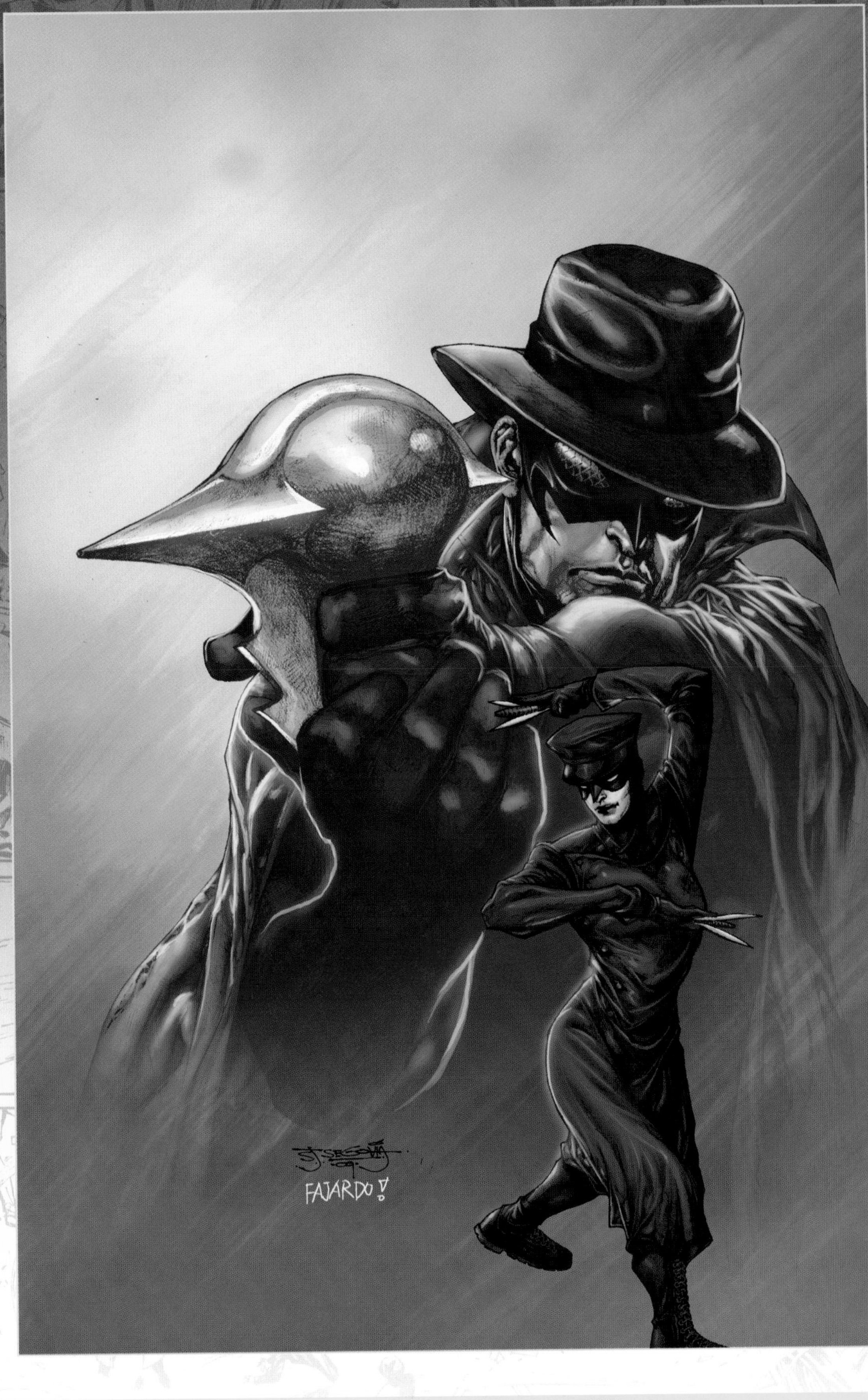
FAJARDO!

Cover to issue #1 by STEPHEN SEGOVIA

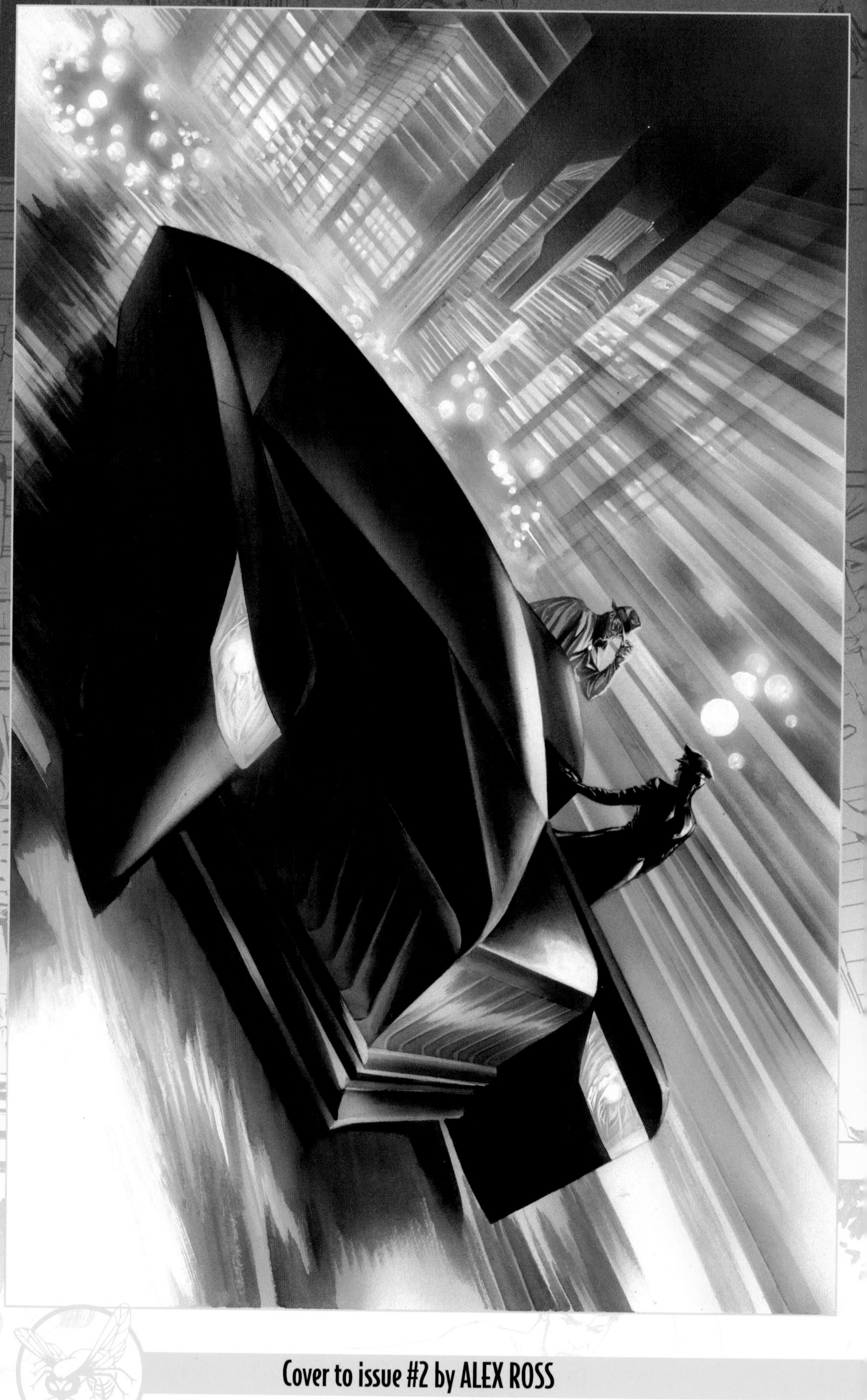

Cover to issue #2 by ALEX ROSS

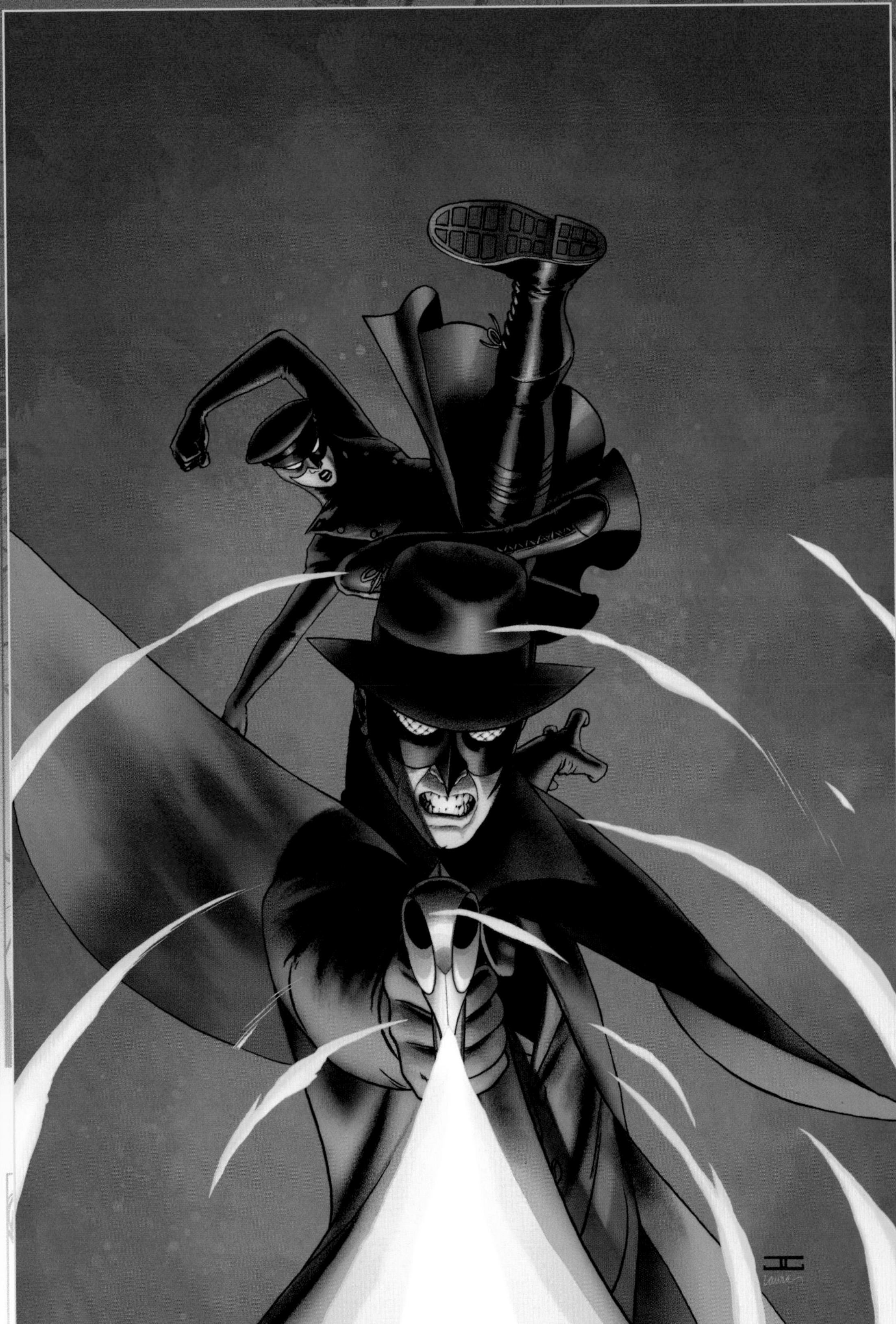

Cover to issue #2 by JOHN CASSADAY

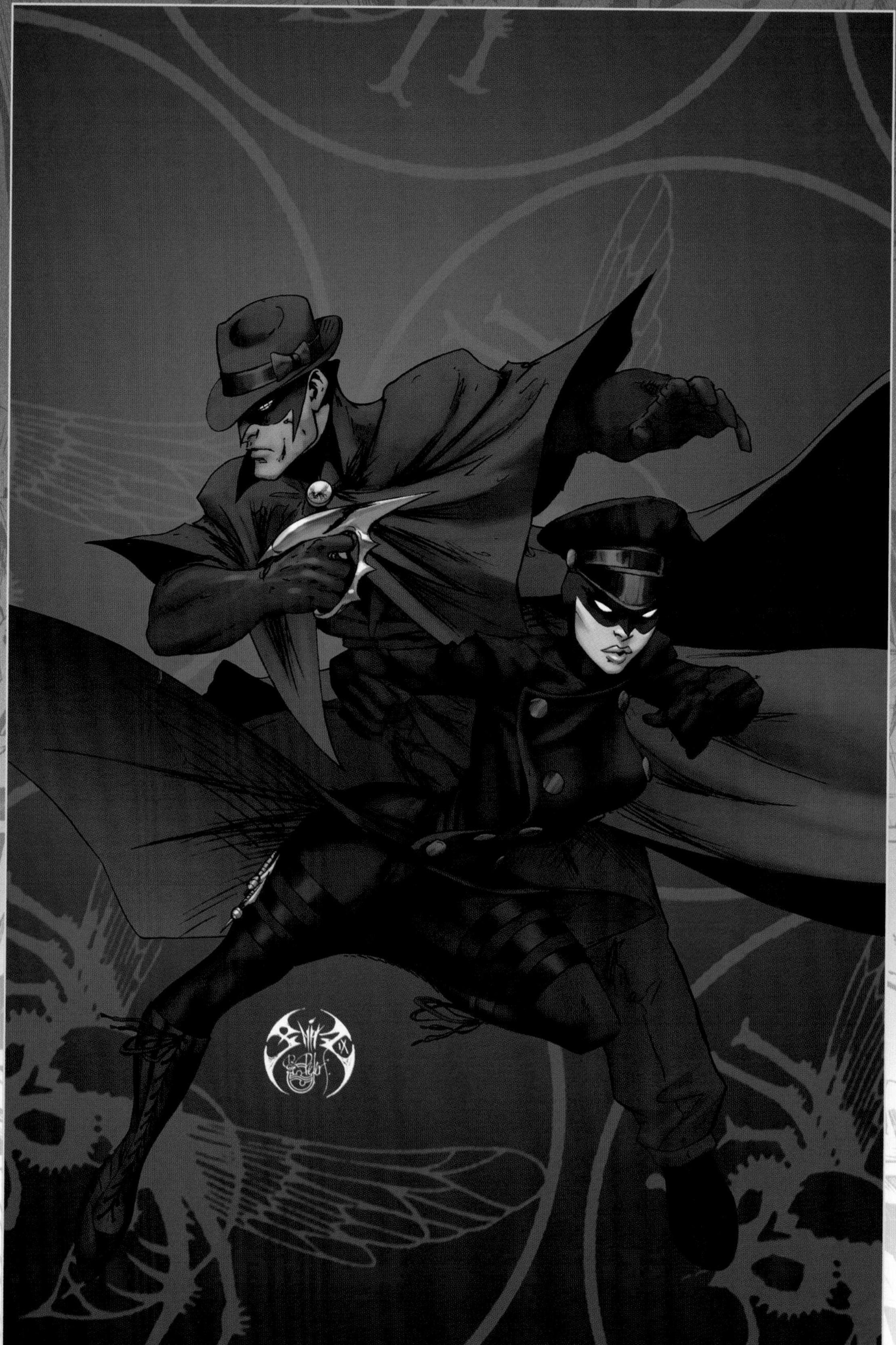

Cover to issue #2 by JOE BENITEZ

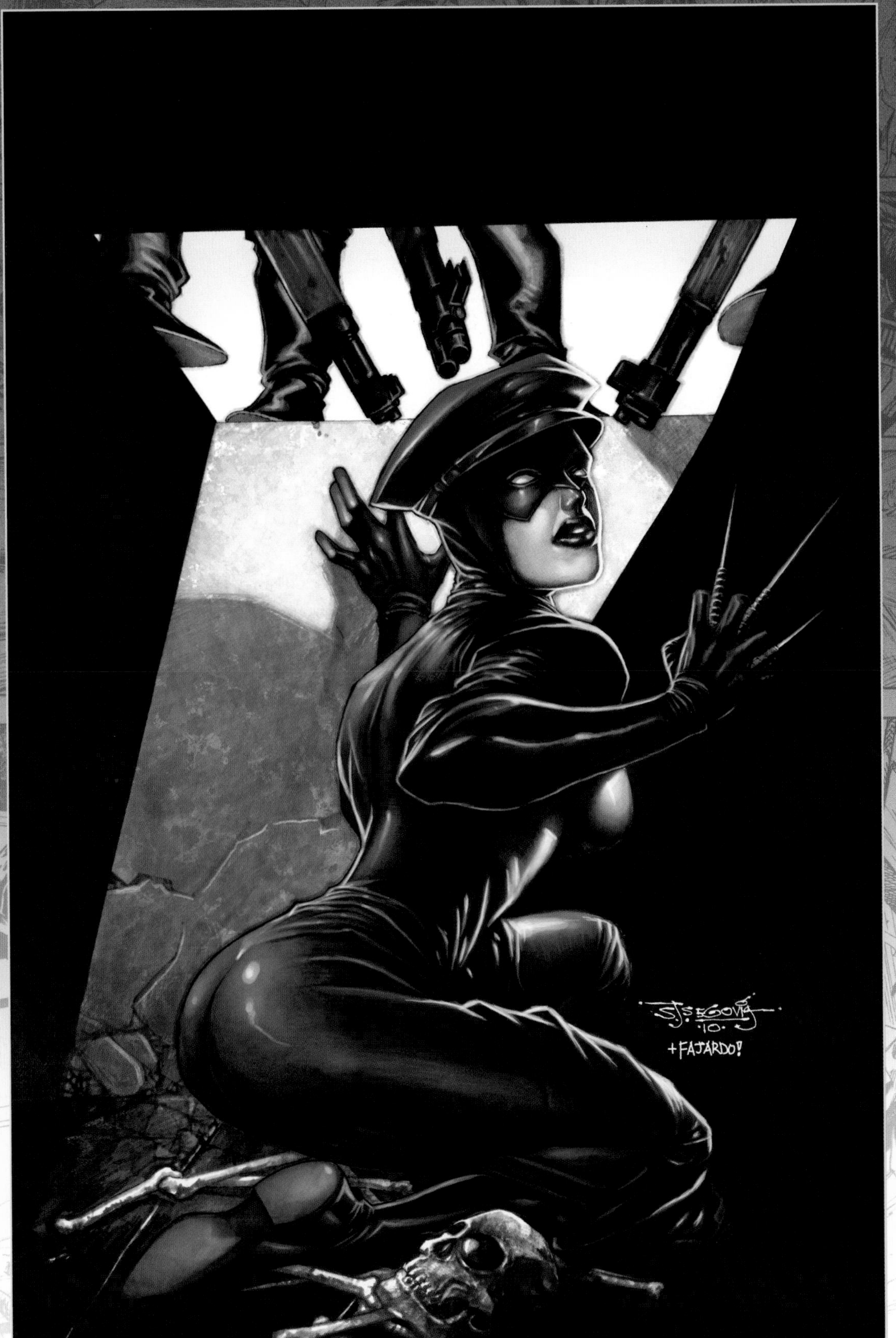
S.J. SEGOVIA '10
+FAJARDO!

Cover to issue #2 by STEPHEN SEGOVIA

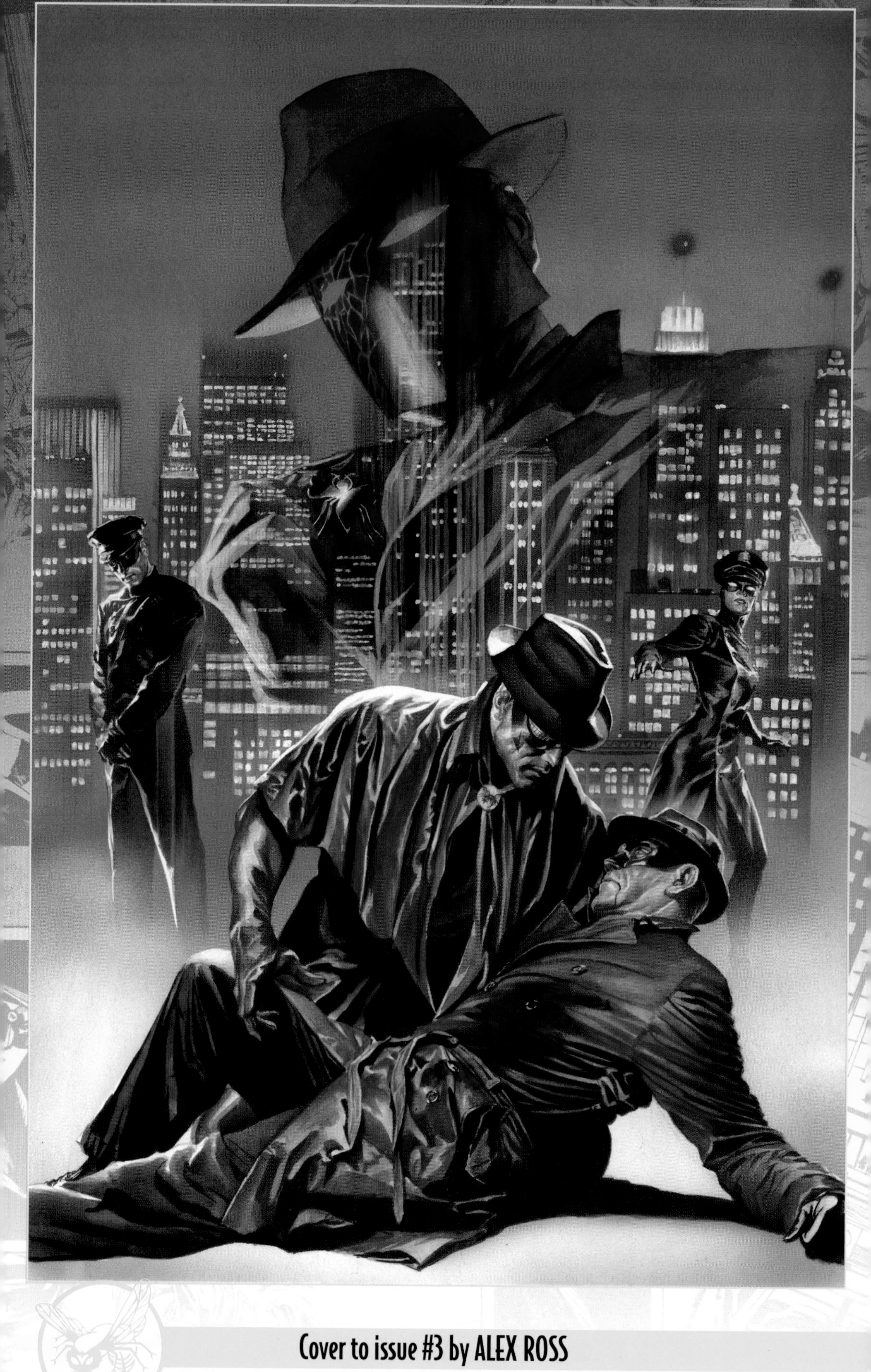

Cover to issue #3 by ALEX ROSS

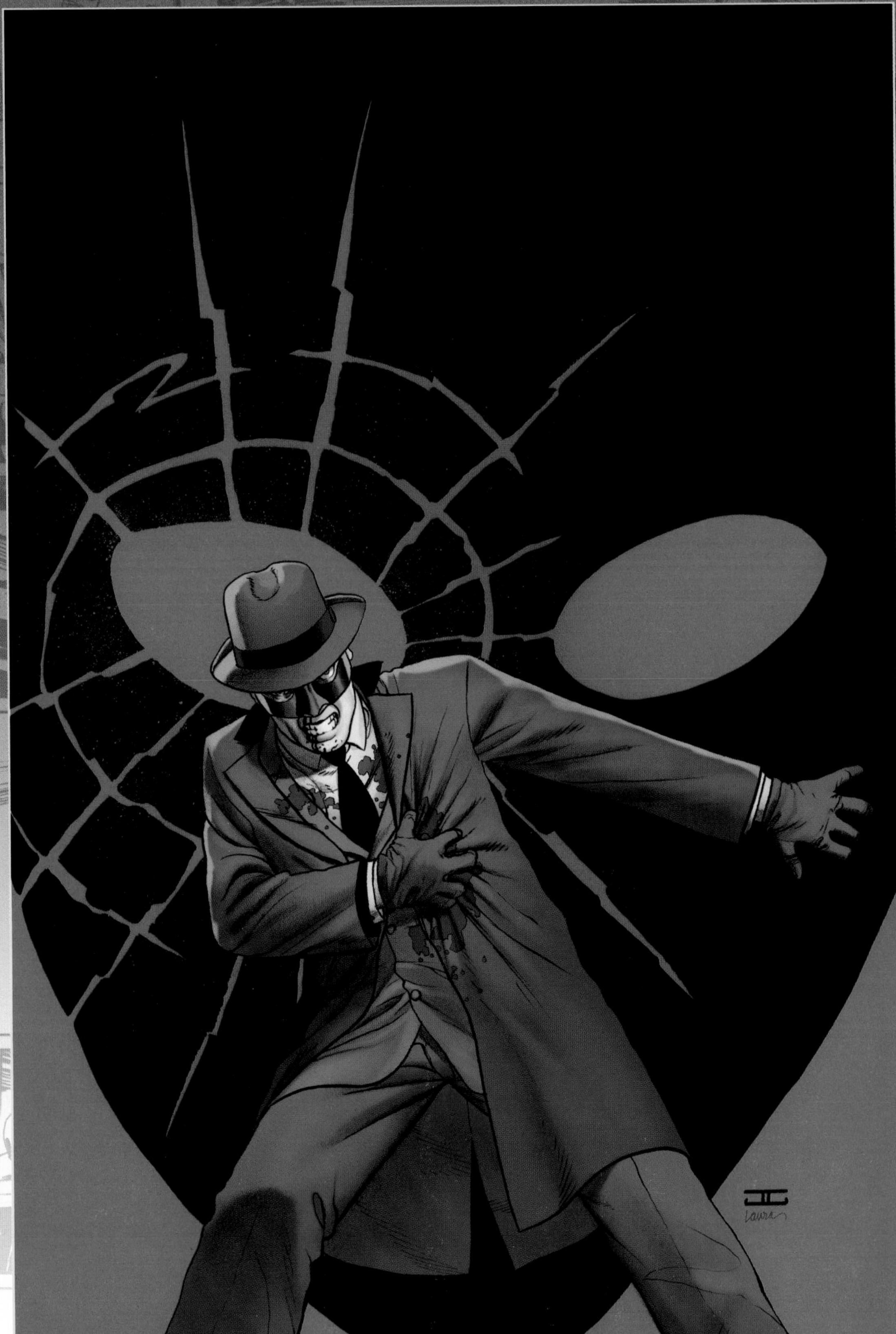

Cover to issue #3 by JOHN CASSADAY

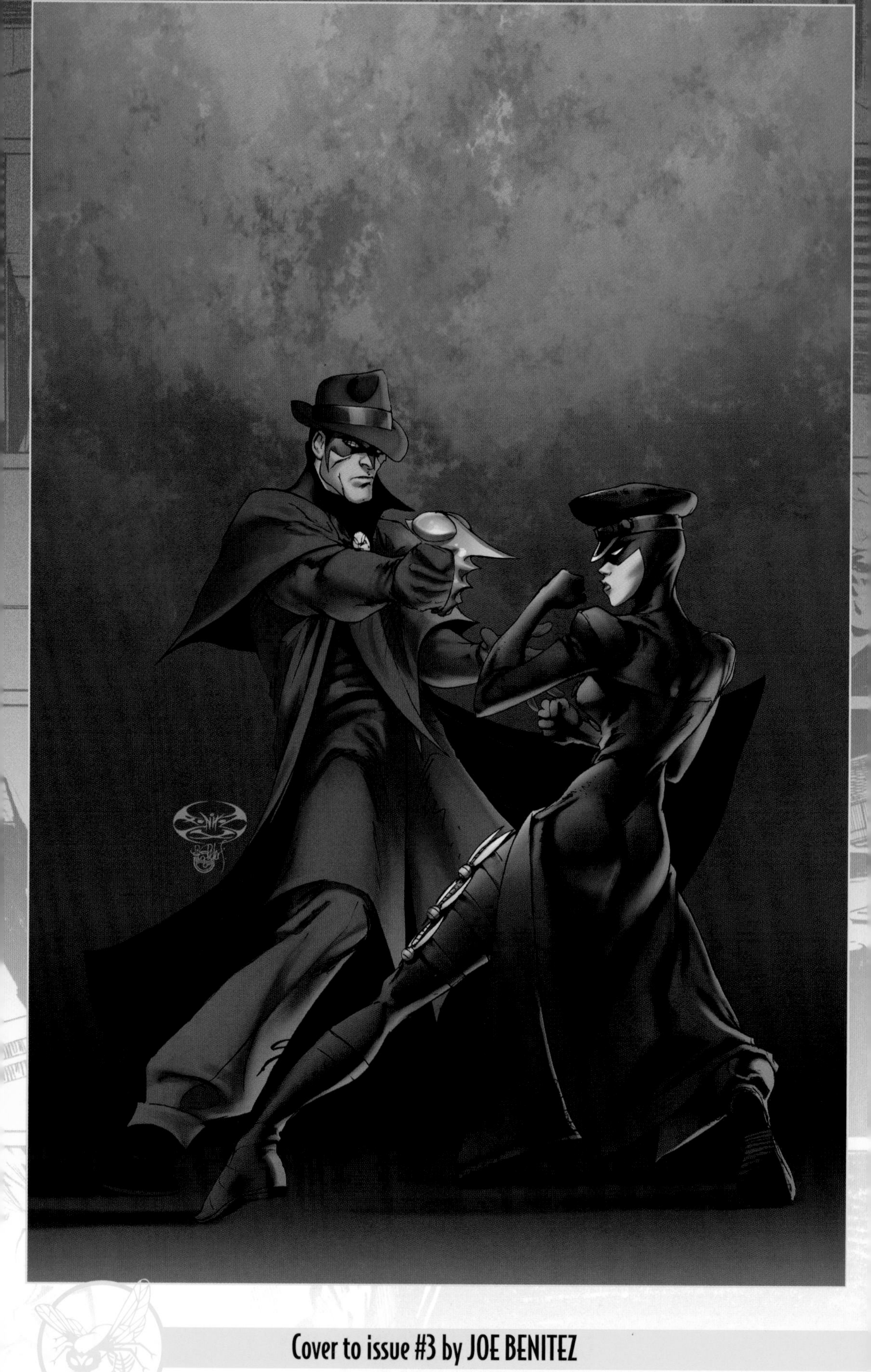

Cover to issue #3 by JOE BENITEZ

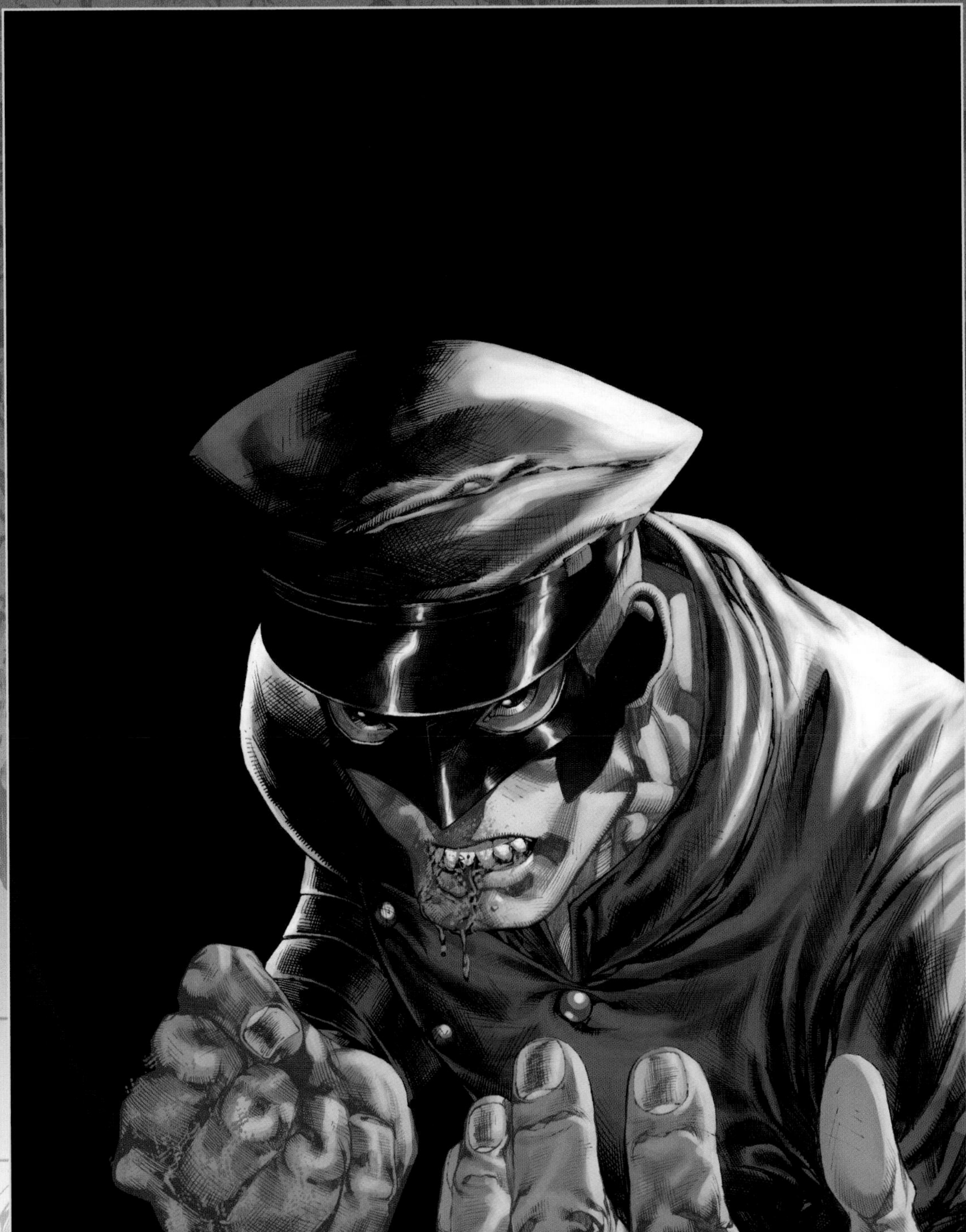
S.J. SEGOVIA ·10·
+
FAJARDO!

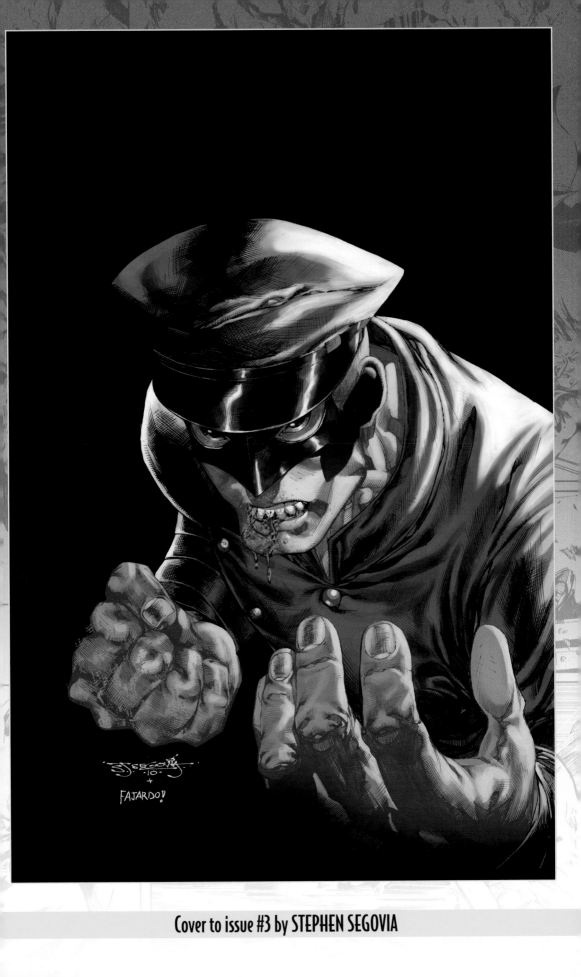

Cover to issue #3 by STEPHEN SEGOVIA

"Actual Death Cover" to issue #3 by MICHAEL NETZER

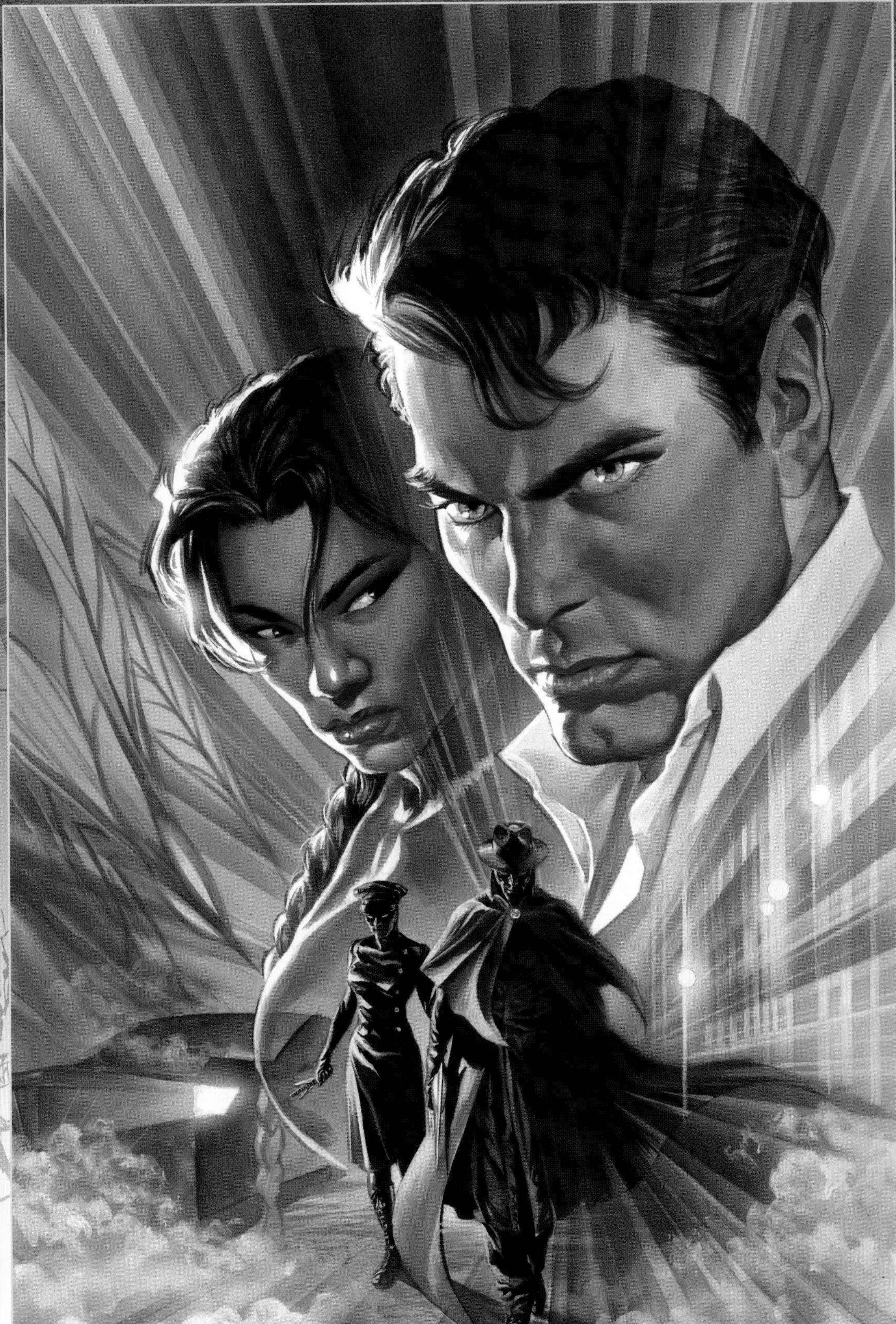

Cover to issue #4 by ALEX ROSS

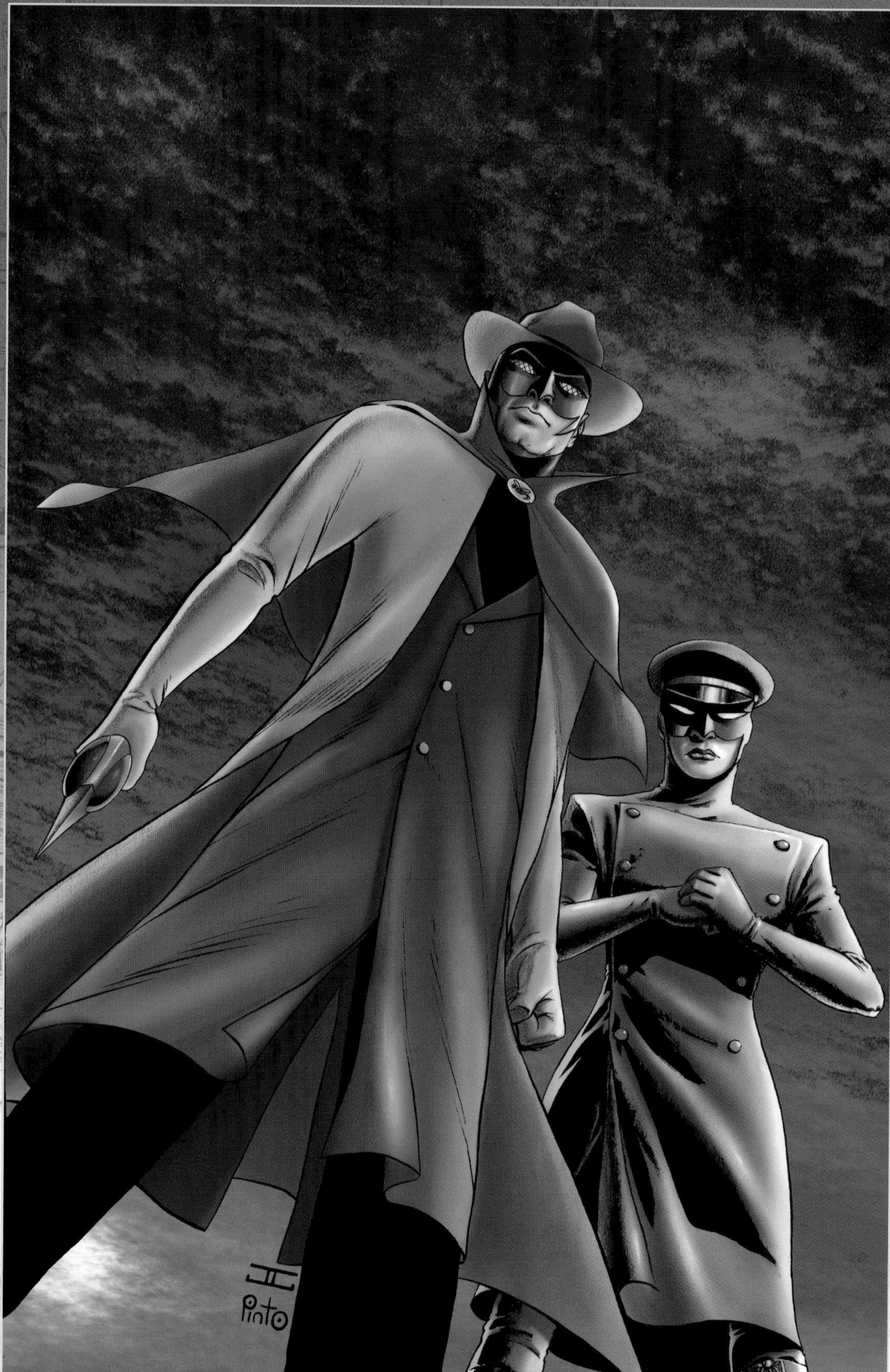
JC
Pinto

Cover to issue #4 by JOHN CASSADAY

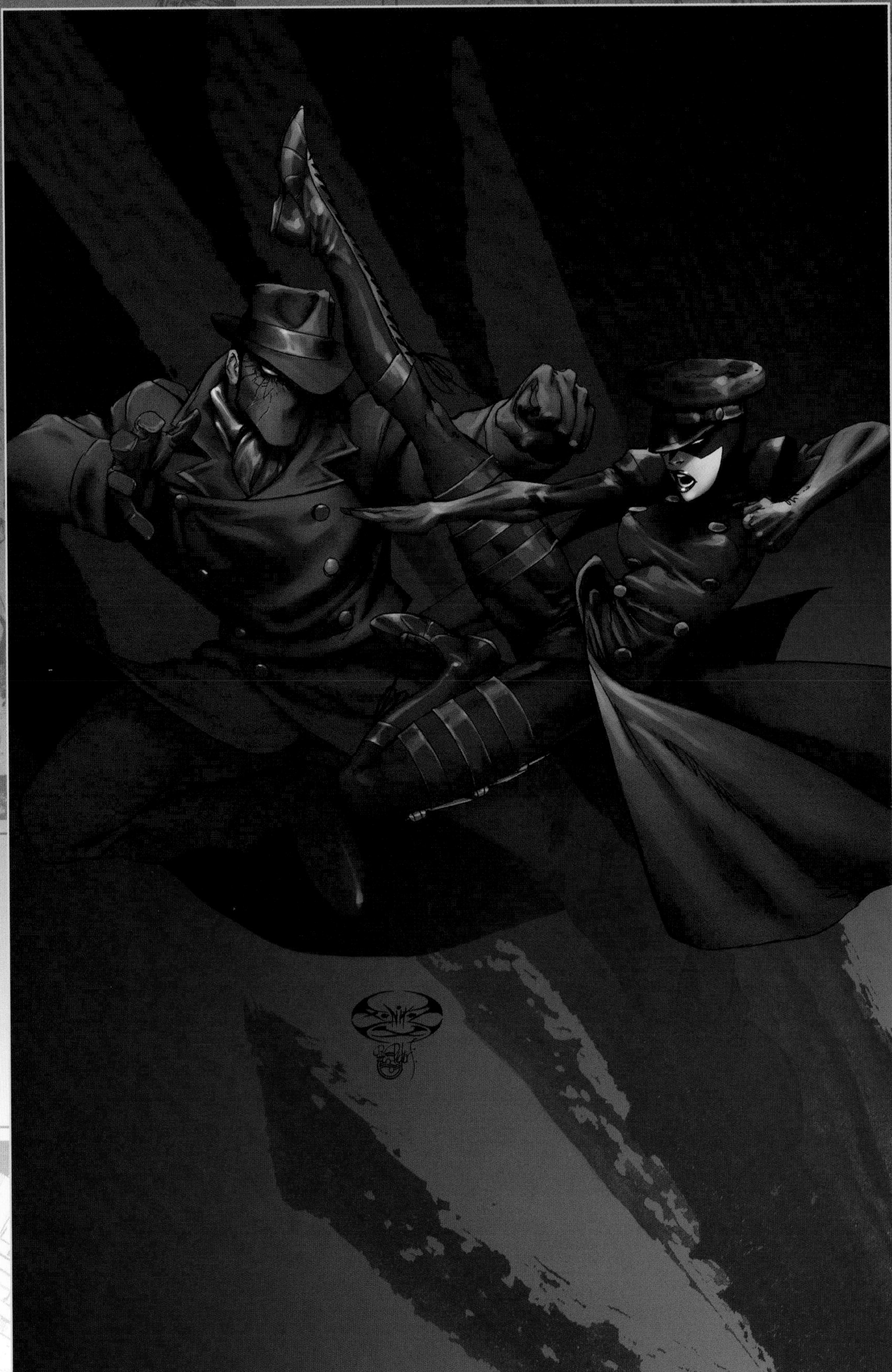

Cover to issue #4 by JOE BENITEZ

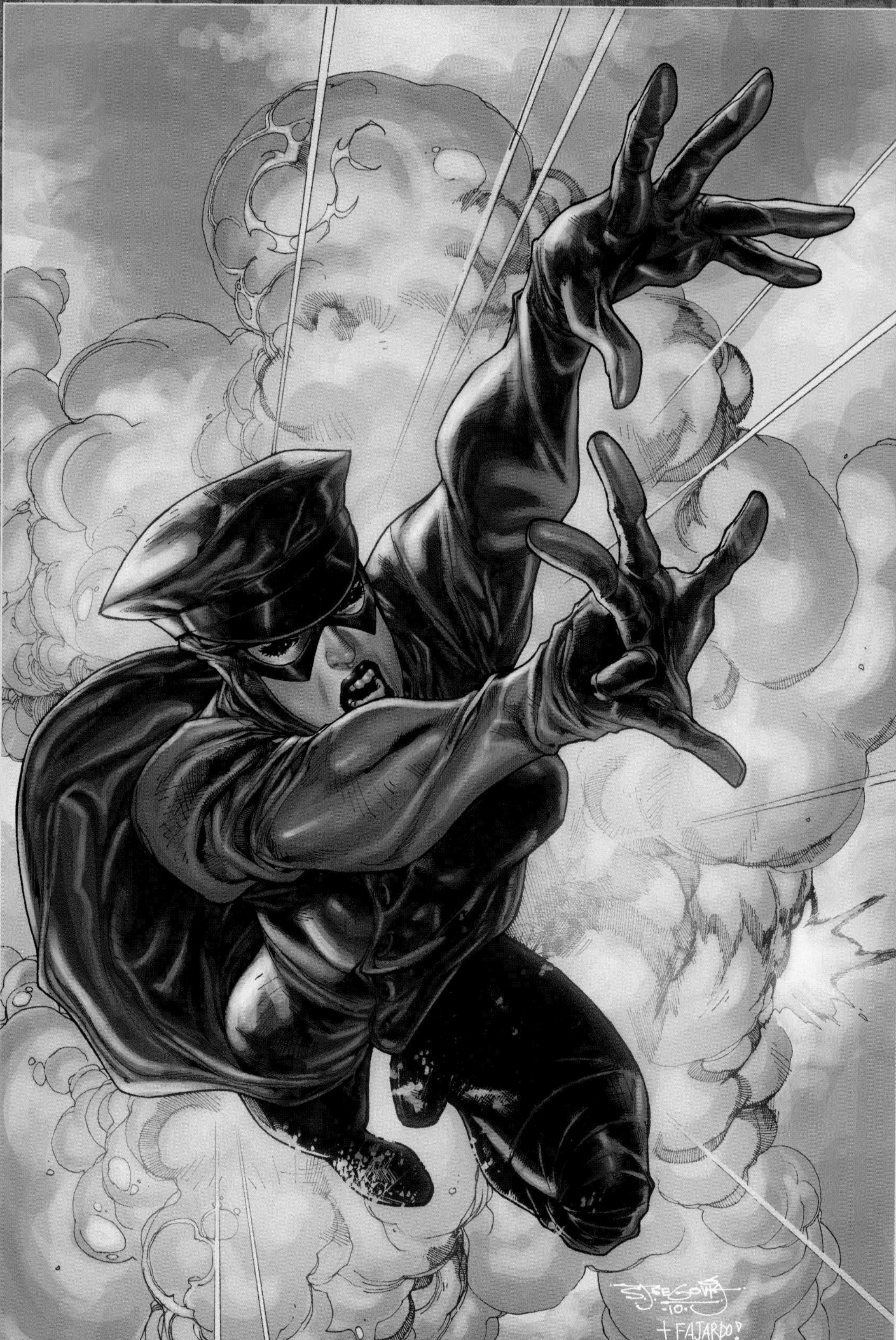
+FAJARDO!

Cover to issue #4 by STEPHEN SEGOVIA

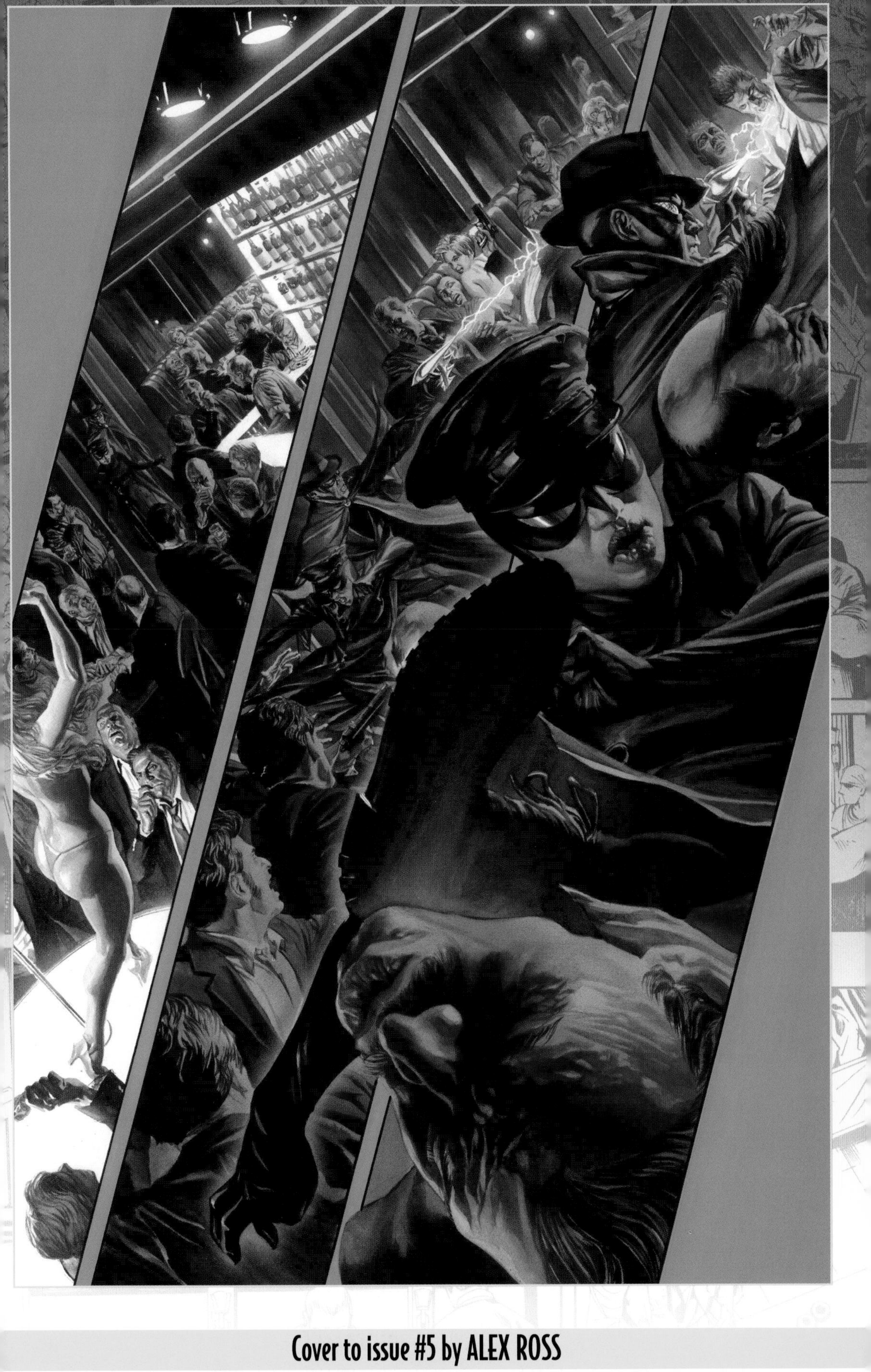

Cover to issue #5 by ALEX ROSS

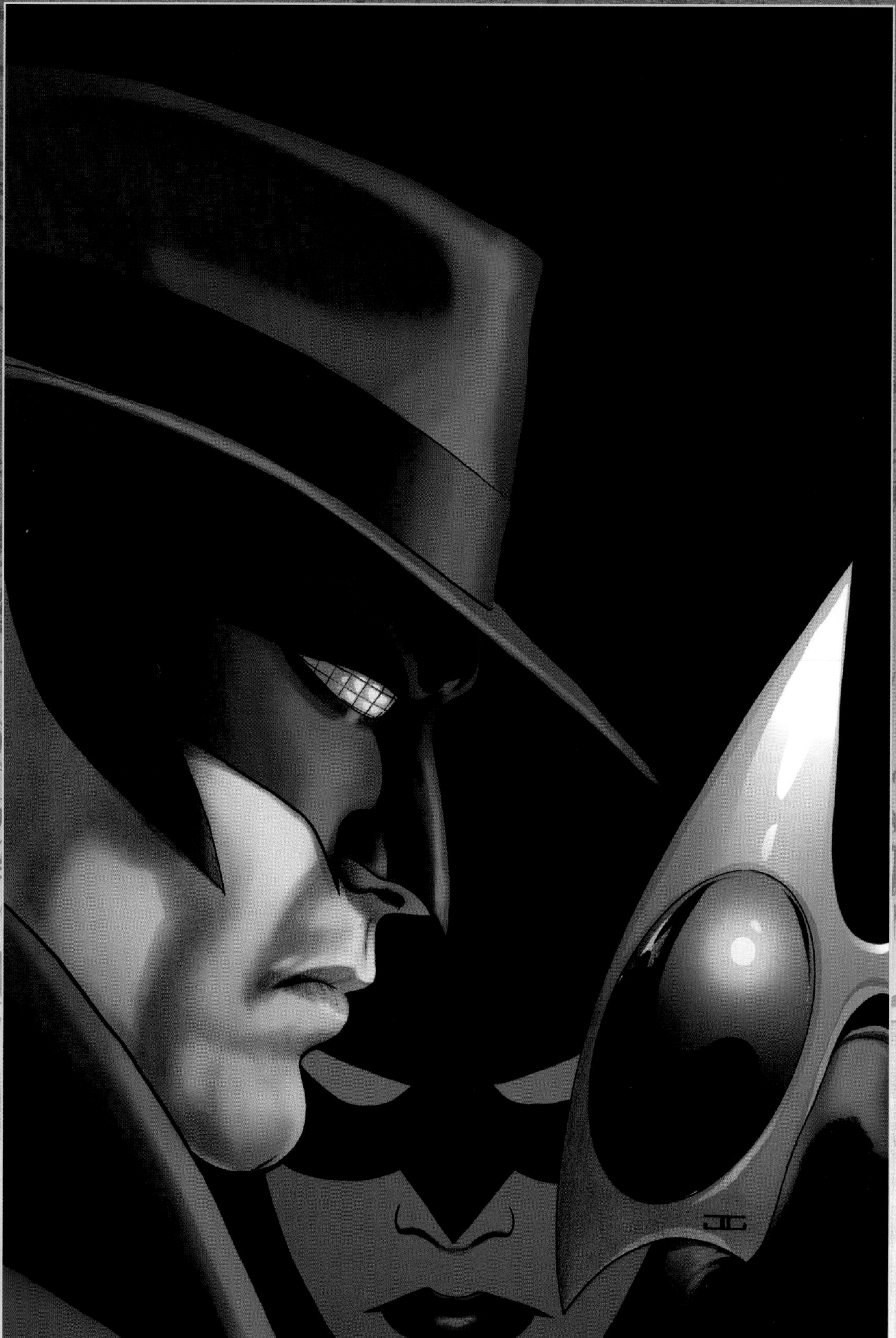

Cover to issue #5 by JOHN CASSADAY

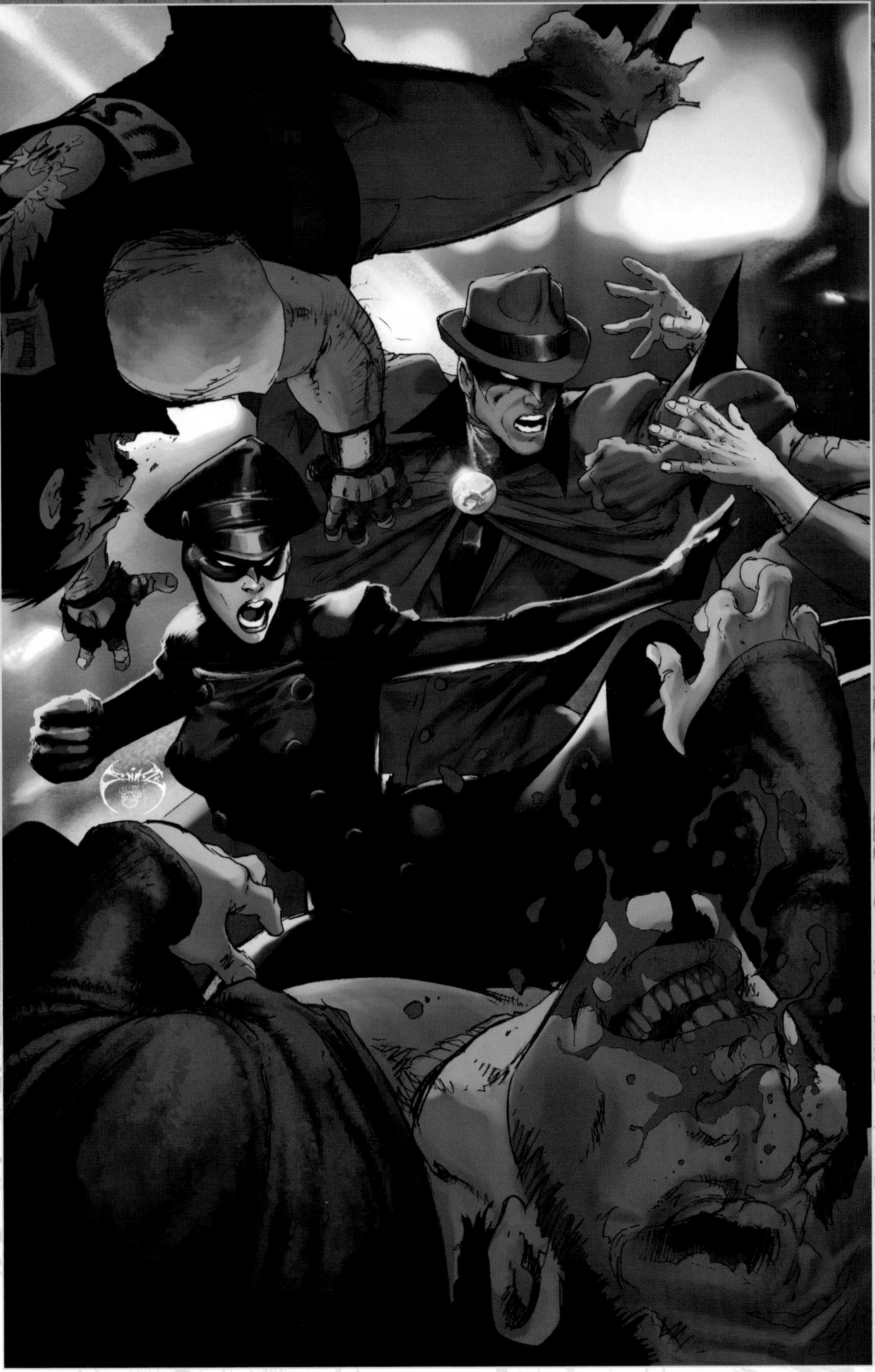

Cover to issue #5 by JOE BENITEZ

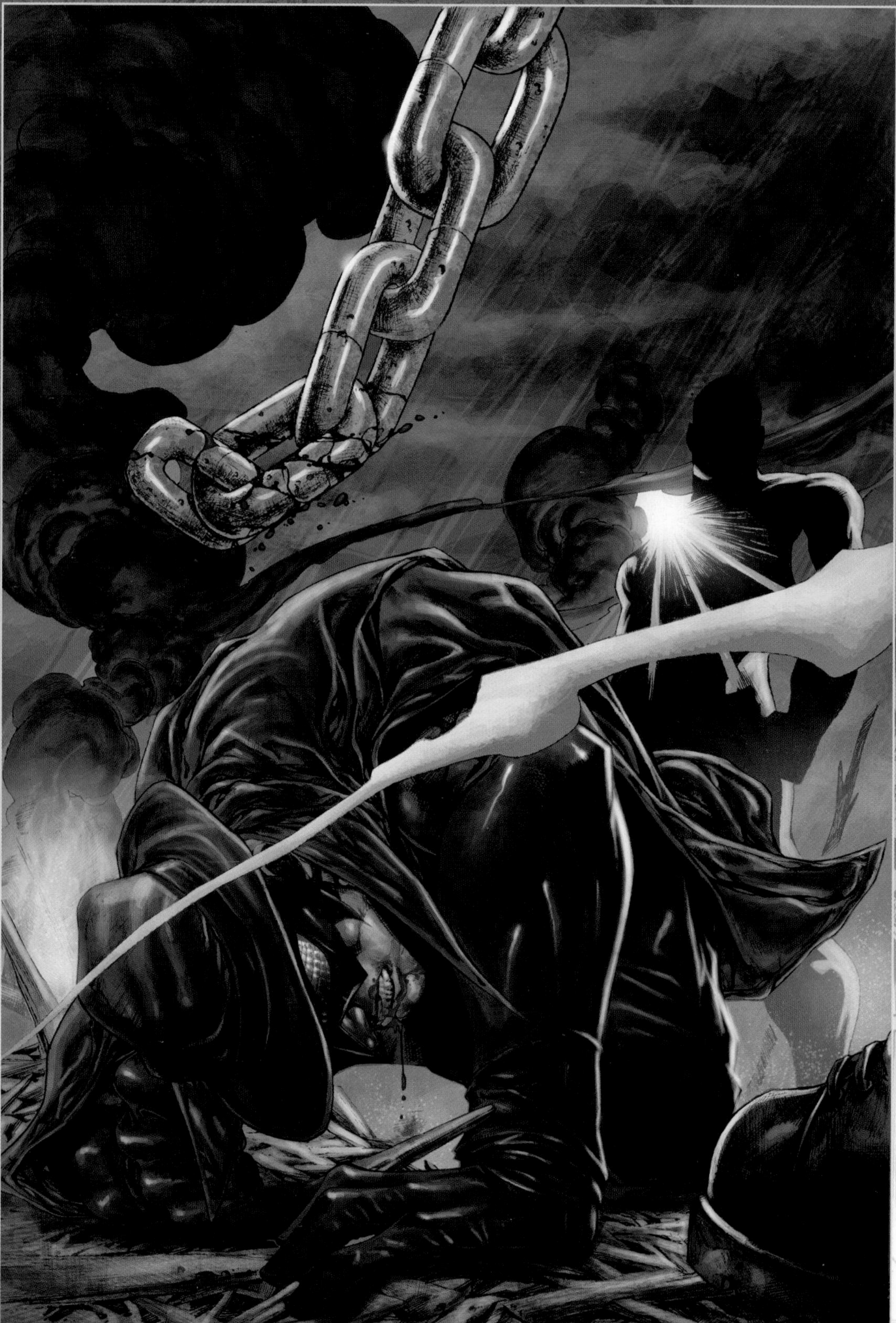

Cover to issue #5 by STEPHEN SEGOVIA